Fodor's InFocus

D1009130

PORTLAND

1st Edition

Where to Stay and Eat
for All Budgets

Must-See Sights
and Local Secrets

Ratings You Can Trust

Excerpted from *Fodor's Pacific Northwest*
Fodor's Travel Publications New York, Toronto, London, Sydney, Auckland
www.fodors.com

FODOR'S InFocus PORTLAND

Series Editor: Douglas Stallings

Editor: Amy B. Wang

Editorial Production: Carolyn Roth

Editorial Contributors: Andrew Collins, Sandy MacDonald

Maps & Illustrations: David Lindroth, *cartographer*; Rebecca Baer, Bob Blake and William Wu, *map editors*

Design: Fabrizio LaRocca, *creative director*; Guido Caroti, *art director*; Ann McBride, *designer*; Melanie Marin, *senior picture editor*

Cover Photo: (Multnomah Falls, Columbia River Gorge National Scenic Area): Ron Niebrugge/Alamy

Production/Manufacturing: Matthew Struble

COPYRIGHT

1st Edition

ISBN 978-1-4000-0748-6

ISSN 1941-0255

SPECIAL SALES

This book is available for special discounts for bulk purchases for sales promotions or premiums. Special editions, including personalized covers, excerpts of existing books, and corporate imprints, can be created in large quantities for special needs. For more information, write to Special Markets/Premium Sales, 1745 Broadway, MD 6-2, New York, NY 10019, or e-mail specialmarkets@randomhouse.com.

AN IMPORTANT TIP & AN INVITATION

Although all prices, opening times, and other details in this book are based on information supplied to us at press time, changes occur all the time in the travel world, and Fodor's cannot accept responsibility for facts that become outdated or for inadvertent errors or omissions. **So always confirm information when it matters,** especially if you're making a detour to visit a specific place. Your experiences—positive and negative—matter to us. If we have missed or misstated something, **please write to us.** We follow up on all suggestions. Contact the Portland editor at editors@fodors.com or c/o Fodor's at 1745 Broadway, New York, NY 10019.

PRINTED IN THE UNITED STATES OF AMERICA

10 9 8 7 6 5 4 3 2 1

Be a Fodor's Correspondent

Your opinion matters. It matters to us. It matters to your fellow Fodor's travelers, too. And we'd like to hear it. In fact, we *need* to hear it. When you share your experiences and opinions, you become an active member of the Fodor's community. Here's how you can help improve Fodor's for all of us.

Tell us when we're right. We rely on local writers to give you an insider's perspective. But our writers and staff editors also depend on you. Your positive feedback is a vote to renew our recommendations for the next edition.

Tell us when we're wrong. We update most of our guides every year. But things change. If any of our descriptions are inaccurate or inadequate, we'll incorporate your changes in the next edition and will correct factual errors at fodors.com *immediately*.

Tell us what to include. You probably have had fantastic travel experiences that aren't yet in Fodor's. Why not share them with a community of like-minded travelers? Share your discoveries and experiences with everyone directly at fodors.com. Your input may lead us to add a new listing or a higher recommendation.

Give us your opinion instantly at our feedback center at www.fodors.com/feedback. You may also e-mail editors@fodors.com with the subject line "Portland Editor." Or send your nominations, comments, and complaints by mail to Portland Editor, Fodor's, 1745 Broadway, New York, NY 10019.

Happy Traveling!

Tim Jarrell, Publisher

CONTENTS

ABOUT THIS BOOK

Our Ratings

We wouldn't recommend a place that wasn't worth your time, but sometimes a place is so experiential that superlatives don't do it justice: you just have to be there to know. These sights, properties, and experiences get our highest rating, **Fodor's Choice**, indicated by orange stars throughout this book. Black stars highlight sights and properties we deem **Highly Recommended**, places that our writers, editors, and readers praise again and again.

Credit Cards

Want to pay with plastic? **AE, D, DC, MC, V** after restaurant and hotel listings indicate whether American Express, Discover, Diners Club, MasterCard, and Visa are accepted.

Restaurants

Unless we state otherwise, restaurants are open for lunch and dinner daily. We mention dress only when there's a specific requirement and reservations only when they're essential or not accepted—it's always best to book ahead.

Hotels

Unless we tell you otherwise, you can assume that the hotels have private bath, phone, TV, and air-conditioning. We always list facilities but not whether you'll be charged an extra fee to use them, so when pricing accommodations, find out what's included.

Many Listings

★	Fodor's Choice
★	Highly recommended
⊠	Physical address
↔	Directions
⌂	Mailing address
☎	Telephone
⊟	Fax
⊕	On the Web
✉	E-mail
✆	Admission fee
☉	Open/closed times
Ⓜ	Metro stations
▭	Credit cards

Hotels & Restaurants

⊡	Hotel
⇥	Number of rooms
⚴	Facilities
†○†	Meal plans
✕	Restaurant
⌲	Reservations
⟍	Smoking
⚑⟊	BYOB
✕⊡	Hotel with restaurant that warrants a visit

Outdoors

⅄	Golf
⚠	Camping

Other

☕	Family-friendly
⇨	See also
⊠	Branch address
☞	Take note

WHEN TO GO

Portland's mild climate is best from June through September. Hotels are often filled in July and August, so it's important to book reservations in advance. Spring and fall are also excellent times to visit. The weather usually remains quite good, and the prices for accommodations, transportation, and tours can be lower (and the crowds much smaller!) in the most popular destinations. In winter, snow is uncommon in the city but abundant in the nearby mountains, making the region a skier's dream.

Climate
Average daytime summer highs are in the 70s; winter temperatures are generally in the 40s. Rainfall varies greatly from one locale to another. In the coastal mountains, for example, 160 inches of rain fall annually, creating temperate rain forests. Portland has an average of only 36 inches of rainfall a year—less than New York, Chicago, or Miami—however, in winter the rain may never seem to end. More than 75% of Portland's annual precipitation occurs from October through March. Portland is equally gray and drizzly in winter.

Forecasts **National Weather Service** (⊕www.wrh.noaa.gov). **Weather Channel** (⊕www.weather.com).

Welcome to Portland

WORD OF MOUTH

"I like wandering NW 23rd Street, or Hawthorne between 30th and 39th streets, Pittock mansion, Chinese or Japanese gardens, the Saturday market, bike riding along the Willamette, browsing the antique and art shops in the Pearl district, shopping at Powell's Bookstore."

—lcuy

By Janna
Mock-
Lopez

WHAT DISTINGUISHES PORTLAND, OREGON, from the rest of America's cityscapes? Or from the rest of the world's urban destinations, for that matter? In a Northwest nutshell: everything. For some, it's the wealth of cultural offerings and never-ending culinary choices; for others, it's Portland's proximity to the ocean and mountains, or simply the beauty of having all these attributes in one place. Strolling through downtown or within one of Portland's numerous neighborhoods, there's an unmistakable vibrancy to this city—one that is encouraged by clean air, infinite trees, and a diverse blend of historic and modern architecture.

Portland's various nicknames—Rose City, Bridgetown, Beervana, Brewtopia—tell its story in a nutshell as well. For a more involved explanation of what "everything" means, though, do what Portlanders would do to immerse themselves in a topic: grab a robust cup of coffee, a pot of steaming tea, or a sudsy mug of microbrew, and read on.

HISTORY

Like many fertile banks and rivers along the West Coast, Portland's first inhabitants were bands of Native Americans. Dating back to more than 10,000 years ago, indigenous tribes created complex thriving communities where they lived off and traded the various natural resources. Thanks to the networks of rivers, including the mighty Columbia, one such resource of abundance was salmon. Tribes such as the Chinook based their entire economies and cultures upon the cycles of salmon runs.

By the late 1700s into the early 1800s, Europeans began to descend from the West, while the famed Lewis and Clark expedition opened up the portal that began to draw settlers from the East. The British Hudson Bay Company, looking to find permanence and expand its fur-trading empire-in-the-making, founded Fort Vancouver, a settlement that resided in the Portland metropolitan area then known as Oregon Country.

With growing interest in the beauty and bounty of the West, both the Oregon Trail and the Barlow Road passages enabled the first large wave of pioneers to create settlements in the early 1840s. As legend has it, two such pioneers were William Overton and Asa Lovejoy. Overton was particularly impressed by the region's commercial prospects and set his sights on obtaining land. Unable to

TOP REASONS TO GO

■ Unleash your inner foodie in a city that has become a hot culinary destination, and experience an amazingly textured range of global delights created with fresh, locally harvested ingredients.

■ Beer "hop" (pun intended) between more than 40 local microbrews and sample offbeat varieties with such names as Hallucinator, Doggie Claws, and Sock Knocker.

■ Get up close and personal with Portland's true quirky nature by staying at or visiting one of the many beautifully restored McMenamin's properties in and around

town, such as a renovated elementary school turned hotel.

■ Spend the day at Washington Park, where you can stroll through the International Rose Test Garden, Japanese Garden, Oregon Zoo, World Forrestry Center, *and* Children's Museum—all within a short distance of one another.

■ Peruse the infinite aisles of more than a million new and used books at Powell's City of Books in the Pearl District. Top off hours of literary wanderlust with a fresh mocha or ginseng tea downstairs at World Cup Coffee and Tea House.

subsidize the 25¢ to file a land claim for the 640-acre site, he borrowed the quarter from Lovejoy in return for half of the claim. They cleared trees, built roads, and constructed this area's first buildings.

The next phase of the region's evolution arrived after Overton sold his portion of their joint claim to former shopkeeper and would-be developer Frances Pettygrove. When it came time to name their new settlement in 1845, Lovejoy and Pettygrove disagreed on what they wanted. Lovejoy, a Massachusetts native wanted "Boston," while Pettygrove, from Maine, preferred "Portland." To settle the matter, they did a coin toss—best of three—in which Pettygrove prevailed.

From the time Pettygrove and Lovejoy built a log store on the southeast corner of Front and Washington, growth moved quickly. Tanneries, saw mills, and even an oxen-driven mill wagon serving as the first public transportation system had been established. By the end of that decade, Portland had 800 residents. The Oregon Territory was officially formed in 1848. It was a vast chunk of real estate that included land north of California all the way south of Canada. Through the help of Congress and the passage of the Oregon Land act, every man or woman became entitled to 320 acres.

With the first of three transcontinental railroads reaching Portland in 1883, the city's fate of becoming a major trading hub was further solidified. In 1887 the Morrison Bridge—not the one visible today, which replaced the original in 1958—had been built across the Willamette River. With more arrivals came more neighborhoods and annexations: by 1900, Portland had become the Northwest's largest city with a population of nearly 100,000. However, it was the nearly 1.5 million visitors that came over the course of several months to take part in the Lewis and Clark Centennial Exposition in 1905, which spurred the next major growth wave. Portland's population doubled in the next five years.

A drive around the city, particularly in the Northeast or Northwest areas, and you'll see the beautiful Victorian-, Edwardian-, and Colonial-style homes built during this time. The Pittock Mansion, one of the most notable, still-standing depictions of Portland's development is now a public museum fully furnished with period artifacts. Belonging to lumber, real estate, and publishing magnates Henry and Georgiana Pittock, and completed in 1914, the 46-acre estate is nestled 1,000 feet directly above the city.

Remarkably, by the mid-1920s, nine of Portland's existing bridges had already been built, including the Steel, Hawthorne, Broadway, Interstate, Sellewood, Burnside, Ross Island, and Vista bridges. Due to the first and then second world wars, and the demand for an army of 100,000 workers to meet demands at the Kaiser Company, one of the largest shipbuilding operations in the world, Portland continued its iconic stature as a place for prosperity.

Ever-progressive even then, Portland housed many of these workers—roughly 40,000 of them—in Vanport, what was considered the first public housing project ever built in the United States. Unfortunately a flood later destroyed Vanport and left many of its residents displaced. The instant swell in homeless coupled with continued regional growth over the next decade prompted the expansion into suburbia. Portland's largest suburbs—Gresham, Beaverton, and Hillsboro—saw the biggest increases in residents.

By the late 1960s into the early 1970s, government stepped in to exercise the people's will and preserve the place Portland-

1

ers knew was special. It is because of the grassroots efforts coupled by what visionary politicians set in motion during this time that Portland is the city it is today. Under Governor Tom McCall, land conservation policies were adopted, including the creation of an urban growth boundary. Under this policy, high-density development was focused in designated urban areas and firm restrictions were placed on farmland. This approach was counter to what most cities across America of this size and growth rate were experiencing: as automobile use became more engrained into suburban culture, most people were abandoning city centers in favor of outlying areas being developed along highways.

Those in favor of this political approach say it has preserved precious farmland, provided an economic base for the farmers—many of whom have been in the area for more than a hundred years—and forced the creation of public transportation options. As a result, over time these circumstances have yielded less overall traffic compared to other cities of this size.

Though not entirely congestion-free today, because of such thoughtful planning Portland is a vibrant, clean, ever-evolving destination, nationally and internationally recognized for its urban planning, sustainability practices, and transportation efficiency.

GETTING AROUND

Most visitors comment about how easy it is to get around Portland. The Willamette River is Portland's east–west dividing line. Burnside Street separates north from south. The city's 200-foot-long blocks make them easy to walk, but you can also explore the downtown core and Nob Hill by MAX light rail, the Portland Streetcar, or TriMet buses (⇨*Portland Essentials*). Closer to the downtown core are the Pearl District and Old Town/Chinatown. Both the Pearl District and Nob Hill have a plethora of restaurants, specialty shops, and nightspots.

Aside from being pedestrian-friendly through inviting sidewalk sights and sounds, you can also explore the entire downtown for free through TriMet's "fareless square" system. Fare is not required when boarding buses, MAX light-rail, or streetcars when traveling within this designated area. Just say "fareless" as you board, and be sure to get off before you pass into a fare zone; drivers really do take note of who is riding for free, and may ask you to get off.

Taking advantage of the Zipcar car-sharing service is also a great way to get around Portland when you want a vehicle without major expense. Obtaining membership is easy: sign up online to become a member (⊕www.zipcar.com) based on a few simple guidelines; once you've applied, it takes only a few days for approval. An individual annual membership fee is $50 and members have use of Zipcars in many other major U.S. cities.

Unlike a car rental agency, car-sharing vehicles are dispersed throughout the city rather than at a single location. Once your reservation is made, you go to your car's location and let yourself in without paperwork or extra charges. Rates start at $8 per hour or $56 per day, and are all-inclusive.

PORTLAND LIFE

As a result of inventive dining, a plethora of cultural offerings, a rich juxtaposition of historic and modern architecture, endless recreational activities, and its friendly feel, Portland has become an alluring destination for just about everyone: whether you're young or old, low budget or extravagant, a novice or a seasoned traveler, there's something about this city that will feel inexplicably right.

It seems that food—or rather the creative applications of ingredients—has become a big deal of late where Portland is concerned, in national gourmet magazines and even the *New York Times*. It's true that Portland's dining scene is filled with amazing choices—though that's not necessarily what is causing all the commotion. Rather, it's the "sustainable" movement—using ingredients that are raised, grown, or foraged within a reasonable distance—that keeps diners and chefs magnetized to the city. Often, diners experience savory fish, fowl, or pasta dishes made with seasonal fruit and vegetable accompaniments that have just been plucked from the vine or ground.

After you're done with a delicious meal, you may find yourself at one of the many unique coffeehouses or local breweries sipping on a cup or mug of something satisfying. Portland is a mecca for both, and dozens of options blanket the city. Stumptown Coffee Roasters is a local favorite

Portland by Bike

1

In the mid-1990s the City of Portland adopted a Bicycle Master Plan to provide direction over a 20-year period for improvements that encourage more bicycles. Thanks to this plan, locals and travelers alike can take advantage of Portland's incredible bicycle-friendliness. If you prefer two nonmotorized wheels for getting around, then Portland will tantalize you with a network of more than 150 mi of bicycle boulevards, lanes, and off-street paths. Add to that thorough, accessible maps, specialized tours, and parking capacity (including lockers and racks downtown), and bicycling becomes not only a feasible but a sought-after mode of transportation.

An active collective of educators, advocates, riding groups, and businesses, along with government support, are working toward making Portland even more bike-friendly and safe. According to TriMet, whose entire bus fleet is equipped with bicycle racks, more than 80,000 bicycles are taken on MAX or bus each year. An intended 400-plus mi of bike paths are to be added over the next decade.

For a wealth of bicycle transportation resources and information, visit ⊕ www.port-landonline.com/transportation.

for a cup of joe; for microbrew possibilities, check out a McMenamins, BridgePort, or Widmer brewery. These sites are frequented by locals, too, and make great hangouts to people-watch or as a pit stop for determining the day's or evening's activities.

Portland has a thriving cultural community and showcases everything from the ballet, opera, symphonies, theater, and art exhibitions both minor and major in scope. Whatever you choose, you can count on several things: relatively affordable ticket prices and crowds dressed in everything from tennis shoes to tuxedos. Portlanders are sometimes accused by outsiders of being "too casual" when it comes to showing up for performances. But it's perhaps this "lower-brow" approach to arts and culture that is why many events are well-attended.

One arts attraction that both locals and tourists alike comfortably frequent is the Portland Art Museum. Its two large buildings house paintings by old-world masters, an impressive collection of Native American art—much from the Northwest—and an expanding collection of modern and contemporary art. Right across the street from the Portland Art Museum is the Oregon Historical Society, which has more than 85,000 artifacts, including ancient objects from the earliest settlements. Displays illuminate Oregon's "growth of business and industry, the development of artwork and crafts, and maritime history."

If smaller galleries are more of your thing, Portland has plenty. Many of the city's galleries and studios are condensed in the swanky Pearl District, just on the fringe of downtown. From print art, fiber art, contemporary art, and photography to glass, performance art, and even 3-D art, you can find an immense selection of edgy talent.

IF YOU LIKE

BIKING

Portland has been called the best city in the country for biking, and with bike lanes galore, mild weather year-round, and a beautiful waterfront to ride along, it's no wonder. With all this encouragement, cyclists in Portland have gotten creative: not only does cycling provide an excellent form of transportation around here, it also has evolved into a medium of progressive politics and public service. Riders gather at least once every month to ride en masse through the streets of the city in an event called Critical Mass to show solidarity as a powerful alternative to an auto-society, and they have been known to gather force for the purpose of political protest. In addition, several bike co-ops have sprung up throughout the city in the past several years, devoted to providing used bikes at decent prices to members of the community, as well as to teaching bike maintenance and the economic and environmental benefits of becoming a commuter on two wheels.

PUB THEATERS

Everyone knows that Oregon loves its microbrews and sipping a pint of local brew is one of Oregon's favorite pastimes, but Portlanders have taken this a step further, creating a recreational venue fondly called the pub theater; that is, a movie theater showing second-run, classic, or cult films for $2 or $3, where you can buy a pitcher of good locally brewed beer and a slice of pizza to enjoy while watching. The McMenamins brothers are largely to thank for this phenomenon, being the masterminds behind such popular spots as the Bagdad Theatre, the Mission Theatre,

CLOSE UP

1

Portland Parks It

Some of the best things about Portland aren't inside the city's restaurants or museums but outside in its parks. If the weather cooperates—and in Portland that isn't always a given—you need to do as city residents do and head outdoors.

When looking toward the hills on the west side of town it's hard to miss the tree-blanketed 5,155 acres of Forest Park. Six times the size of New York City's Central Park and deemed the nation's largest urban wilderness, Forest Park a carless haven for runners, hikers, bikers, and nature enthusiasts. The park is home to more than 60 mammals, including elk, deer, and bobcats, and more than 110 bird species.

Another popular park is Washington Park—one of Oregon's oldest, acquired in 1871—which has picnic areas, playgrounds, and hiking trails; located within the park are Hoyt Arboretum and the International Rose Test and Japanese Gardens. Waterfront Park is right downtown and lies on the west bank of the Willamette River. This local favorite hosts many of Portland's major annual festivals and concerts such as the Rose Festival and

Waterfront Blues Festival.

A few other natural havens outside of the downtown area attract nature lovers: Mt. Tabor Park, actually an extinct volcanic cinder cone, has miles of trails meandering through its trees toward the top, where impressive downtown and Mt. Hood views are the reward. The other is Laurelhurst Park, a wonderful mix of large shady trees and open green spaces. There are plenty of enclaves for sunny afternoon picnics, and paths for admiring nature and for allowing kids to run around.

If you have kids in tow you'll appreciate that, in addition to plenty of outdoor parks, there are scores of indoor family-friendly activities. Landmark destinations to spend a few hours or an entire day are the Oregon Zoo—adjacent Portland Children's Museum and World Forestry Center Discovery Museum—and the Oregon Museum of Science and Industry (fondly referred to as OMSI), on the east side of the Willamette River across from downtown. Each museum has fascinating permanent and touring exhibits sure to keep kids learning and loving the fact they're on vacation.

and the St. John's Pub, but unaffiliated establishments like the Laurelhurst Theatre and the Clinton Street Theater manage to edge in on the action as well.

CLOSE UP

The Portland Attractions Pass

To keep wallets under cost control, there's the **Portland Attractions Pass,** for sale at the visitor information center in Pioneer Courthouse Square. Each pass gains free admission to Portland's top 10 attractions: the End of the Oregon Trail Interpretive Center, Oregon Historical Society, Oregon Museum of Science and Industry (OMSI), Oregon Zoo, Pittock Mansion, Portland Art Museum, Portland Children's Museum, Portland Classical Chinese Garden, Portland Japanese Garden, and the World Forestry Center Discovery Museum. Passes are good for a five-day period and cost $35 for adults, $29 for children.

BRIDGES

With a river running through the center of the city, Portland has one of the most interesting urban landscapes in the country, due in no small part to the several unique bridges that span the width of the Willamette River. Five of the city's 10 bridges are drawbridges, frequently raised to let barges go through, and there's something awe-inspiring and anachronistic in watching a portion of a city's traffic and hubbub stand still for several minutes as a slow-moving vessel floats through still water. Each bridge is beautiful and different: the St. John's Bridge has elegant 400-foot towers, the Broadway Bridge is a rich red hue, the arches of the huge two-level Fremont Bridge span the river gracefully, and the Steel Bridge has a pedestrian walkway just 30 feet above the water, allowing walkers and bikers to get a fabulous view of the river.

Exploring Portland

WORD OF MOUTH

"[Portland] is one of the most lively U.S. cities with lots to see and do—gardens, theater, great dining—staying in a downtown area hotel will let you step out your door and take free transportation on the streetcars, light rail, and buses in the downtown area."

—norahs

Updated
by Janna
Mock-
Lopez

ONE OF THE GREATEST THINGS ABOUT PORTLAND is that there's so much to explore. This city rightfully boasts that there's something for everyone. What makes discovering Portland's treasures even more enticing is that its attractions, transportation options, and events are all relatively accessible and affordable.

Younger singles will appreciate that Portland has long been considered a hub for indie music. Hundreds of bands flock to become part of the creative flow of alternative, jazz, blues, and rock, which dominate the nightclub scene seven nights a week. Factor in an outrageous number of independent brewpubs and coffee shops—with snowboarding, windsurfing, or camping within an hour's drive—and it's easy to see why so many younger singles take advantage of Portland's eclectic indoor and outdoor offerings.

Couples can double the romance and intrigue, with strolls through never-ending parks, dimmed dining rooms for savoring innovative regional cuisine, and gorgeous cruises along the Willamette River aboard the *Portland Spirit*. If it's hiking, climbing, biking, running, and skiing that are a basis for kindred spirit-hood, then paired people have a built-in playground to renew shared interests with unlimited access to nature's bounty.

Families can explore first-rate museums and parks designed for kids of all ages, such as the Children's Museum, the Oregon Museum of Science and Industry, and Oaks Park. Many of these attractions offer permanent displays as well as nationally touring exhibits. At most libraries, parks, and recreational facilities, expect to find hands-on activities, music, story times, plays, and special performances for children. Many restaurants in and around Portland are family-friendly, and with immediate access to the MAX and street car, toting kids around downtown is easy. Between Portland's rich scope of exposure to both culture and nature, parents will be delighted by the meaningful interactivity to be shared.

DOWNTOWN

Portland has one of the most attractive, inviting downtown urban cores in the United States. It's clean, compact, and filled with parks, plazas, and fountains. With a mix of new and historic buildings, architecture aficionados will find plenty to admire. Hotels, shops, museums, restaurants,

PORTLAND TOP FIVE EXPERIENCES

■ Gaze at Portland's gorgeous skyline in the afternoon light, while gently gliding down the Willamette River aboard the *Portland Spirit*.

■ Walk or ride the street car downtown and mindfully observe the interesting juxtapositions of modern and historical architecture.

■ Take in the true cultural and social flavor of Portland by participating in either the First Thursday Gallery Walk in the Pearl District or the Last Thursday art event on Alberta Street.

■ Discover what "sustainability" means by trying one of Portland's many eco-conscious restaurants offering locally harvested ingredients on their menus.

■ Spend a leisurely afternoon strolling one of the many local farmers' markets and taste-testing locally baked breads, goat cheeses, fruits, and vegetables.

and entertainment can all be found here, and the entire downtown area is part of the Tri-Met transit system's Fareless Square, within which you can ride MAX, the Portland Streetcar, or any bus for free.

Numbers in the text correspond to numbers in the margin and on the Downtown, the Pearl District, and Old Town/ Chinatown map.

WHAT TO SEE

❷ **Central Library.** The elegant, etched-graphite central staircase and elaborate ceiling ornamentation make this no ordinary library. With a gallery space on the second floor and famous literary names engraved on the walls, this building is well worth a walk around. ✉*801 S.W. 10th Ave., Downtown 97205* ☎*503/988–5123* ✆*Free* ☉*Mon. and Thurs.–Sat. 10–6, Tues. and Wed. 10–8, Sun. noon–5.*

❶⑦ **Chapman and Lownsdale squares.** During the 1920s, these parks were segregated by sex: Chapman, between Madison and Main streets, was reserved for women, and Lownsdale, between Main and Salmon streets, was for men. The elk statue on Main Street, which separates the parks, was given to the city by former mayor David Thompson. It purportedly honors an elk that grazed here in the 1850s.

GREAT ITINERARIES

IF YOU HAVE 1 DAY

Spend the morning exploring downtown. Visit the Portland Art Museum or the Oregon History Center, stop by the historic First Congregational Church and Pioneer Courthouse Square, and take a stroll along the Park Blocks or Waterfront Park. Eat lunch and do a little shopping along Northwest 23rd Avenue in the early afternoon, and be sure to get a look at the beautiful historic homes in Nob Hill. From there, drive up into the northwest hills by the Pittock Mansion, and finish off the afternoon at the Japanese Garden and the International Test Rose Garden in Washington Park. If you still have energy, head across the river for dinner on Hawthorne Boulevard; then drive up to Mt. Tabor Park for Portland's best sunset.

IF YOU HAVE 3 DAYS

On your first day, follow the itinerary above, but stay on the west side for dinner, and take your evening stroll in Waterfront Park. On your second morning, visit the Portland Classical Chinese Garden in Old Town, and then head across the river to the Sellwood District for lunch and antiquing. Stop by the Crystal Springs Rhododendron Garden; then head up to Hawthorne District in the afternoon. Wander through the Hawthorne and Belmont neighborhoods for a couple hours, stop by Laurelhurst Park, and take a picnic dinner up to Mt. Tabor Park. In the evening, catch a movie at the Bagdad Theatre, or get a beer at one of the east side brewpubs. On Day 3, take a morning hike in Hoyt Arboretum or Forest Park; then spend your afternoon exploring shops and galleries in the Pearl District and on northeast Alberta Street. Drive out to the Grotto, and then eat dinner at the Kennedy School or one of the other McMenamins brewpubs.

IF YOU HAVE 7 DAYS

With a full week, you have time to slow down and take your time in the city. Follow the suggestions outlined above, but spread them out over four days instead of three. Then it's time to get out of town. Whether you drive through the beautiful Columbia Gorge, head to the coast, or explore the Oregon wine country, there's plenty to see within a few hours drive. See Chapter 8, "Side Trips from Portland," for inspiration and help in planning the rest of your week.

20 City Hall. Portland's four-story, granite-faced City Hall, which was completed in 1895, is an example of the Renaissance Revival style popular in the late 19th century. Italian influences can be seen in the porch, the pink scagliola columns, the cornice embellishments, and other details. Much beauty was restored when the building was renovated in the late 1990s. The ornate interior—with intricate scrollwork, decorative tile, sunny atrium, and art exhibits—provides a fine shortcut between Southwest 4th and 5th avenues. ⊠ *1220 S.W. 5th Ave., Downtown 97204* ☎ *503/823–4000* ⊙ *Weekdays 8–5.*

4 First Congregational Church. This Venetian Gothic church, modeled after Boston's Old South Church, was completed in 1895, and you still can hear its original bell, purchased in 1871, ringing from its 175-foot tower. The church provided much of the land on which the Portland Center for the Performing Arts was built. ⊠ *1126 S.W. Park Ave., Downtown 97205* ☎ *503/228–7219* ⊡ *Free* ⊙ *Weekdays 9–2.*

12 Governor Tom McCall Waterfront Park. The park named for a former governor of Oregon revered for his statewide land-use planning initiatives stretches north along the Willamette River for about a mile to Burnside Street. Broad and grassy, it yields a fine ground-level view of downtown Portland's bridges and skyline. The park, on the site of a former expressway, hosts many events, among them the Rose Festival, classical and blues concerts, and the Oregon Brewers Festival. The four-day **Cinco de Mayo Festival** in early May celebrates Portland's sister-city relationship with Guadalajara, Mexico. Next to the Rose Festival, this is one of Portland's biggest get-togethers. Food and arts-and-crafts booths, stages with mariachi bands, and a carnival complete with a Ferris wheel line the riverfront for the event. Bikers and joggers enjoy the area year-round. The arching jets of water at the **Salmon Street Fountain** change configuration every few hours and are a favorite cooling-off spot during the dog days of summer. ⊠ *S.W. Naito Pkwy. (Front Ave.) from south of Hawthorne Bridge to Burnside Bridge, Downtown.*

18 Justice Center. This modern building houses the jail, county courts, and police support offices. Visitors are welcome to browse the **Police Museum** (☎ *503/823–0019* ⊡ *Free* ⊙ *Tues.–Fri. 10–3*) on the 16th floor, which has uniforms, guns, and badges worn by the Portland Police Bureau.

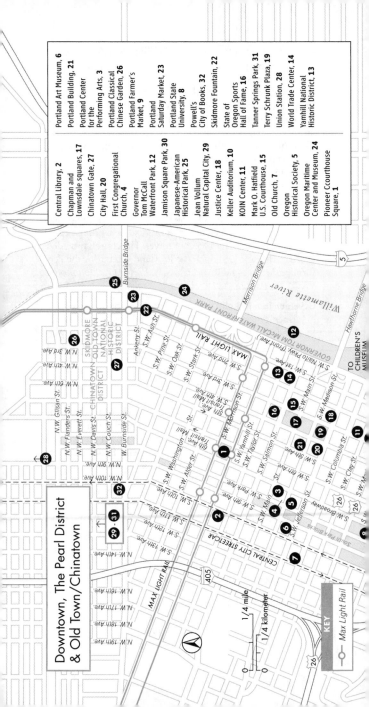

Downtown, The Pearl District & Old Town/Chinatown

Central Library, **2**
Chapman and Lownsdale squares, **17**
Chinatown Gate, **20**
City Hall, **4**
First Congregational Church, **4**
Governor Tom McCall Waterfront Park, **12**
Jamison Square Park, **30**
Japanese-American Historical Park, **25**
Jean Vollum Natural Capital City, **29**
Justice Center, **18**
Keller Auditorium, **10**
KOIN Center, **11**
Mark O. Hatfield U.S. Courthouse, **15**
Old Church, **7**
Oregon Historical Society, **5**
Oregon Maritime Center and Museum, **24**
Pioneer Courthouse Square, **1**

Portland Art Museum, **6**
Portland Building, **21**
Portland Center for the Performing Arts, **3**
Portland Classical Chinese Garden, **26**
Portland Farmer's Market, **9**
Portland Saturday Market, **23**
Portland State University, **8**
Powell's City of Books, **32**
Skidmore Fountain, **22**
State of Oregon Sports Hall of Fame, **16**
Tanner Springs Park, **31**
Terry Schrunk Plaza, **19**
Union Station, **28**
World Trade Center, **14**
Yamhill National Historic District, **13**

KEY

○── Max Light Rail

There's a security check to get in, and photo ID is required. ✉ *1111 S.W. 2nd Ave., Downtown.*

❿ **Keller Auditorium.** Home base for the Portland Opera, the former Civic Auditorium also hosts traveling musicals and other theatrical extravaganzas. The building itself, part of the Portland Center for the Performing Arts, is not particularly distinctive, but the **Ira Keller Fountain,** a series of 18-foot-high stone waterfalls across from the front entrance, is worth a look. ✉ *S.W. 3rd Ave. and Clay St., Downtown 97201* ☎ *503/274–6560* ⊕ *www.pcpa.com.*

⓫ **KOIN Center.** An instant landmark after its completion in 1984, this handsome pink tower with a tapering form and a pyramidal top takes its design cues from early art deco skyscrapers. Made of brick with limestone trim and a blue metal roof, the tower has offices (including those of the CBS-TV affiliate and a radio station) and, on its top floors, expensive condominiums. ✉ *S.W. Columbia St. and S.W. 3rd Ave., Downtown.*

⓯ **Mark O. Hatfield U.S. Courthouse.** Portland's BOORA Architects and the New York architectural firm Kohn Pedersen Fox designed this skyscraper, which was completed in 1997. The sophisticated exterior is clad in Indiana limestone, and the courtroom lobbies have expansive glass walls. Whimsical bronze critters make light of the justice system in a piece entitled "Law of Nature," the centerpiece of a ninth-floor sculpture garden that has grand city views. Visitors must pass through a security screening and show photo ID. ✉ *S.W. 3rd Ave. between Main and Salmon Sts., Downtown 97204* ⊟ *Free* ☉ *Weekdays.*

❼ **Old Church.** This building erected in 1882 is a prime example of Carpenter Gothic architecture. Tall spires and original stained-glass windows enhance its exterior of rough-cut lumber. The acoustically resonant church hosts free classical concerts at noon each Wednesday. If you're lucky you'll get to hear one of the few operating Hook and Hastings tracker pipe organs. ✉ *1422 S.W. 11th Ave., Downtown 97201* ☎ *503/222–2031* ⊕ *www.oldchurch.org* ⊟ *Free* ☉ *Weekdays 11–3.*

❺ **Oregon Historical Society.** Impressive eight-story-high trompe
★ l'oeil murals of Lewis and Clark and the Oregon Trail (the route the two pioneers took from the Midwest to the Oregon Territory) cover two sides of this downtown museum, which follows the state's story from prehistoric times to

the present. A pair of 9,000-year-old sagebrush sandals, a covered wagon, and an early chainsaw are displayed inside "Oregon My Oregon," a permanent exhibit that provides a comprehensive overview of the state's past. Other spaces host large traveling exhibits and changing regional shows. The center's research library is open to the public; its bookstore is a good source for maps and publications on Pacific Northwest history. ✉ *1200 S.W. Park Ave., Downtown 97205* ☎ *503/222–1741* ⊕ *www.ohs.org* ⊠ *$10* ☾ *Mon.– Sat. 10–5, Sun. noon–5.*

❶ Pioneer Courthouse Square. Considered by most to be the living room, public heart, and commercial soul of Downtown Portland, Pioneer Square is not entirely square but rather centered in this amphitheatrical brick piazza. Special seasonal, charitable, and festival-oriented events often take place in this premier people-watching venue. On Sunday **vintage trolley** (☎ *503/323–7363*) cars run from the MAX station here to Lloyd Center, with free service every half hour between noon and 6 PM. Call to check on the current schedule. You can pick up maps and literature about the city and the state here at the **Portland/Oregon Information Center** (☎ *503/275–8355* ⊕ *www.pova.com* ☾ *Mar.– Oct., weekdays 8:30–5:30, Sat. 10–4, Sun. 10–2*). Directly across the street is one of downtown Portland's most familiar landmarks, the classically sedate **Pioneer Courthouse.** Built in 1869, it's the oldest public building in the Pacific Northwest. ✉ *701 S.W. 6th Ave., Downtown.*

❻ Portland Art Museum. The treasures at the Pacific North-
★ west's oldest visual- and media-arts facility span 35 centuries of Asian, European, and American art. A high point is the Center for Native American Art, with regional and contemporary art from more than 200 tribes. **The Jubitz Center for Modern and Contemporary Art** contains six floors devoted entirely to modern art, which rotates and has more than 400 works of art from the Museum's permanent collection. The film center presents the annual Portland International Film Festival in February and the Northwest Film Festival in early November. Also take a moment to linger in the peaceful outdoor sculpture garden. ✉ *1219 S.W. Park Ave., Downtown 97205* ☎ *503/226–2811, 503/221–1156 film schedule* ⊕ *www.pam.org* ⊠ *$10* ☾ *Tues., Wed., and Sat. 10–5, Thurs. and Fri. 10–8, Sun. noon–5.*

㉑ Portland Building. *Portlandia,* the second-largest hammered-copper statue in the world, surpassed only by the Statue of Liberty, kneels on the second-story balcony of one of the first postmodern buildings in the United States. The design of the building itself was considered controversial. As architect Michael Graves's first major design commission, it's buff-color, with brown-and-blue trim and exterior decorative touches. A huge fiberglass mold of Portlandia's face is exhibited in the second-floor Public Art Gallery, which provides a good overview of Portland's 1% for Art Program, and the hundreds of works on display throughout the city. ⊠*1120 S.W. 5th Ave., Downtown* ⊡*Free* ◷ *Weekdays 8–6.*

❸ Portland Center for the Performing Arts. The "old building" and the hub of activity here is the **Arlene Schnitzer Concert Hall,** host to the Oregon Symphony, musical events of many genres, and lectures. Across Main Street, but still part of the center, is the 292-seat **Delores Winningstad Theater,** used for plays and special performances. Its stage design and dimensions are based on those of an Elizabethan-era stage. The 916-seat **Newmark Theater** is also part of the complex. ⊠*S.W. Broadway and S.W. Main St., Downtown 97205* ☎*503/274–6560* ⊕*www.pcpa.com* ◷*Free tours Wed. at 11* AM, *Sat. every ½ hr 11–1, and 1st Thurs. of month at 6* PM.

❾ Portland Farmer's Market. On Saturday from April through mid-December, local farmers, bakers, chefs, and entertainers converge at the South Park Blocks near the PSU campus for Oregon's largest open-air farmer's market. It's a great place to sample the regional bounty of seasonal and organic produce, and to witness an obsession for local food that's revolutionizing Portland's culinary scene. There's also a Wednesday market. ⊠*South Park Blocks at S.W. Park Ave. and Montgomery St., Downtown* ☎*503/241–0032* ⊕*www.portlandfarmersmarket.org* ◷*Apr.–mid-Dec., Sat. 8:30–2; May–Oct., Wed. 10–2.*

❽ Portland State University. The state's only university in a major metropolitan area takes advantage of downtown's South Park Blocks to provide trees and greenery for its 15,000 students. The compact campus, between Market Street and I–405, spreads west from the Park Blocks to 12th Avenue and east to 5th Avenue. Seven schools offer undergraduate, masters, and doctoral degrees. ⊠*Park Ave. and Market St., Downtown 97207* ☎*503/725–3000* ⊕*www.pdx.edu.*

⑯ State of Oregon Sports Hall of Fame. This museum has two multimedia theaters and sports memorabilia associated with prominent Oregonian athletes and organizations such as Heisman Trophy winner Terry Baker, long-distance runner Mary Slaney, the Portland Trail Blazers professional basketball team, and baseball player Mickey Lolich, who pitched for the Detroit Tigers in three World Series. ✉*321 S.W. Salmon St., Downtown 97204* ☎*503/227–7466* ⊕*www. oregonsportshall.org* ⊡*$4* ⊙*Tues.–Sat. noon–5.*

⑲ Terry Schrunk Plaza. A terraced amphitheater of green lawn and brick, shaded by flowering cherry trees, the plaza is a popular lunch spot for the office crowd. Up by Southwest 4th Avenue there's a Suzhou stone, a valuable limestone boulder received as a sister-city gift from Suzhou, China. ✉*Between S.W. 3rd and 4th Aves. and S.W. Madison and Jefferson Sts., Downtown.*

⑭ World Trade Center. The three sleek, handsome World Trade Center buildings, designed by the Portland architectural firm Zimmer Gunsel Frasca, are connected by sky bridges. Banks, retail stores, a deli, coffee shops, and a hair salon occupy the ground floors. ✉*Salmon St. between S.W. 2nd Ave. and S.W. Naito Pkwy., Downtown.*

⑬ Yamhill National Historic District. Trains glide by many examples of 19th-century cast-iron architecture on the MAX line between the Skidmore and Yamhill stations, where the streets are closed to cars. Take a moment at the Yamhill station to glance around at these old buildings, which have intricate rooflines and facades. Nearby, on Southwest Naito Parkway at Taylor Street is **Mill Ends Park,** which sits in the middle of a traffic island. This patch of whimsy, at 24 inches in diameter, has been recognized by *Guinness World Records* as the world's smallest official city park. ✉*Between S.W. Naito Pkwy. and S.W. 3rd Ave. and S.W. Morrison and S.W. Taylor Sts., Downtown.*

THE BERRY BOTANIC GARDEN. There are no berries to pick at this public garden and research center, which contains an extraordinary collection of rare and native plants cultivated by accomplished gardener Rae Selling Berry. Tranquil paths wind through many habitats including native plants, rhododendrons, and unusual alpine flora on a wooded 6¼-acre estate near Lewis & Clark College. Due to a local ordinance the garden can only receive visitors by appointment, so call a day ahead. ✉*15505*

S.W. Summerville Ave., Downtown ☎ *503/636–4112* ⊕ *www.berrybot.org* 🎫 *$5* ⊙ *Daily by appointment only, dawn–dusk.*

PEARL DISTRICT & OLD TOWN/ CHINATOWN

2

The Skidmore Old Town National Historic District, commonly called Old Town/Chinatown, is where Portland was born. The 20-square-block section, bounded by Oak Street to the south and Everett Street to the north, includes buildings of varying ages and architectural designs. Before it was renovated, this was skid row. Vestiges of that condition remain in parts of Chinatown; however, renovations underway along Northwest 3rd and 4th avenues should help make it more inviting. The Portland Classical Chinese Garden is also here. MAX serves the area with a stop at the Old Town/Chinatown station.

Bordering Old Town to the northwest is the Pearl District. Formerly a warehouse area along the railroad yards, the Pearl District is the fastest-growing part of Portland. Midrise residential lofts have sprouted on almost every block, and boutiques, outdoor retailers, galleries, and trendy restaurants border the streets. The Portland streetcar line passes through here on its way from Nob Hill to downtown and Portland State University, with stops at two new, ecologically themed city parks.

Numbers in the text correspond to numbers in the margin and on the Downtown, the Pearl District & Old Town/Chinatown map.

WHAT TO SEE

㉗ Chinatown Gate. Recognizable by its 5 roofs, 64 dragons, and 2 huge lions, the Chinatown Gate is the official entrance to the **Chinatown District.** During the 1890s, Portland had the second-largest Chinese community in the United States. Today's Chinatown is compressed into a handful of blocks with a few restaurants (many prefer Chinese eateries outside the district), shops, and grocery stores. ⊠ *N.W. 4th Ave. and Burnside St., Old Town/Chinatown.*

㉚ Jamison Square Park. This gently terraced park surrounded by tony Pearl District lofts contains a soothing fountain that mimics nature. Rising water gushes over a stack of basalt blocks, gradually fills the open plaza, and then sub-sides. Colorful 30-foot tiki totems by pop artist Kenny Scharf stand along the park's west edge. Take the street-car to Jamison Square. ⊠ *N.W. 10th Ave. and Lovejoy St., Pearl District.*

㉕ Japanese-American Historical Plaza. Take a moment to study the evocative figures cast into the bronze columns at the plaza's entrance; they show Japanese-Americans before, during, and after World War II—living daily life, fighting in battle for the United States, and marching off to intern-ment camps. Simple blocks of granite carved with haiku poems describing the war experience powerfully evoke this dark episode in American history. ⊠ *N.W. Naito Pkwy. and Davis St., in Waterfront Park, Old Town/Chinatown.*

㉙ Jean Vollum Natural Capital Center. Known to most locals as the Ecotrust Building, this building has a handful of organic and environment-friendly businesses and retail including Hot Lips Pizza, World Cup Coffee, and Patagonia (outdoor clothes). Built in 1895 and purchased by Ecotrust in 1998, the building has been significantly adapted to serve as a landmark in sustainable, "green" building practices. Grab a "field guide" in the lobby and take the self-guided tour of the building, which begins with the original "remnant wall" on the west side of the parking lot; proceeds throughout the building; and ends on the "eco-roof," a grassy rooftop with a great view of the Pearl District. ⊠ *721 N.W. 9th Ave., Pearl District 97200* ☎ *503/227–6225* ⊕ *www.ecotrust.org* ⊠ *Free* ☉ *Weekdays 7–6; ground-floor businesses also eve-nings and weekends.*

㉔ Oregon Maritime Center and Museum. Local model makers created most of this museum's models of ships that plied the Columbia River. Contained entirely within the stern-wheeler steamship *Portland,* docked at the foot of South-west Pine Street on the seawall in Tom McCall Waterfront Park, this small museum provides an excellent overview of Oregon's maritime history. Starting spring 2008 visitors will benefit by the museum's extensive remodels. ⊠ *On steam-ship at end of S.W. Pine St., in Waterfront Park, Skidmore District 97204* ☎ *503/224–7724* ⊕ *www.oregonmaritime museum.org* ⊠ *$5* ☉ *Wed.–Sun. 11–4.*

★ Fodor'sChoice **Portland Classical Chinese Garden.** In a twist on ㉖ the Joni Mitchell song, the city of Portland and private donors took down a parking lot and unpaved paradise, as it were, when they created this wonderland neighboring the Pearl District and Old Town/Chinatown. It's the largest Suzhou-style garden outside China, with a large lake, bridged and covered walkways, koi- and water lily–filled ponds, rocks, bamboo, statues, waterfalls, and courtyards. A team of 60 artisans and designers from China literally left no stone unturned—500 tons of stone were brought here from Suzhou—in their efforts to give the windows, roof tiles, gateways, including a "moongate," and other architectural aspects of the Garden some specific meaning or purpose. Also on the premises are a gift shop and a two-story teahouse overlooking the lake and garden. ⊠ *N. W. 3rd Ave. and Everett St., Old Town/Chinatown 97209* ☎ *503/228–8131* ⊕ *www.portlandchinesegarden.org* ☞ *$7* ⊘ *Nov.–Mar., daily 10–5; Apr.–Oct., daily 9–6. Tours daily at noon and 1.*

★ FodorsChoice **Portland Saturday Market.** On weekends from
㉓ March to Christmas, the west side of the Burnside Bridge and the Skidmore Fountain environs has North America's largest open-air handicraft market. If you're looking for a diverse blend of jewelry, yard art, housewares, and decorative goods made from every material under the sun, you'll enjoy perusing an amazing collection of talent in a favorite local pastime. Entertainers and food and produce booths add to the festive feel. ⊠ *Under west end of Burnside Bridge, from S.W. Naito Pkwy. to Ankeny Sq., Skidmore District 97209* ☎ *503/222–6072* ⊕ *www.saturdaymarket. org* ⊘ *Mar.–Dec., Sat. 10–5, Sun. 11–4:30.*

★ FodorsChoice **Powell's City of Books.** The largest independent
㉜ bookstore in the world, with more than 1.5 million new and used books, Powell's is a Portland landmark that can easily consume several hours. It's so big it has its own map, and rooms are color-coded according to the types of books, so you can find your way out again. Be sure to espy the pillar bearing signatures of prominent sci-fi authors who have passed through the store—the scrawls are protected by a jagged length of Plexiglas. At the very least, stop into Powell's for a peek or grab a cup of coffee at the adjoining branch of World Cup Coffee. ⊠ *1005 W. Burnside St., Pearl District 97209* ☎ *503/228–4651* ⊕ *www.powells. com* ⊘ *Daily 9 AM–11 PM.*

㉒ **Skidmore Fountain.** This unusually graceful fountain built in 1888 is the centerpiece of **Ankeny Square**, a plaza around which the Portland Saturday Market takes place. Two nymphs uphold the brimming basin on top; citizens once quenched their thirst from the spouting lions' heads below, and horses drank from the granite troughs at the base of the fountain. ⊠*On MAX line at S.W. Ankeny St. and 1st Ave., Skidmore District.*

㉛ Tanner Springs Park. Tanner Creek, which once flowed through the area, lends its name to Portland's newest park, created in 2005. Today this creek flows underground, and this quiet, manmade wetland and spring with alder groves was built in the middle of the Pearl District as a reminder of Portland's vanishing watersheds. ⊠*N.W. 10th Ave. and Marshall St., Pearl District.*

㉘ Union Station. You can always find your way to Union Station by heading toward the huge neon GO BY TRAIN sign that looms high above the station. The vast lobby area, with high ceilings and marble floors, is worth a brief visit if you hold any nostalgia for the heyday of train travel in the United States. ⊠*800 N.W. 6th Ave., Old Town/Chinatown 97209.*

NOB HILL & VICINITY

The showiest example of Portland's urban chic is Northwest 23rd Avenue—sometimes referred to with varying degrees of affection as "trendy-third"—a 20-block thoroughfare that cuts north–south through the neighborhood known as Nob Hill. Fashionable since the 1880s and still filled with Victorian residential architecture, the neighborhood is a mixed-use cornucopia of old Portland charm and new Portland hip. With its cafés, restaurants, galleries, and boutiques, it's a delightful place to stroll, shop, and people-watch. More restaurants, shops, and nightspots can be found on Northwest 21st Avenue, a few blocks away. The Portland Streetcar runs from Legacy Good Samaritan Hospital in Nob Hill, through the Pearl District on 10th and 11th avenues, connects with MAX light rail near Pioneer Courthouse Square downtown, and then continues on to Portland State University and River Place on the Willamette River.

Numbers in the text correspond to numbers in the margin and on the Nob Hill & Vicinity map.

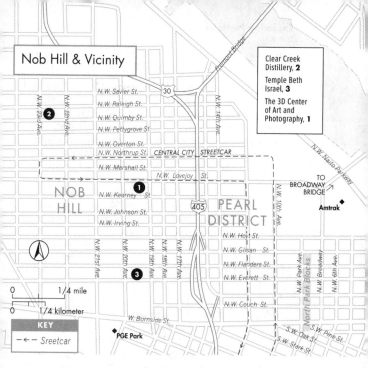

Nob Hill & Vicinity

Clear Creek
Distillery, **2**

Temple Beth
Israel, **3**

The 3D Center
of Art and
Photography, **1**

N.W. Savier St.
N.W. Raleigh St.
N.W. Quimby St.
N.W. Pettygrove St.
N.W. Overton St.
N.W. Northrup St.   CENTRAL CITY STREETCAR
N.W. Marshall St.
N.W. Lovejoy   St.

NOB
HILL
N.W. Kearney   St.

N.W. Johnson St.

N.W. Irving St.

PEARL
DISTRICT
N.W. Hoyt St.
N.W. Glisan   St.
N.W. Flanders St.
N.W. Everett   St.
N.W. Couch St.

TO
BROADWAY
BRIDGE

Amtrak

North Park Blocks

W. Burnside St.

PGE Park

S.W. Oak St.
S.W. Pine St.
S.W. Stark St.

0   1/4 mile
0   1/4 kilometer

KEY
← – Sreetcar

WHAT TO SEE

❷ Clear Creek Distillery. The distillery keeps such a low profile
that it's practically invisible. But ring the bell and someone
will unlock the wrought-iron gate and let you into a dim,
quiet tasting room where you can sample Clear Creek's
world-famous Oregon apple and pear brandies and grap-
pas. ✉ *1430 N.W. 23rd Ave., near Quimby St., Nob Hill
97210* ☎ *503/248–9470* ⊕ *www.clearcreekdistillery.com*
☽ *Weekdays 9–5, Sat. noon–5.*

NEED A BREAK? **Vivace Coffee** (✉ *1400 N.W. 23rd Ave.* ☎ *503/228–
3667*) is inside Pettygrove House, a restored Victorian gin-
gerbread house built in 1892 that was once home to Francis
Pettygrove, the man who named Portland as a prize in a coin-
toss. Today it's a creperie and coffeehouse with colorful walls
and comfortable chairs.

❸ Temple Beth Israel. The imposing sandstone, brick, and stone
structure with a massive domed roof and Byzantine styling

was completed in 1928 and still serves a congregation first organized in 1858. ✉ *1972 N.W. Flanders St., Nob Hill.*

❶ **The 3D Center of Art and Photography.** Half gallery and half museum, this center devoted to three-dimensional imagery exhibits photographs best viewed through red-and-blue glasses, in addition to artifacts on the history of stereoscopic art. A collection of rare Nazi-era stereo-cards is displayed next to Viewmasters and 3-D snapshot cameras. A three-dimensional rendering of famous classical paintings is one of many changing 3-D slide shows you might see in the backroom Stereo Theatre. ✉ *1928 N.W. Lovejoy St., Nob Hill 97209* ☎ *503/227–6667* ⊕ *www.3dcenter.us* ▣ *$4* ☉ *Thurs.–Sat. 11–5, Sun. 1–5; also 1st Thurs. of month* 6 PM–9 PM.

WASHINGTON PARK & FOREST PARK

The best way to get to Washington Park is via MAX light rail, which travels through a tunnel deep beneath the city's West Hills. Be sure to check out the Washington Park station, the deepest (260 feet) transit station in North America. Graphics on the walls depict life in the Portland area during the past 16.5 million years. There's also a core sample of the bedrock taken from the mountain displayed along the walls. Elevators to the surface put visitors in the parking lot for the Oregon Zoo, the World Forestry Center Discovery Museum, and the Children's Museum.

Numbers in the text correspond to numbers in the margin and on the Washington Park & Forest Park map.

WHAT TO SEE

❸ **Children's Museum.** Colorful sights and sounds offer a feast of sensations for kids of all ages where hands-on play is the order of the day. Visit nationally touring exhibits, catch a storytime, a sing-along, or a puppet show in the Play It Again theater, create sculptures in the clay studio, splash hands in the water works display, or make a creation from junk in the Garage. To reach the zoo, take the "Zoo" exit off U.S. 26. ✉ *4015 S.W. Canyon Rd., Washington Park 97221* ☎ *503/223–6500* ▣ *$6* ☉ *Tues.–Sat. 9–5, Sun. 11–5.*

❾ Forest Park. The nation's largest (5,000 acres) urban wilderness, this city-owned park, with more than 50 species of birds and mammals, has more than 70 mi of trails. Running the length of the park is the 24½-mi Wildwood Trail, which extends into Washington Park. The 11-mi Leif Erikson Drive, which picks up from the end of Northwest Thurman Street, is a popular place to jog or ride a mountain bike. The **Portland Audubon Society** (✉*5151 N.W. Cornell Rd.* ☏*503/292–9453*) supplies free maps and sponsors a bevy of bird-related activities including guided bird-watching events. There's a hospital for injured and orphaned birds as well as a gift shop stocked with books and feeders. ✉*Past Nob Hill in Northwest district. Take N.W. Lovejoy St. west to where it becomes Cornell Rd. and follow to park* ☏*503/823–7529* 🎫*Free* ⊙*Daily dawn–dusk.*

❹ Hoyt Arboretum. Ten miles of trails wind through the arboretum, which has more than 1,000 species of plants and one of the nation's largest collections of coniferous trees; pick up trail maps at the visitor center. Also here are the Winter Garden and a memorial to veterans of the Vietnam War. ✉*4000 S.W. Fairview Blvd., Washington Park 97221* ☏*503/228–8733* ⊕*www.hoytarboretum.org* 🎫*Free* ⊙*Arboretum daily dawn–dusk, visitor center daily 9–4.*

❺ International Rose Test Garden. Despite the name, these
★ grounds are not an experimental greenhouse laboratory but three terraced gardens, set on 4 acres, where 10,000 bushes and 400 varieties of roses grow. The flowers, many of them new varieties, are at their peak in June, July, September, and October. From the gardens, you can see highly photogenic views of the downtown skyline and, on fine days, the Fuji-shaped slopes of Mt. Hood, 50 mi to the east. Summer concerts take place in the garden's amphitheater. Take MAX light rail to Washington Park station and transfer to Bus No. 63. ✉*400 S.W. Kingston Ave., Washington Park 97221* ☏*503/823–3636* ⊕*www.portlandonline.com* 🎫*Free* ⊙*Daily dawn–dusk.*

★ Fodor'sChoice **Japanese Garden.** The most authentic Japanese
❻ garden outside Japan is nestled among 5½ acres of Washington Park above the International Rose Test Garden. This serene spot, designed by a Japanese landscape master represents five separate garden styles: Strolling Pond Garden, Tea Garden, Natural Garden, Sand and Stone Garden, and Flat Garden. The Tea House was built in Japan and reconstructed here. The west side of the Pavilion has a majestic

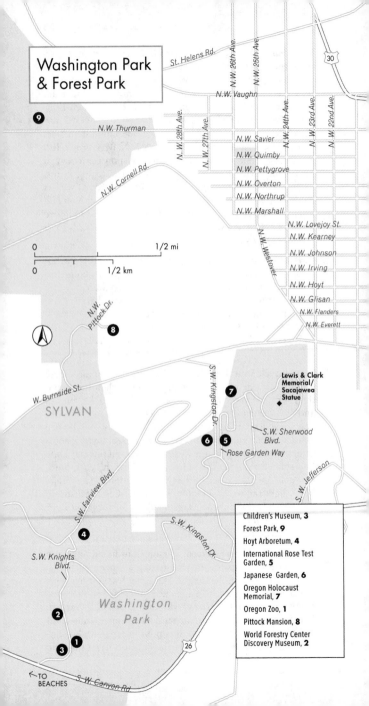

Washington Park & Forest Park

❾

St. Helens Rd.

N.W. 26th Ave.
N.W. 25th Ave.

30

N.W. Vaughn

N.W. 24th Ave.
N.W. 23rd Ave.
N.W. 22nd Ave.

N.W. Thurman

N.W. 28th Ave.
N.W. 27th Ave.

N.W. Savier
N.W. Quimby
N.W. Pettygrove
N.W. Overton
N.W. Northrup
N.W. Marshall

N.W. Cornell Rd.

N.W. Lovejoy St.
N.W. Kearney
N.W. Johnson
N.W. Irving
N.W. Hoyt
N.W. Glisan
N.W. Flanders
N.W. Everett

N.W. Westover

0   1/2 mi
0   1/2 km

N.W. Pittock Dr.

❽

Lewis & Clark
Memorial/
Sacajawea
Statue ◆

W. Burnside St.

SYLVAN

S.W. Kingston Dr.

❼

S.W. Sherwood
Blvd.

❻ ❺

Rose Garden Way

S.W. Fairview Blvd.

S.W. Kingston Dr.

S.W. Jefferson

❹

S.W. Knights
Blvd.

Washington
Park

❷

❸ ❶

26

Children's Museum, **3**
Forest Park, **9**
Hoyt Arboretum, **4**
International Rose Test
Garden, **5**
Japanese Garden, **6**
Oregon Holocaust
Memorial, **7**
Oregon Zoo, **1**
Pittock Mansion, **8**
World Forestry Center
Discovery Museum, **2**

← TO
BEACHES

S.W. Canyon Rd.

view of Portland and Mt. Hood. Take MAX light rail to Washington Park station and transfer to Bus No. 63. ⊠*611 S.W. Kingston Ave., Washington Park 97221* ☎*503/223– 1321* ⊕*www.japanesegarden.com* ☎*$6.75* ☉*Oct.–Mar., Mon. noon–4, Tues.–Sun. 10–4; Apr.–Sept., Mon. noon–7, Tues.–Sun. 10–7.*

❼ **Oregon Holocaust Memorial.** This memorial to those who perished during the Holocaust bears the names of surviving families who live in Oregon and Southwest Washington. A bronzed baby shoe, a doll, broken spectacles, and other strewn possessions await notice on the cobbled courtyard. Soil and ash from six Nazi concentration camps is interred beneath the black granite wall. Take MAX light rail to Washington Park station, and transfer to Bus No. 63. ⊠*S.W. Wright Ave. and Park Pl., Washington Park 97221* ☎*503/352–2930* ⊕*http://ohrc.pacificu.edu* ☎*Free* ☉*Daily dawn–dusk.*

❶ **Oregon Zoo.** This beautiful animal park in the West Hills is
☺ famous for its Asian elephants. Major exhibits include an
★ African section with rhinos, hippos, zebras, and giraffes. Steller Cove, a state-of-the-art aquatic exhibit, has two Steller sea lions and a family of sea otters. Other exhibits include polar bears, chimpanzees, an Alaska Tundra exhibit with wolves and grizzly bears, a penguinarium, and habitats for beavers, otters, and reptiles native to the west side of the Cascade Range. In summer a 4-mi round-trip narrow-gauge train operates from the zoo, chugging through the woods to a station near the International Rose Test Garden and the Japanese Garden. Take the MAX light rail to the Washington Park station. ⊠*4001 S.W. Canyon Rd., Washington Park 97221* ☎*503/226–1561* ⊕*www.oregonzoo. org* ☎*$9.75, $2 2nd Tues. of month* ☉*Mid-Apr.–mid-Sept., daily 9–6; mid-Sept.–mid Apr., daily 9–4.*

❽ **Pittock Mansion.** Henry Pittock, the founder and publisher
★ of the *Oregonian* newspaper, built this 22-room, castlelike mansion, which combines French Renaissance and Victorian styles. The opulent manor, built in 1914, is filled with art and antiques. The 46-acre grounds, north of Washington Park and 1,000 feet above the city, have superb views of the skyline, rivers, and the Cascade Range. There's a teahouse and a small hiking trail. ⊠*3229 N.W. Pittock Dr., from W. Burnside St. heading west, turn right on N.W. Barnes Rd. and follow signs, North of Washington Park 97210* ☎*503/823–3623* ⊕*www.pittockmansion.com*

$7 ☉ *June–Aug., daily 11–4; Sept.–Dec. and Feb.–May, daily noon–4.*

❷ **World Forestry Discovery Center Museum.** Visitors will find
☾ interactive and multimedia exhibits that teach forest sustainability. A white-water raft ride, smoke-jumper training simulator, and Timberjack tree harvester all provide different perspectives on Pacific Northwest forests. On the second floor the forests of the world are explored in various travel settings. A canopy lift ride hoists visitors to the 50-foot ceiling to look at a Douglas fir. A $1 parking fee is collected upon entry. Or take MAX light rail to the Washington Park station. ✉ *4033 S.W. Canyon Rd., Washington Park 97221* ☎ *503/228–1367* ⊕ *www.worldforestry. org* $7 ☉ *Daily 10–5.*

EAST OF THE WILLAMETTE RIVER

Portland is known as the City of Roses, but the 10 distinctive bridges spanning the Willamette River have also earned it the name Bridgetown. The older drawbridges, near downtown, open several times a day to allow passage of large cargo ships and freighters. You can easily spend a couple of days exploring the attractions and areas on the east side of the river.

Numbers in the text correspond to numbers in the margin and on the East of the Willamette River map.

WHAT TO SEE

❻ **Crystal Springs Rhododendron Garden.** For much of the year this 7-acre retreat near Reed College is used by bird-watchers and those who want a restful stroll. But starting in April, thousands of rhododendron bushes and azaleas burst into flower. The peak blooming season for these woody shrubs is May; by late June the show is over. ✉ *S.E. 28th Ave., west side, 1 block north of Woodstock Blvd., Sellwood/ Woodstock area* ☎ *503/771–8386* ⊕ *www.portlandonline. com* $3 Mar.–Labor Day, Thurs.–Mon. 10–6; otherwise free ☉ *Daily dawn–dusk.*

NEED A BREAK? At the **Bagdad Theatre and Pub** (✉ *3702 S.E. Hawthorne Blvd., Hawthorne District* ☎ *503/236–9234*) you can buy a pint of beer, a slice of pizza, and watch a movie.

3 Hawthorne District. This neighborhood stretching from the foot of Mt. Tabor to 30th Avenue tends to attract a more college-age, "bohemian," crowd than downtown or Nob Hill. With many bookstores, coffeehouses, taverns, restaurants, antiques stores, used-CD shops, and boutiques filling the streetfront, it's easy to spend a few hours wandering the street. ⊠*S.E. Hawthorne Blvd. between 30th and 42nd Aves., Hawthorne District 97214.*

5 Laurelhurst Park. Manicured lawns, stately trees, and a wildfowl pond make this 25-acre southeast Portland park a favorite urban hangout. **Laurelhurst,** one of the city's most beautiful neighborhoods, surrounds the park. ⊠*S.E. 39th Ave. between S.E. Ankeny and Oak Sts., Laurelhurst* ⊕*www.portlandparks.org* ☉*Daily dawn–dusk.*

4 Mt. Tabor Park. Dirt trails and asphalt roads wind through forested hillsides and past good picnic areas to the top of Mt. Tabor, an extinct volcano with a panoramic view of Portland's West Hills and Cascade mountains. This butte and the conical hills east of the park are evidence of the gigantic eruptions that formed the Cascade Range millions of years ago. One of the best places in the city to watch the sunset, the park is also a popular place to bike, hike, picnic, or just throw a Frisbee. ⊠*S.E. 60th Ave. and Salmon St., Just east of Hawthorne District* ⊕*www.portlandonline. com* ☉*Daily dawn–dusk.*

THE GROTTO. Owned by the Catholic Church, the National Sanctuary of Our Sorrowful Mother, as it's officially known, displays more than 100 statues and shrines in 62 acres of woods. The grotto was carved into the base of a 110-foot cliff and has a replica of Michelangelo's *Pietà*. The real treat is found after ascending the cliff face via elevator, as you enter a wonderland of gardens, sculptures, and shrines, and a glass-walled cathedral with an awe-inspiring view of the Columbia River and the Cascades. There's a dazzling Festival of Lights at Christmastime (late November and December), with 250,000 lights, and holiday concerts in the 600-seat chapel. Sunday masses are held here, too. ⊠*Sandy Blvd. at N.E. 85th Ave., Near Airport 97294* ☎*503/254–7371* ⊕*www.thegrotto.org* ☎*Plaza level free; elevator to upper level $3* ☉*Mid-May–Labor Day, daily 9–7:30; Labor Day–late Nov. and Feb.–mid-May, daily 9–6:30; late Nov.–Jan., daily 9–4.*

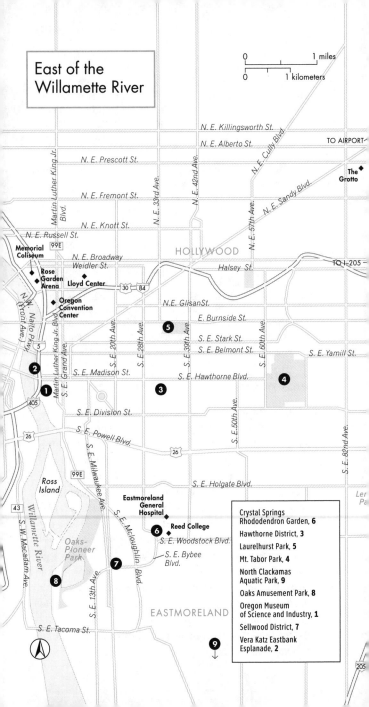

East of the Willamette River

0 ————————— 1 miles
0 ————————— 1 kilometers

N. E. Killingsworth St.
N. E. Alberto St.
N.E. Cully Blvd.
TO AIRPORT

N. E. Prescott St.

The Grotto

N. E. Fremont St.

N. E. Sandy Blvd.

N. E. Knott St.

N. E. Russell St.

Memorial Coliseum 99E

N. E. Broadway
Weidler St.

HOLLYWOOD

Rose Garden Arena

Lloyd Center
30 84

Halsey St.

TO I-205

Oregon Convention Center

N.E. Glisan St.

N.W. Naito Pkwy. (Front Ave.)

5

E. Burnside St.

Martin Luther King Jr. Blvd.

S. E. Stark St.
S. E. Belmont St.

S. E. Yamill St.

5

S. E. 20th Ave.

S. E. 28th Ave.

S. E. 39th Ave.

S. E. 60th Ave.

2

S. E. Grand Ave.

S. E. Madison St.

3

4

S. E. Hawthorne Blvd.

1

405

S. E. Division St.

S. E. 50th Ave.

S. E. 82nd Ave.

26

S. E. Powell Blvd.

26

Ross Island

99E

S. E. Holgate Blvd.

43

S. E. Milwaukee Ave.

Eastmoreland General Hospital

6

Reed College

Willamette River

Oaks-Pioneer Park

S. E. McLoughlin Blvd.

S. E. Woodstock Blvd.

S. E. Bybee Blvd.

Ler Pa

S. W. Macadam Ave.

8

7

S. E. 13th Ave.

EASTMORELAND

S. E. Tacoma St.

9

Crystal Springs
Rhododendron Garden, **6**

Hawthorne District, **3**

Laurelhurst Park, **5**

Mt. Tabor Park, **4**

North Clackamas
Aquatic Park, **9**

Oaks Amusement Park, **8**

Oregon Museum
of Science and Industry, **1**

Sellwood District, **7**

Vera Katz Eastbank
Esplanade, **2**

205

N. E. 33rd Ave.

N. E. 42nd Ave.

N. E. 57th Ave.

2

❾ North Clackamas Aquatic Park. If you're visiting Portland with kids any time of the year and are looking for a great way to cool off—especially on one of Portland's hot July or August days—check out this 45,000-square-foot, all-indoor attraction, whose main pool has 4-foot waves and three super slides. There's also a 25-yard-long lap pool, a wading pool, an adults-only hot whirlpool, and a café. Children under age 8 must be accompanied by someone 13 or older. ✉ *7300 S.E. Harmony Rd., Milwaukie 97222* ☎ *503/557–7873* ⊕ *www.clackamas.us/ncprd/aquatic* ✍ *$9.99* ☉ *Open swim mid-June–Labor Day, weekdays noon–4 and 7–9, weekends 11–3 and 4–8; Labor Day–mid-June, Sat. noon–7, Sun. noon–5.*

North Mississippi Street. Four blocks of old storefronts reinvented as eco-cafés, collectives, shops, and music venues along this north Portland street showcase the indie spirit of the city's do-it-yourselfers and creative types. Bioswale planter boxes, found-object fences, and café tables built from old doors are some of the innovations you'll see around this hip new district. At the hub of it all is the ReBuilding Center, an outlet for recycled building supplies that has cob (clay-and-straw) trees and benches built into the facade. Take MAX light rail to the Albina/Mississippi station. ✉ *Between N. Fremont and Shaver Sts., off N. Interstate Ave.*

Northeast Alberta Street. Quirky handicrafts by local artists are for sale inside the galleries, studios, coffeehouses, restaurants, and boutiques lining this street in the northeast Portland neighborhood. It's a fascinating place to witness the intersection of cultures and lifestyles in a growing city. Shops unveil new exhibits during an evening event called the Last Thursday Art Walk. The Alberta Street Fair in September showcases the area with arts-and-crafts displays and street performances. ✉ *Between Martin Luther King Jr. Blvd. and 30th Ave., Alberta District.*

❽ Oaks Amusement Park. There's a small-town charm to this park, with bumper cars, thrill rides and roller-skating year-round. A 360-degree loop roller coaster and other high-velocity, gravity-defying contraptions border the midway, along with a carousel and Ferris wheel. The skating rink, built in 1905, is the oldest continuously operating one in the United States, and features a working Wurlitzer organ. There are outdoor concerts in summer. ✉ *S.E. Spokane St. east of Willamette River; from S.E. Tacoma St. on* *east side of Sellwood Bridge, take S.E. 6th Ave. north and Spokane west, Sellwood 97202* ☎*503/233–5777* ⊕*www. oakspark.com* ✄*Park free, multiride bracelets $11.25– 14, individual-ride tickets $2.25* ⊙*Mid-June–Labor Day, Tues.–Thurs. noon–9, Fri. and Sat. noon–10, Sun. noon–7; late-Apr.–mid-June and Labor Day–Oct., weekends noon– 7; late-Mar.–late-Apr., weekends noon–5.*

❶ **Oregon Museum of Science and Industry** *(OMSI).* Hundreds
ᵔ of hands-on exhibits draw families to this interactive sci-
★ ence museum, which also has an Omnimax theater and the Northwest's largest planetarium. The many permanent and touring exhibits are loaded with enough hands-on play for kids to fill a whole day exploring robotics, ecology, rockets, computers, animation, and outer space. Moored in the Willamette as part of the museum is a 240-foot submarine, the USS *Blueback,* which can be toured for an extra charge. ✉*1945 S.E. Water Ave., south of Morrison Bridge, Under Hawthorne Bridge 97214* ☎*503/797–6674 or 800/955– 6674* ⊕*www.omsi.edu* ✄*Full package $19, museum $9, planetarium $5.50, Omnimax $8.50, submarine $3.50* ⊙*Mid-June–Labor Day, daily 9:30–7; Labor Day–mid-June, daily 9:30–5.*

❼ **Sellwood District.** The browseable neighborhood that begins east of the Sellwood Bridge was once a separate town. Annexed by Portland in the 1890s, it retains a modest charm. On weekends the antiques stores along 13th Avenue do a brisk business. Each store is identified by a plaque that tells the date of construction and the original purpose of the building. More antiques stores, specialty shops, and restaurants are near the intersection of Milwaukie and Bybee. ✉*S.E. 13th Ave. between Malden and Clatsop Sts., Sellwood.*

❷ **Vera Katz Eastbank Esplanade.** A stroll along this 1½-mi
★ pedestrian and cycling path across from downtown is one of the best ways to experience the Willamette River and Portland's bridges close-up. Built in 2001 the esplanade runs along the east bank of the Willamette River between the Hawthorne and Steele bridges, and features a 1,200-foot walkway that floats atop the river, a boat dock, and public art. Pedestrian crossings on both bridges link the esplanade to Waterfront Park, making a 3-mi loop. Take MAX light rail to the Rose Quarter station. ✉*Parking at east end of Hawthorne Bridge, between Madison and Salmon Sts.*

Where to Eat

WORD OF MOUTH

"Portland is a hot restaurant town right now, with myriad cuisines to choose from. There are a plethora of options in terms of budget; from street carts to 4[-star] dining, and everything in between. I am the happy hour queen and like to sample the more expensive restaurants this way. Portland has tons of great happy hours, if that's your thing.
                                    —vlcgoddess

Updated
by Janna
Mock-
Lopez

THESE DAYS, PORTLAND IS TO DINING what Angelina Jolie is to the movies. Rising star chefs are flocking to this playground of sustainability and creativity: a major portion of Portland's hottest new restaurants change menus weekly—sometimes even daily—depending upon the ingredients they have delivered to their door that morning from local farms. A combination of fertile soils, temperate weather, nearby waters, and an urban growth boundary means that a bountiful harvest (of anything from lettuces to hazelnuts, mushrooms to salmon) is within any Portland chef's reach.

And these chefs are not shy about putting new twists on old favorites. Restaurants like LePigeon (yes, they serve pigeon), Beast, Rocket, Hoyt 23, Roux, Fife, and Paley's Place have all taken culinary risks to delight diners by presenting an exciting blend of menu offerings based on sustainable ingredients. Because there's such a nearly-fanatical willingness for chefs to explore their creative boundaries, one's palette hardly knows what to expect from restaurant to restaurant, season to season.

The other benefit of this culinary craze is that menus extend across nations and continents. First-time visitors to Portland always seem to be impressed by the diversity of its restaurants. Lovers of ethnic foods have their pick of Chinese, French, Indian, Peruvian, Italian, Japanese, Polish, Middle Eastern, Tex-Mex, Thai, and Vietnamese specialties. Of course, Northwest cuisine is prevalent, taking advantage of the availability of fresh salmon, halibut, crab, oysters, and mussels due to the proximity of rivers and the Pacific Ocean.

Most of the city's trendier restaurants and reliable classics are concentrated in Nob Hill, the Pearl District, and downtown. But an incredible smattering of cuisines can be found on the east side of town as well, near Fremont, Hawthorne Boulevard, Sandy Boulevard, Alberta Street, and tucked away in myriad neighborhoods in between. True food enthusiasts will also be well rewarded by doing a little research to find some of the out-of-the-way places.

HOURS, PRICES & DRESS

Compared to other major cities, Portland restaurants may not be open quite as late, and it's unusual to see many diners after 11 PM even on weekends; there are a handful of restaurants and popular bars that do serve late if you happen to be out on the town.

One aspect to Portland's dining scene that many locals and out-of-towners find appealing is how reasonably priced top-notch restaurants are; well. Particularly welcome in Portland is happy hour, when both inventive cocktails as well as small plates of food can be a good value; you can easily put together a fine early dinner by grazing from the happy hour menu at one of the city's fine restaurants that also happens to have a popular bar scene.

Portland's come-as-you-are flair will either be refreshing or annoying to those who prefer (or abhor) how casually diners show up at even the higher-end establishments. Jeans are acceptable almost everywhere.

3

WHAT IT COSTS

RESTAURANTS

¢	$	$$	$$$	$$$$
under $10	$10–$15	$16–$20	$21–$30	over $30

Restaurant prices are per person for a main course at dinner and do not include any service charges or taxes.

DOWNTOWN

Finding a fabulous place to dine downtown is as easy and closing your eyes and pointing on the map. From casual to classy, daring to distinguished, there are never-ending choices to pick from. One thing visitors appreciate about the downtown dining scene at lunch is the plethora of food carts that stripe the streets. Smells of Greek, Russian, Japanese, Lebanese, and Mexican food permeate the air as the noon hour approaches. Lines of people, mostly downtown workers, hover around makeshift kitchen trailers waiting to get their mid-day fill of inexpensive, authentic selection of food. Be sure to stop by one of these food carts and try what's being offered.

AMERICAN

$$–$$$$ ✕**Portland City Grill.** On the 30th floor of the US Bank Tower, Portland City Grill has one of the best views in town. You can sit at a windowside table and enjoy the Portland sky-line while eating fine steak and seafood with an Asian flair; it's no wonder that this restaurant is a favorite hot spot for the city's jet set. The adjoining bar and lounge has comfort-

PORTLAND TOP 5 DINING TIPS

■ Savor the memorable Pad Thai and garlic basil chicken—or any number of cooked-to-order Thai dishes—at Lemongrass.

■ Sophisticated service, a glamorous setting, and an enticing menu make a visit to Gracie's, inside the movie startlet–themed Hotel DeLuxe, a must-do in Portland.

■ Dimly lit dining rooms and impeccable service go surprisingly well with mouth-watering steak, roasted sweet corn, and Mississippi mud cake at El Gaucho.

■ Enjoy one of the best skyline views in the city from the 30th-floor windows of Portland City Grill, over Asian-influenced dishes or a happy hour cocktail.

■ Take advantage of the vastest, freshest selection of Pacific Northwest catches of the day at McCormick & Schmick's, along with wines from regional California and Oregon vineyards.

able arm chairs all along its windowed walls, which are the first to get snatched up during the extremely popular happy hour each day. ⊠*111 S.W. 5th Ave., Downtown 97204* ☎*503/450–0030* ⊟*AE, D, MC, V* ⊘*No lunch weekends.*

★ FodorsChoice ✕**Gracie's.** Stepping into this dining room is
$$$ like stepping into a swanky, prestigious 1940s supper club. Dazzling chandeliers, beautifully rich floor-to-ceiling draperies, velvet couches, and marble-topped tables exude class. Dishes like grilled swordfish and stuffed pork loin are perfectly seasoned and served with seasonal vegetables. On weekends, there's a brunch menu that includes fresh fruit, waffles, omelets, and more. ⊠*Hotel DeLuxe, 729 S.W. 15th Ave., Downtown 97205* ☎*503/222–2171* ⊟*AE, D, MC, V.*

$$$ ✕**Veritable Quandary.** Brunch, lunch, and dinner, oh my! There are so many delicious options at this long-standing local favorite: the tantalizing French toast and revered chocolate soufflé pair well with the equally delicious beautiful outdoor patio, where you're surrounded by roses, fuschias, and hanging begonia baskets. The menu emphasizes fresh, flavorful produce and seafood; prices are reasonable for the quality and the wine list is one of the best in town. ⊠*1220 S.W. 1st Ave., Downtown 97201* ☎*503/227–7342* ⊟*AE, D, DC, MC, V.*

★ Fodor'sChoice ×**Higgins.** Chef Greg Higgins, former execu-
$$–$$$ tive chef at the Heathman Hotel, focuses on ingredients
from the Pacific Northwest and on organically grown herbs
and produce while incorporating traditional French cooking styles and other international influences into his menu.
Start with a salad of warm beets, asparagus, and artichokes
or the country-style terrine of venison, chicken, and pork
with dried sour cherries and a roasted-garlic mustard.
Main courses change seasonally and might include dishes
made with Alaskan spot prawns, halibut, duck, or pork
loin. Vegetarian items are available. A bistro menu is available in the adjoining bar, where comfortable leather booths
and tables provide an alternative to the main dining room.
⊠*1239 S.W. Broadway, Downtown 97205* ☎*503/222–
9070* ⊟*AE, D, DC, MC, V* ⊘*No lunch weekends.*

$–$$$ ×**Jake's Grill.** Not to be confused with the Jake's of seafood
fame, this eatery in the Governor Hotel has more turf than
surf. Steaks and the Sunday brunch are popular draws. Pri-
vate booths with green velvet curtains make for a cozy,
intimate dinner. The bar is famous for its Bloody Marys.
⊠*611 S.W. 10th Ave., Downtown 97205* ☎*503/220–1850*
⊟*AE, D, DC, MC, V.*

$–$$$ ×**Red Star Tavern & Roast House.** Cooked in a wood-burning
oven, smoker, rotisserie, or grill, the cuisine at Red Star can
best be described as American comfort food inspired by
the bounty of the Pacific Northwest. Spit-roasted chicken,
maple-fired baby-back ribs with a brown-ale glaze, charred
salmon, and crayfish étouffée are some of the better entrées.
The wine list includes regional and international vintages,
and 10 microbrews are on tap. The spacious restaurant,
in the 5th Avenue Suites Hotel, has tufted leather booths,
murals, and copper accents. ⊠*503 S.W. Alder St., Downtown 97204* ☎*503/222–0005* ⊟*AE, D, DC, MC, V.*

¢–$$ ×**Mother's Bistro.** The menu is loaded with home-style
favorites—macaroni and cheese with extra ingredients of
the day, soups, pierogi, matzo ball soup, pot roast, and
meat loaf. For vegetarians there's a couscous stew. The high
ceilings in the well-lit dining room lend an air of spacious-
ness, but the tables are a bit close together. The bar is open
late Friday and Saturday. ⊠*409 S.W. 2nd Ave., Downtown
97204* ☎*503/464–1122* ⊟*AE, D, MC, V* ⊘*Closed Mon.
No dinner Sun.*

¢–$$ ×**Rock Bottom Brewing Co.** Some locals might balk at the
idea of a corporate brewpub in a city that prides itself on

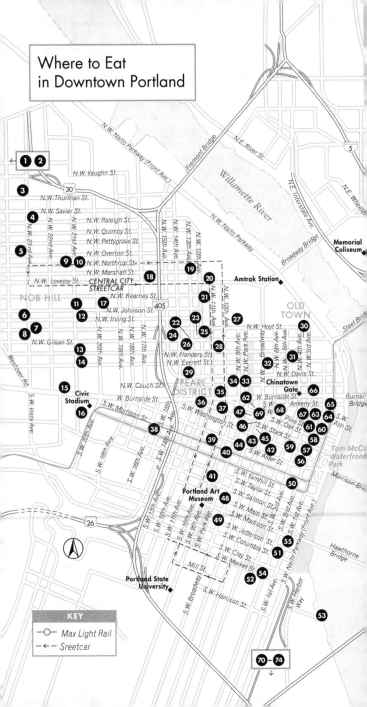

Where to Eat
in Downtown Portland

N.W. Nalto Parkway (Front Ave.)

Fremont Bridge

Willamette River

N.E. River St.

←

1 2

N.W. Vaughn St.

3

30

N.W. Thurman St.

N.W. Savier St.

4

N.W. Raleigh St.

N.W. Quimby St.

N.W. Pettygrove St.

N.W. Overton St.

5

9 10

N.W. Northrup St.

N.W. Marshall St.

19

N.W. Lovejoy St.

CENTRAL CITY
STREETCAR

18

Amtrak Station

20

N.E. Interstate Ave.

Broadway Bridge

Memorial
Coliseum

NOB HILL

N.W. Kearney St.

21

N.W. Johnson St.

11

17

405

OLD
TOWN

Steel Bri

6

N.W. Irving St.

12

N.W. Hoyt St.

27

30

7

8

N.W. Glisan St.

13

14

22 23

24

25

26

28

N.W. Broadway

32

31

N.W. Davis St.

Chinatown
Gate

66

N.W. Couch St.

29

PEARL
DISTRICT

35

34 33

62

W. Burnside St.

68

67 63

65

Burnsi
Bridg

15

Civic
Stadium

16

W. Burnside St.

36

37

47

69

S.W.

Ankeny St.

64

Westover Rd.

S.W. Morrison St.

S.W. Vista Ave.

38

39

46

45

Pine St.

S.W. Oak St.

61 60

58

57

Tom McCa
Waterfront
Park

40

43 44

42

S.W. Alder St.

59

56

41

S.W. Yamhill St.

S.W. Taylor St.

50

Morrison Brid

48

Portland Art
Museum

S.W. Salmon St.

S.W. Main St.

49

S.W. Madison St.

S.W. Jefferson St.

55

S.W. Columbia St.

51

Hawthorne
Bridge

S.W. Clay St.

Portland State
University

Mill St.

S.W. Market St.

54

52

S.W. Harrison St.

26

S.W. Harbor
Way

53

KEY

○— Max Light Rail

-←- Sreetcar

70 - 74

↓

N.E. Siskiyou

N.E. Knott St.
N.E. Russell St.

N.E. Martin Luther King Jr. Blvd.

N.E. Thompson St

N.E. Hancock St

N.E. Schuyler St.
N.E. 2nd Ave.
N.E. Broadway
N.E. Weidler St.
N.E. Halsey St.

LLOYD
DISTRICT

Lloyd Center

N.E. Wasco St.
N.E. Multnomah St.

Rose
Garden
Arena

N.E. 1st Ave.
N.E. Holladay St.
Oregon
Convention
Center

N.E. Lloyd Blvd.

84
N.E. Glisan St.

N.E. Everett St.

E. Burnside St.
S.W. Ankeny St.
S.E. Ash St.
S.E. 1st Ave.
S.E. 2nd Ave.
S.E. Grand Ave.
S.E. 7th Ave.
S.E. 8th Ave.
99E
Sandy Blvd.
S.E. Stark St.
S.E. 11th Ave.
S.E. Washington St.

S.E. Belmont St.

S.E. Martin Luther King Jr. Blvd.
S.E. 3rd Ave.
S.E. Grand Ave.

BUCKMAN
DISTRICT

S.E. Main St.

TO HAWTHORNE→
DISTRICT

S.E. Madison St.
S.E. Hawthorne Blvd.
S.E. Water Ave.
S.E. Clay St.
S.E. Market St.

23 Hoyt, **8**
Al-Amir, **58**
Alexis, **66**
Andina, **22**
Aquariva, **70**
Bastas, **13**
BeWon, **5**
Bijou Café, **63**
Blue Hour, **29**
Bo Restobar, **45**
BridgePort BrewPub & Restaurant, **19**
Bush Garden, **40**
Caffé Mingo, **11**
Carafe, **54**
Cha! Cha! Cha!, **26**
Chart House, **71**
Clyde Common, **37**
Dan & Louis's Oyster Bar, **30**
El Gaucho, **62**
Eleni's Philoxenia, **34**
Fenouil, **21**
Fong Chong, **31**
The Gilt Club, **32**
Giorgio's, **25**
Gracie's, **38**
The Heathman, **48**
Higgins, **49**
Hot Lips Pizza, **27**
Hurley's, **17**
Jake's Famous Crawfish, **36**
Jake's Grill, **39**
Kells Irish Restaurant and Pub, **64**
Ken's Artisan Bakery, **14**
Kornblatt's, **7**
Le Bouchon, **24**
Le Happy, **18**
London Grill, **47**
Lucy's Table, **12**
MacTarnahan's Taproom, **2**

Mama Mia Trattoria, **56**
Mandarin Cove, **51**
Marina Fish House, **53**
McCormick & Schmick's, **60**
Meriwether's, **1**
Mother's Bistro, **57**
Murata, **52**
Oba!, **23**
Old Spaghetti Factory, **72**
Olea, **30**
Original Pancake House, **73**
Paley's Place, **10**
Papa Haydn/Jo Bar, **6**
Pastini, **4**
Pazzo, **43**
Pearl Bakery, **33**
Pine Street Bistro & Wine Bar, **61**
Pizzicato, **44**
Plainfield's Mayur, **16**
Portland City Grill, **68**
Portland Steak & Chophouse, **67**
Red Star Tavern & Roast House, **42**
The Ringside, **15**
Rock Bottom Brewing Co., **50**
Saucebox, **69**
Silk, by Pho Van, **28**
Southpark Seafood Grill & Wine Bar, **41**
St. Honoré Boulangerie, **3**
Sungari Pearl, **20**
Ten01, **35**
Three Square Grill, **74**
Typhoon!, **46**
Veganopolis Cafeteria, **59**
Veritable Quandary, **55**
Wildwood, **9**

0   1/2 mile
0   1/2 kilometer

its outstanding local microbrews, but this slightly upscale establishment manages to do just fine and serves some tasty dinner options, including burgers, pasta, and salads. With a full bar, pool upstairs, and rustic decor, there is plenty to please the after-work crowd. Brewery tours are available. ✉ *210 S.W. Morrison St., 97204* ☎ *503/796–2739* ▭ *AE, D, MC, V.*

¢–$ ✕ **Bijou Cafe.** This spacious, sunny, high-ceiling restaurant has some of the best breakfasts in town: French-style crepes and oyster hash are a few popular favorites, along with fabulous pancakes and French toast. Breakfast is served all day, and at lunch there are burgers, sandwiches, and soups, as well as delectable daily specials. ✉ *132 S.W. 3rd Ave., Downtown 97204* ☎ *503/222–3187* ▭ *MC, V* ⊙ *No dinner.*

ASIAN

$–$$$ ✕ **Mandarin Cove.** One of Portland's better Chinese restaurants has Hunan- and Szechuan-style beef, chicken, pork, seafood, and vegetarian dishes. There are almost two dozen seafood choices. Try the sautéed scallops simmered in spicy tomato sauce. ✉ *111 S.W. Columbia St., 97201* ☎ *503/222–0006* ▭ *AE, DC, MC, V* ⊙ *No lunch.*

$$ ✕ **Sungari Pearl.** Tantalizing dishes of the east meet the stylistic panache of the west at this highly polished establishment. Beauty is in the details, from stainless steel chopsticks to delicate orchids; it's also present in the artful twists of traditional favorites, such as crispy prawns with honeyed walnuts or spicy sesame beef served with sweet sauce and topped with roasted sesame seeds. ✉ *1105 N.W. Lovejoy St., 97209* ☎ *971/222–7327* ▭ *AE, MC, V.*

CONTINENTAL

$$$–$$$$ ✕ **London Grill.** The plush, dimly lit dining room in the historic Benson Hotel serves classic dishes made with fresh, seasonal local ingredients. Try the cedar-smoked salmon with juniper-berry sauce. With one of the longest wine lists around and a good chance of live jazz guitar or piano music, this a place to truly indulge. Breakfast is also available. Jackets are encouraged, but not required, for men. ✉ *309 S.W. Broadway, 97205* ☎ *503/295–4110* ▭ *AE, D, DC, MC, V.*

3

$-$$$ ✕**The Heathman.** Chef Philippe Boulot revels in fresh ingre-
★ dients of the Pacific Northwest. His menu changes with the
season and includes entrées made with grilled and braised
fish, fowl, veal, lamb, and beef. Among the chef's North-
west specialties are a delightful Dungeness crab, mango,
and avocado salad and a seafood paella made with mus-
sels, clams, shrimp, scallops, and chorizo. Equally creative
choices are available for breakfast and lunch. The dining
room, scented with wood smoke and adorned with Andy
Warhol prints, is a favorite for special occasions. ✉*Heath-
man Hotel, 1001 S.W. Broadway, Downtown 97205*
☎*503/790–7752* ▭*AE, D, DC, MC, V.*

$-$$ ✕**Clyde Common.** If you want to experience "community,"
then this bustling, contemporary spot is for you. Visi-
tors from all walks of life—politicians, quasi-celebrities,
socialites, the hip and trendy, straight and gay—frequent
this newer establishment. Big tables dominate this restaurant, which means you'll never know who you'll end up
sitting next to or what interesting conversations you may
have. The open kitchen allows you to see what's going on
from any vantage point. The edgy menu includes frogs'
legs, chicken livers, and sardines, accompanied by a host
of interesting ingredients such as horseradish, nettles, and
refried peanuts. There's no shortage of invention on the
drink menu, either: try the "Ace Gibson" with Medoyeff
vodka and house pickled onion, or the "Anemic Mary"
with serrano chili and sun-dried tomato vodka, celery
juice, and sour mix. ✉*1014 S.W. Stark St., Downtown
97205* ☎*503/228–3333* ▭*AE, D, MC, V.*

FRENCH

$$$ ✕**Carafe.** Straightforward French favorites and proximity
to the Keller Auditorium make this quaint bistro a popular
choice. Confit of albacore tuna niçoise served with heir-
loom tomatoes, haricots verts, and hard-boiled egg, as
well as crispy duck leg confit with pickled apricots, squash
ribbons, and balsamic, are a few of the dishes to choose
from. If you're in the mood for lighter fare, there are also
plenty of pastas, sandwiches, and soups. Since this is across
from Keller Auditorium, call ahead. If there's a show going
on, there could be crowds and longer waits. ✉*200 S.W.
Market St., 97201* ☎*503/248–0004* ▭*AE, DC, MC, V*
☉*Closed Sun.*

IRISH

¢–$$ ✕ **Kells Irish Restaurant and Pub.** Step into cool, dark Kells for a pint of Guinness and such authentic pub fare as fish-and-chips, Guinness stew, shepherd's pie, and Irish soda bread. Burgers and vegetarian sandwiches round out the bar menu, and there's breakfast on weekends. Live Irish music plays every night of the week. Be sure and ask the bartender how all those folded-up dollar bills got stuck to the ceiling. ⊠ *112 S.W. 2nd Ave., 97204* ☎ *503/227–4057* ⊟ *AE, D, MC, V.*

ITALIAN

¢–$$$ ✕ **Pazzo.** The aromas of roasted garlic and wood smoke greet patrons of the bustling, street-level dining room of the Hotel Vintage Plaza. Pazzo's menu relies on deceptively simple new Italian cuisine—creative pastas, risottos, and grilled meats, fish, and poultry as well as antipasti and appetizers. All the baked goods are made in the Pazzoria Bakery & Cafe next door. The decor is a mix of dark wood, terra-cotta, and dangling garlands of garlic. Breakfast is served daily. ⊠ *627 S.W. Washington St., Downtown 97205* ☎ *503/228–1515* ⊟ *AE, D, DC, MC, V.*

$–$$ ✕ **Mama Mia Trattoria.** Warmth and comfort are the specialties of Mama's, which is the place to come to if you're in the mood for spaghetti with meatballs, lasagna, or potato gnocchi. Don't let the sultry red interior, sparkly chandeliers, and starched tablecloths fool you. This mildly boisterous place allows you to be more casual than it is (just like mom), and the bar is open late into the night. ⊠ *439 S.W. 2nd Ave., 97204* ☎ *503/295–6464* ⊟ *AE, D, DC, MC, V* ⊘ *No lunch. Open late.*

JAPANESE

$$–$$$$ ✕ **Murata.** Slip off your shoes and step inside one of the tatami rooms at Murata, Portland's best Japanese restaurant. You can also pull up a chair at the corner sushi bar. So ordinary looking it barely stands out among the office towers near Keller Auditorium, the restaurant draws a crowd of locals, celebrities, and Japanese businesspeople who savor the sushi, sashimi, tempura, hamachi, and teriyaki. Grilled salmon cheeks stand out among many seafood specialties. ⊠ *200 S.W. Market St., 97201* ☎ *503/227–0080* ⊟ *AE, MC, V* ⊘ *Closed Sun. No lunch Sat.*

$-$$$ ×**Bush Garden.** This authentic Japanese restaurant, which opened in 1960, is known for its sashimi and sukiyaki but also offers traditional favorites such as udon noodles, bento, tempura, and teriyaki. There is karaoke singing Monday–Saturday. ⊠ *900 S.W. Morrison St., 97205* ☎ *503/226–7181* ⊟ *AE, D, DC, MC, V* ⊙ *Closed Sun.*

LEBANESE

$-$$ ×**Al-Amir.** Upon entering the restaurant and moving beyond the small bar in the front, through the elaborately large and ornate Middle Eastern gateway into a dark, stylish dining room, choose between excellent broiled kebabs, falafel, hummus, tabbouleh, and baba ghanoush. There's live music and belly dancing on Friday and Saturday. ⊠ *223 S.W. Stark St.* ☎ *503/274–0010* ⊟ *AE, D, MC, V* ⊙ *No lunch weekends.*

¢–$ ×**Pine Street Bistro & Wine Bar.** More than half the menu is vegetarian, but the leg of lamb served on a bed of rice with lentil soup or a full salad is a favorite. A special menu of meals low in saturated fats targets health-conscious diners. The laid-back restaurant's two dining areas are decorated simply, with white linen and dark wood. You can dine outside on sidewalk tables in summer. ⊠ *221 S.W. Pine St., Downtown 97204* ☎ *503/223–5058* ⊟ *AE, MC, V* ⊙ *No lunch Sun.*

PAN-ASIAN

$-$$ ×**Saucebox.** Creative pan-Asian cuisine and many creative cocktails draw the crowds to this popular restaurant and nightspot near the big downtown hotels. Inside the long and narrow space with closely spaced tables draped with white cloths, Alexis Rockman's impressive and colorful 24-foot painting *Evolution* spans the wall over your head, and mirrored walls meet your gaze at eye level. The menu includes Korean baby-back ribs, Vietnamese pork tenderloin, and Indonesian roasted Javanese salmon. An excellent late-night menu is served after 10 PM. ⊠ *214 S.W. Broadway, Downtown 97205* ☎ *503/241–3393* ⊟ *AE, DC, MC, V* ⊙ *Closed Sun. and Mon. No lunch.*

$ ×**Bo Restobar.** Combining the trend of tapas and chic cocktails, this "restobar" located in the Hotel Lucia brings both to delicious heights. Considered a hot spot for mingling, the stylish dark walls accented by colorful modern art create a sleek setting in which to sip a specialty martini made with chili-infused liquor. For nibbling, try the lemongrass clam chowder, the twice-cooked beef strips, or the Koreadilla—a quesadilla with spicy pork and goat cheese. ✉*400 S.W. Broadway, Downtown 97205* ☎*503/222–2688* 🖃*AE, DC, MC, V.*

PIZZA

¢ ✕**Pizzicato.** This local chain serves pies and slices topped by inventive combinations such as chanterelles, shiitakes, and portobellos, or andouille sausage, shrimp, and smoked mozzarella. The menu includes large salads to share, antipasti, and panini. The restaurant interiors are clean, bright, and modern. Beer and wine are available. ✉*705 S.W. Alder St., Downtown 97205* ☎*503/226–1007* ✉*505 N.W. 23rd Ave., Nob Hill* ☎*503/242–0023* 🖃*AE, D, DC, MC, V.*

SEAFOOD

$–$$$ ✕**Jake's Famous Crawfish.** Diners have been enjoying fresh Pacific Northwest seafood in Jake's warren of wood-paneled dining rooms for more than a century. The back bar came around Cape Horn during the 1880s, and the chandeliers hanging from the high ceilings date from 1881. The restaurant gained a national reputation in 1920 when crawfish was added to the menu. White-coat waiters take your order from an almost endless sheet of daily seafood specials year-round, but try to come during crawfish season (May–September), when you can sample the tasty crustacean in pie, cooked Creole style, or in a Cajun-style stew over rice. ✉*401 S.W. 12th Ave., Downtown 97205* ☎*503/226–1419* 🖃*AE, D, DC, MC, V* ⊘*No lunch Sun.*

$–$$$ ✕**Marina Fish House.** When it comes to river, bridge, and city-skyline views, there's not a bad seat in this circular glass dining room, which floats on the Willamette River. The regional chain's menu includes seafood and chicken salads, seasonal specials, and creative seafood fare. The oven-roasted jumbo prawns are stuffed with crab, Brie, and roasted garlic and topped with béarnaise sauce. Upstairs, a comfortable lounge has a popular happy hour every day in the late afternoon and before closing. ✉*RiverPlace, 425 S.W. Montgomery St., Downtown 97201* ☎*503/227–3474* 🖃*AE, D, DC, MC, V.*

$–$$$ ✕McCormick & Schmick's. The seafood is flawless at this lively restaurant, where you can dine in a cozy, private wooden booth downstairs or upstairs overlooking the bar. Fresh Pacific Northwest oysters and Alaskan halibut are favorites; specialties include Dungeness crab cakes with roasted red-pepper sauce. A new menu is printed daily with a list of more than two dozen fresh seasonal choices. Oregon and California vineyards take center stage on the wine list. The popular bar has bargain happy-hour appetizers and a wide selection of top-shelf, single-malt scotches. ✉ *235 S.W. 1st Ave., Downtown 97204* ☎ *503/224–7522* ☐ *AE, D, DC, MC, V* ⊘ *No lunch.*

3

$–$$ ✕Southpark Seafood Grill & Wine Bar. Wood-fired seafood is served in this comfortable, art deco–tinged room with two bars. Chef Ronnie MacQuarrie's Mediterranean-influenced menu includes grilled grape-leaf-wrapped salmon with pomegranate and sherry glaze as well as tuna au poivre with mashed potatoes and red-wine demi-glace. There's a wide selection of fresh Pacific Northwest oysters and fine regional wines available by the glass. Some of the desserts are baked to order. ✉ *901 S.W. Salmon St., Downtown 97205* ☎ *503/326–1300* ☐ *AE, D, MC, V.*

¢–$$ ✕Dan & Louis's Oyster Bar. Oysters at this Portland landmark near the river come fried, stewed, or on the half shell. The clam chowder is tasty, but the crab stew is a rare treat. Combination dinners let you mix your fried favorites. The collection of steins, plates, and marine art has grown since the restaurant opened in 1907 to fill beams, nooks, crannies, and nearly every inch of wall. ✉ *208 S.W. Ankeny St., Downtown 97204* ☎ *503/227–5906* ☐ *AE, D, DC, MC, V.*

STEAK

★ Fodor's Choice ✕El Gaucho. Three dimly lit dining rooms with
$$$–$$$$ blue walls and striped upholstery invite those with healthy pocketbooks. The specialty here is 28-day, dry-aged, certified Angus beef, but chops, ribs, and chicken entrées are also cooked in the open kitchen. The chateaubriand for two is carved tableside. Seafood lovers might want to try the tomato fennel bouillabaisse. Service is impeccable at this Seattle transplant in the elegant Benson Hotel. Each night live Latin guitar music serenades the dinner guests. ✉ *319 S.W. Broadway, Downtown 97205* ☎ *503/227–8794* ☐ *AE, DC, MC, V* ⊘ *No lunch.*

¢–$$$$ ×**Portland Steak & Chophouse.** Expensive cuts of steak and prime rib are the draw at this steak house in the Embassy Suites hotel. The menu includes wood-fired pizzas, pasta, and café meals. Surf lovers can choose the Hawaiian ahi, cioppino, or seafood linguine. The bar menu draws a loyal happy-hour crowd. ⊠ *121 S.W. 3rd Ave., Downtown 97204* ☎*503/223–6200* ⊟*AE, D, MC, V.*

THAI

$–$$$ ×**Typhoon!** A Buddha statue with burning incense watches over diners at this popular restaurant in the Lucia Hotel. Come enjoy the excellent food in a large, modern dining room filled with colorful art and sleek red booths. The spicy chicken or shrimp with crispy basil, the curry and noodle dishes, and the vegetarian spring and salad rolls are standouts. If tea is your thing, 145 varieties are available, from $2 a pot to $55 for some of the world's rarest. ⊠*400 S.W. Broadway, Downtown 97205* ☎*503/224–8285* ⊟*AE, D, DC, MC, V.*

VEGETARIAN

¢ ×**Veganopolis Cafeteria.** Everything on the menu here is meat-, dairy-, and egg-free, right down to house-made cheeses (made from nuts), baked goods, and organic beer and wine. Chill music swirls through the sleek, airy interior, filled at lunchtime with office workers queued up for such sophisticated sandwiches as quinoa burgers, corned seitan Reubens, and vegan BLTs. It also has soups, salads, hot dishes, and fair-trade coffee. In the evenings there's a dinner buffet, and breakfast is served Saturday mornings. ⊠*412 S.W. 4th Ave., 97204* ☎*503/226-3400* ⊟*AE, D, DC, MC, V* ☉*Closed Sun.*

PEARL DISTRICT & OLD TOWN/ CHINATOWN

The Pearl District, once a microcosm of Portland's industrial past—where worn, empty warehouses prevailed—is now the city's most bustling destination for arts and dining. Many of these same warehouses have been refurbished into hot spots to gather for drinks and food. On any given day or night, visitors can comb the scene for a perfectly selected glass of wine or a lush designer cocktail. Within this small area are global selections of Greek, French, Italian, Peruvian, Japanese, and more. Restaurants here tend to be slightly more upscale, though there are plenty of causal bakeries, coffee shops, and places to grab sandwiches. Be aware that on the first Thursday of the month, these restaurants are jammed because of the city's First Thursday gallery walk.

AMERICAN

3

$$$–$$$$ ✕**Ten01.** Soft light, endless ceilings, and clean architectural lines make for a very chic dining room at Ten01. Start with the sweet onion–cauliflower soup with spicy lamb sausage, almonds, golden raisins, and curry. Then indulge in practically plucked-off-the-farm bacon-wrapped jumbo quail wrapped in bacon, or a sautéed Alaskan halibut with maitake mushroom, pancetta, and truffle-mushroom sauce. Save room for the signature Oregon honey crisp apple with lavender tuile for dessert. The wine list is among the city's best. ⊠*1001 N.W. Couch St., Pearl District 97209* ☎*503/226–3463* ⊙*Closed Sun.* ⊟*AE, DC, MC, V.*

¢ ✕**BridgePort BrewPub & Restaurant.** The hops- and ivy-covered, century-old industrial building seems out of place among its neighbors, but once inside you'll be clear about the business here: frothy pints of BridgePort's ale, brewed on the premises. The India Pale Ale is a specialty, but a treat for the indecisive is the seven-glass sampler that might also include "Old Knucklehead," the brewery's barley wine–style ale. Seafood, chicken, steak, pasta, salads, and small plates are served for lunch and dinner, as well as pub favorites. In summer the flower-festooned loading dock is transformed into a beer garden. ⊠*1313 N.W. Marshall St., Pearl District 97209* ☎*503/241–3612* ⊟*MC, V.*

CAFÉS

¢ ✕**Pearl Bakery.** A light breakfast or lunch can be had at this popular spot known for its excellent fresh breads, pastries, cakes, and sandwiches. The cakes, cookies, croissants, and Danish are some of the best in the city. ⊠*102 N.W. 9th Ave., Pearl District 97209* ☎*503/827–0910* ⊙*No dinner* ⊟*MC, V.*

CHINESE

¢–$ ✕ **Fong Chong.** Although it looks run-down, Fong Chong is considered by some to serve the best dim sum in town. The family-style eatery has dumplings filled with shrimp, pork, or vegetables, accompanied by plenty of different sauces. If you haven't eaten dim sum before, just take a seat: the food is brought to you on carts and you pick what you want as it comes by. ✉ *301 N.W. 4th Ave., Chinatown 97209* ☎ *503/228–6868* ═ *AE, MC, V.*

CONTINENTAL

$$$ **The Gilt Club** Cascading gold curtains, ornate show-piece
★ chandeliers, and high-back booths complement a swanky rich-red dining room. The food is equally lush, with buttercup pumpkin gnocchi topped with an Oregon venison ragu, and a truffle, red quinoa, and goat cheese custard with roasted autumn baby vegetables. The drink menu is loaded with flavor-embellished drinks such as "Tracy's First Love," with house-infused cucumber vodka, cucumber, basil, and fresh lime. ✉ *306 N.W. Broadway, 97209* ☎ *503/ 222–4458* ☉ *Closed Sun.* ═ *AE, MC, V.*

FRENCH

$$$ ✕ **Le Bouchon.** A warm, jovial waitstaff make Francophiles feel right at home at this French bistro in the Pearl District, which serves classic French cuisine for lunch and dinner. Duck confit, truffle chicken, bouillabaisse, and escargot are all cooked to perfection by chef Claude Musquin. And for dessert, chocolate mousse is a must-try. ✉ *517 N.W. 14th Ave., Pearl District 97209* ☎ *503/248–2193* ═ *AE, MC, V* ☉ *Closed Sun.–Mon.*

$$$ ✕ **Fenouil.** The large stone fireplace, expansive bar bistro menu, and widely-revered French onion soup are a few of the reasons patrons keep coming back to this warm and elegant two-story restaurant. Notable entrée choices vary by season, but two reliable crowd pleasers are the wood-fired duck breast with Armagnac soaked prunes and the grilled Kobe sirloin. There's live music on Friday nights. At the end of each month the chef creates an all-inclusive priced "regional dinner" that explores foods from a unique culinary region. ✉ *900 N.W. 11th Ave., Pearl District 97209* ☎ *503/525–2225* ═ *AE, DC, MC, V.*

¢–$$ ✗**Le Happy.** This tiny creperie just outside of the hubbub of the Pearl District can serve as a romantic dinner-date spot or just a cozy place to enjoy a drink and a snack. You can get sweet crepes with fruit, cheese, and cream or savory ones with meats and cheeses; in addition, the dinner menu is rounded out with steaks and salads. It's a classy joint, but not without a sense of humor: Le Trash Blanc is a bacon and cheddar crepe, served with a can of Pabst. ⊠*1011 N.W. 16th Ave., Pearl District 97209* ☎*503/226–1258* ▭*MC, V* ⊘*Closed Sun. No lunch.*

3

GREEK

$ ✗**Alexis.** The Mediterranean furnishings here consist only of white walls and basic furnishings, but the authentic Greek flavor keeps the crowds coming for *kalamarakia* (deep-fried squid served with *tzatziki,* a yogurt dip), *horiatiki* (a Greek salad combination with feta cheese and kalamata olives), and other traditional dishes. If you have trouble making up your mind, the gigantic Alexis platter includes a little of everything. ⊠*215 W. Burnside St., Old Town 97209* ☎*503/224–8577* ▭*AE, D, MC, V* ⊘*Closed Sun. No lunch Sat.*

$ ✗**Eleni's Philoxenia.** This upscale version of its sister restaurant in Sellwood offers an extensive menu of Mediterranean specialties. The chef's personal favorite is the *kalatsounia* (spinach, fresh dill, and green onions rolled inside philo dough). Other surprising standouts are the *Lahano Salata* (thinly sliced cabbage and shaved fennel, toasted almonds, and lemon paprika dressing) and the *Makaronia me Kima* (ground beef simmered with peppers, onion, tomatoes, zucchini, and garlic served over spaghetti). ⊠*112 N.W. 9th Ave., Pearl District 97209* ☎*503/227–2158* ▭*AE, D, MC, V* ⊘*Closed Sun. and Mon. No lunch.*

ITALIAN

$$$$ ✗**Giorgio's.** Here, elegance overtakes trends and quality trumps appearance. In an intimate, classic setting, diners enjoy French-influenced, intricately prepared Italian cooking. Local ingredients dictate daily menu offerings but you might expect entrées such as lamb with arugula and roasted cardoncello mushrooms or homemade celery root ravioli. Finales include the ever-revolving choices of fresh sorbets.

⊠*1131 N.W. Hoyt St., 97209* ☎*503/221–1888* ⊘*Closed Sun.* ⊟*AE, MC, V.*

$–$$ ✕**Caffé Mingo.** Straightforward, flavorful and fresh is what you'll find from this diverse Italian menu featuring some of the best pizza around. There are also fish and chicken entrées, as well as nightly soup and pasta specials. Don't miss out on the rich chocolate mousse with fresh berries and cream for dessert. ⊠*807 N.W. 21st Ave., 97209* ☎*503/226–4646* ⊘*No lunch* ⊟*AE, DC, MC, V.*

LATIN

$$–$$$ ✕**Oba!** Many come to Oba! for the upscale bar scene, but this Pearl District salsa hangout also serves excellent Latin American cuisine, including coconut prawns, roasted vegetable enchiladas and tamales, and other seafood, chicken, pork, and duck dishes. The bar is open late Friday and Saturday. ⊠*555 N.W. 12th Ave., Pearl District 97209* ☎*503/228–6161* ⊟*AE, D, DC, MC, V* ⊘*No lunch.*

MEDITERRANEAN

$$$–$$$$ ✕**Blue Hour.** The wait staff here are as sophisticated as the white tablecloths and floor-to-ceiling curtains in this vast, towering restaurant. The menu changes daily based on available ingredients and the chef's whims. Four-course prix fixe menus are available for lunch and dinner. Ongoing appetizers to try are the "20 greens" salad and sea scallops wrapped in applewood-smoked bacon with celery root purée. Top the meal off with a bittersweet chocolate chestnut torte with honey cream. ⊠*250 N.W. 13th Ave., Pearl District 97209* ☎*503/226–3394* ⊟*AE, D, MC, V.*

$$$–$$$$ ✕**Olea.** A visit to Olea is like taking of a tour around the Mediterranean coast. From the Moroccan chicken with pureed pistachios and sultana grapes, to salads with heirloom tomatoes, fresh feta, cucumbers, and mint, you'll find much of what your heart desires. The dining room has lots of skylights which enable an abundance of natural light and an open, welcoming environment even on the restaurant's most crowded days. On summer nights it's a great location to sit outside and people watch. ⊠*1338 N.W. Hoyt St., Pearl District 97209* ☎*503/274–0800* ⊟*AE, D, DC, MC, V.*

MEXICAN

¢ ✕**Cha! Cha! Cha!** Burritos and tacos are so tasty at this lively taqueria that if it wasn't always shoehorned with customers, patrons would probably get up and dance. Part of a local chain, Cha! Cha! Cha! takes cuisine you'd expect to find on a taco truck in southern Mexico and puts it on a plate in the Pearl. The extensive menu includes *machaca* (a burrito with shredded beef, sautéed vegetables, scrambled eggs, and Spanish rice) and fish tacos filled with fresh pollack. ✉*1208 N.W. Glisan St., Pearl District 97209* ☎*503/221–2111* ▭*AE, D, MC, V.*

PERUVIAN

$$–$$$ ✕**Andina.** Portland's sleekest, trendiest, and most brightly colored restaurant gives an artful presentation to designer and traditional Peruvian cuisine. Asian and Spanish flavors are the main influences on this cuisine, evident in an extensive seafood menu that includes five kinds of ceviche, grilled octopus, and pan-seared scallops with black quinoa. There are also entrées with poultry, beef, and lamb. A late-night bar swills with sangria, small plates, and cocktails, and a shrinelike wine shop hosts private multicourse meals downstairs. ✉*1314 N.W. Glisan St., Pearl District 97209* ☎*503/228–9535* ▭*AE, D, MC, V* ⊘*No lunch Sun.*

PIZZA

¢ ✕**Hot Lips Pizza.** A favorite of Portland's pizza-lovers, Hot Lips bakes organic and regional ingredients into creative pizzas, available whole or by the slice. Seasonal variations might feature apples, squash, wild mushrooms, and blue cheese. It also has soups, salads, and sandwiches. Beverages include house-made berry sodas, a large rack of wines, and microbrew six-packs. Dine inside the Ecotrust building, outside on the eco-roof, or take it all across the street for an impromptu picnic in Jamison Square. ✉*721 N.W. 9th Ave., Pearl District 97209* ☎*503/595–2342* ▭*AE, D, MC, V.*

VIETNAMESE

¢–$$ ✕ **Silk, by Pho Van.** This spacious, minimalist restaurant is the newer and trendier of the two Pho Van locations in Portland—the less expensive twin is on the far east side, on 82nd Avenue. A big bowl of pho noodle soup is delicious, enough to fill you up, and costs only $8 or $9. The friendly waitstaff will help you work your way through the menu and will make suggestions to give you the best sampling of Vietnamese cuisine. ✉ *1012 N.W. Glisan St., Pearl District 97209* ☎ *503/248–2172* ▭ *AE, D, MC, V* ⊘ *Closed Sun.* ✉ *1919 S.E. 82nd Ave.* ☎ *503/788–5244.*

WEST OF DOWNTOWN

Beyond downtown to the west are a handful of restaurants worth visiting. Without parking to worry about, the 5- to 15-minute drive will reward you with some delicious dining surprises, from pancakes to pizza, and some of the best tapas in Portland. Several of these establishments are located right alongside the Willamette River so there are also lovely views to be had. During the summer months, many offer deck seating. Be aware that these seats are in high demand—but watching the boats sail by on a warm summer night while indulging in a round of tasty appetizers is totally worth the wait.

AMERICAN

$$–$$$ ✕ **Chart House.** On a hill high above the Willamette River, the Chart House has a stunning view of the city and the surrounding mountains from almost all of its tables. Prime rib is a specialty, but the seafood dishes, including coconut-crunchy shrimp deep-fried in tempura batter and the Cajun spiced yellowfin ahi, are just as tempting. ✉ *5700 S.W. Terwilliger Blvd., 97239* ☎ *503/246–6963* ▭ *AE, D, DC, MC, V* ⊘ *No lunch weekends.*

$$ ✕ **Three Square Grill.** Hidden within an older shopping plaza ☺ in the Hillsdale neighborhood you'll discover the best place in Portland to go on Tuesdays for fried chicken and waffle night. Indulge in healthy portions of comfort food's finest including Louisiana-style bouillabaisse with shrimp, crab, oysters and crawfish, to the more refined 21-day dry aged New York steak with truffle butter. Dishes focus on organic ingredients, some deriving from the chef's own home gar-

Eco Fruit of the Vine: Organic Wine

When it comes to the dining scene, Portland is already globally recognized for its sustainability practices. Another trend putting this region in the spotlight is the production of organic wine. Although Oregon has only about 13,000 acres of wine grapes compared to California's 450,000-plus acres, it's estimated that nearly 50 percent of Oregon's vineyards are sustainable or organic compared to California's one percent. Twenty-three percent of its vineyards have met very stringent certification guidelines and are LIVE-certified sustainable or organic, or Demeter-certified biodynamic. (LIVE—Low Input Viticulture & Enology—is just one of two sustainable certification agencies in the United States, established in 1997, that recognizes farms and vineyards for sustainable agricultural practices. Demeter is an international certification body.)

The goals of organic wine production are to reduce reliance on synthetic chemicals and fertilizers with the purpose of protecting the farmer and the environment, and ensure land protection by maintaining natural, chemical-free soil fertility. Perhaps the biggest hindrance in producing organic wine is preserving the wine with a sulfite-free preservative. Wines require long periods of storage so standardized methods of preserving wines includes adding sulfites. Even though yeast naturally produces sulfites during fermentation, adding sulfites goes against certification standards.

People with allergies, including sulfite sensitivities, often seek out organic wines. The FDA requires warning labels for wines with sulfites more than 10 parts per million (ppm). Most red wines contain approximately 40 ppm sulfite. There's also the term "no detectable sulfite" which means that wine constitutes less than one milligram per liter. Many wineries create wine made from organic grapes and label it as such, so long as the detectable sulfite level remains below 100 ppm.

100% certified organic wine labels are still uncommon as the preservation and storage challenges remain in conflict with the strict certification requirements. However, many of the wineries in Portland's neighboring communities of Yamhill and Washington counties are turning new soil on best practices for farming and cultivating some of the most respected wines in the industry.

den, and everything from the bread to desserts are baked fresh daily. Weekend brunches and live music in the evenings are a big hit at this kid-friendly place. ⊠*6320 S.W. Capitol Hwy., 97239* ☎*503/244–4467* ⊟*MC, V.*

¢–$ ✕**Original Pancake House.** Not to be confused with any chain imitations, this pancake house is the real deal. Faithful customers have been coming for close to 50 years to wait for a table at this bustling, cabin-like local landmark, and you can expect to find a contented crowd of locals and tourists alike from the time the place opens at 7 AM until afternoon. With pancakes starting at $7.25, it's not the cheapest place to get a stack, but with 20 varieties and some of the best waffles and crepes around, it's worth the trip. ⊠*8601 S.W. Barbur Blvd., Burlingame 97219* ☎*503/246–9007* ⚲*Reservations not accepted* ⊟*No credit cards* ⊙*Closed Mon. and Tues. No dinner.*

ITALIAN

$ ✕**Aquariva.** Choose from a vast selection of innovative Italian tapas—such as the spinach gnocchi covered in tomoto-basil fondue or Oregon mushroom risotto with white truffle oil—in one of the most prime dining locations in Portland. Gaze out the windows at the Willamette River while sipping on a glass of Italian Syrah chosen from an impressive wine list. There are plenty of cushy couches to lounge in for happy hour, but if the weather's nice, sit outside on the deck. ⊠*470 S.W. Hamilton Ct., South Waterfront 97239* ☎*503/802–5850* ⊟*AE, DC, MC, V.*

¢–$ ✕**Old Spaghetti Factory.** An old trolley car, oversize velvet chairs, dark wood, and fun antiques fill this huge restaurant overlooking the Willamette River. With a lounge upstairs, room for 500 diners, and a great view of the river, the flagship location of this nationwide restaurant chain is a great place for families, with basic pasta dishes and a kids' menu. ⊠*715 S.W. Bancroft St., 97239* ☎*503/222–5375* ⚲*Reservations not accepted* ⊟*AE, D, DC, MC, V.*

NOB HILL & VICINITY

The northwest area of Portland is one of the most ideal spots in town to sample the broadest scope of this city's food scene. From the finest of the fine (Paley's Place, Wildwood, Papa Haydn, and Hoyt 23) to the come-as-you-are-casual (McMenamins Blue Moon, Pizza Schmizza, and Rose's Deli), there's something for everyone within a handful of blocks. Most restaurants in the Nob Hill area are open for lunch and dinner and on the weekends; reservations are recommended for the higher-end establishments. This neighborhood draws an eclectic crowd of people from progressive to conservative, lifetime residents to recent transplants, higher-end income to struggling students. There are numberous retail shops and galleries in the neighborhood, so work up an appetite before or after your meal.

AMERICAN

$$–$$$$ ✕**The Ringside.** This Portland institution has been famous for its beef for more than 50 years. Dine in cozy booths on rib eye, prime rib, and New York strip, which come in regular- or king-size cuts. Seafood lovers will find plenty of choices: a chilled seafood platter with an 8-ounce lobster tail, Dungeness crab, oysters, jumbo prawns, and Oregon bay shrimp. The onion rings, made with Walla Walla sweets, are equally renowned. ⊠*2165 N.W. Burnside St., close to Nob Hill 97210* ☎*503/223–1513* ☰*AE, D, MC, V* ⊙*No lunch.*

¢–$$$ ✕**Papa Haydn/Jo Bar.** Many patrons come to this bistro just for the luscious desserts or for the popular Sunday brunch (reservations essential). Favorite dinner items include pan-seared scallops, dinner salads, and grilled flatiron steak. Wood-fired, rotisserie-cooked meat, fish, and poultry dishes plus pasta and pizza are available next door at the jazzy **Jo Bar.** ⊠*701 N.W. 23rd Ave., Nob Hill 97210* ☎*503/228–7317 Papa Haydn, 503/222–0048 Jo Bar* ☰*AE, MC, V.*

¢–$ ✕**MacTarnahan's Taproom.** The copper beer-making equipment at the door tips you off to the specialty of the house: beer. This restaurant in the Northwest industrial district is part of a 27,000-square-foot MacTarnahan's brewery complex. Start with a tasting platter featuring seven different beers. The haystack back ribs with garlic-rosemary fries are popular, and the fish-and-chips use a butter made with Mac's signature ale. Asparagus-artichoke lasagna is a good vegetarian option. Eat it all on the patio overlooking the landscaped grounds. ⊠*2730 N.W. 31st Ave., off N.W. Yeon St., 97210* ☎*503/228–5269* ☰*AE, DC, MC, V.*

CAFÉS

¢ ✕**Ken's Artisan Bakery.** Golden crusts are the trademark of Ken's rustic breads, croissants, tarts, and puff pastries, good for breakfast, lunch, and light evening meals. Sandwiches, barbecue pulled pork, and croque monsieur are served on thick slabs of freshly baked bread, and local berries fill the flaky pastries. And if the dozen tables inside the vibrant blue bakery are always crammed, sit outside at one of the sidewalk café tables. On Monday nights they serve pizza, and the bakery stays open to 9 PM. ⊠*338 N.W. 21st Ave., 97209* ☎*503/248–2202* ▭*MC, V* ☉*No dinner Tues.–Sun.*

¢ ✕**St. Honoré Boulangerie.** Light meals and pastries are avail-
★ able at this authentic French bakery, named for the patron saint of bakers. Start the day off with plain or chocolate croissant, or café au lait. For lunch and dinner there's quiche, savory puff pastries and tarts, croque monsieur, and a variety of fresh salads. Or simply unwind from shopping with a glass of wine and a luscious dessert at one of the sidewalk café tables. ⊠*2335 N.W. Thurman St., 97210* ☎*503/445–4342* ▭*MC, V.*

CONTINENTAL

$$–$$$$ ✕**Wildwood.** The busy center bar, stainless-steel open kitchen, and blond-wood chairs set the tone at this restaurant serving fresh Pacific Northwest cuisine. Chef Dustin Clark's entrées include dishes made with lamb, pork loin, chicken, steak, and seafood. There's also a vegetarian selection. Wildwood also has a family-style Sunday supper menu with selections for two or more people. ⊠*1221 N.W. 21st Ave., Nob Hill 97209* ☎*503/248–9663* ▭*AE, MC, V.*

$$–$$$ ✕**Meriwether's.** A fabulous garden patio adorns this quaint, higher-end—yet unpretentious—restaurant. The outdoor seating area is covered and heated so during cooler months you can still enjoy Tuscan seafood stew or celery root ravioli while basking in a beautiful garden where something is always in bloom. Dishes are prepared with fruits and vegetables harvested from Meriwether's own farm just 20 minutes away. The always-changing dessert menu features tasty seasonal treats. ⊠*2601 N.W. Vaughn, 97210* ☎*503/228–1250* ▭*AE, D, MC, V.*

$$–$$$ ✕**23 Hoyt.** From the pronounced antler chandelier to the owner's private collection of contemporary art adorning

walls and glass cases, an eclectic mix of fun and flavors in a chic, contemporary setting is what this place is about. The restaurant has received national accolades for its interpretation of Northwest cuisine, which changes seasonally. Items may include a mixed grill dish with juniper-rubbed quail, rabbit boudin blanc, and smoky bacon or Moroccan couscous with Alaskan halibut, manila clams, squid, and sea scallops. If it's in season, don't miss the streudel made with crispy filo layered with poached pears and caramel custard, served with black pepper ice cream. ⊠ *529 N.W. 23rd Ave., 97210* ☎ *503/445–7400* ⊙ *Closed Sun. and Mon. No lunch.* ⊟ *AE, MC, V.*

$–$$$ ✕ **Lucy's Table.** Amid this corner bistro's regal purple and gold interior, chef Michael Conklin creates Northwest cuisine with a mix of Italian and French accents. The seasonal menu includes lamb, steak, pork, and seafood dishes. For dessert try the *boca negra,* chocolate cake with Frangelico whipped cream and cherries poached with port and walnut Florentine. Valet parking is available Wednesday–Saturday. ⊠ *706 N.W. 21st Ave., Nob Hill 97209* ☎ *503/226–6126* ⊟ *AE, DC, MC, V* ⊙ *Closed Sun. No lunch.*

DELICATESSEN

¢ ✕ **Kornblatt's.** This kosher deli and bagel bakery evokes a 1950s diner. Thick sandwiches are made with fresh bread and lean fresh-cooked meats, and the tender home-smoked salmon and pickled herring are simply mouthwatering. For breakfast try the poached eggs with spicy corned-beef hash, blintzes, or potato latkes. ⊠ *628 N.W. 23rd Ave., Nob Hill 97210* ☎ *503/242–0055* ⊟ *AE, MC, V.*

FRENCH

$$$ ✕ **Hurley's.** The most notable dish on this quaint, dimly lit restaurant's French-rooted menu is a $28 hamburger. For burger lovers, take note: this is not the average spin on an old favorite. This ¾-pound spectacle is crafted from ground spiced Kobe short ribs topped with seared foie gras. It's accompanied by housemade potato chips cooked in truffle oil and coated with asiago cheese. Finalize the decadence with a molten chocolate cake with vanilla bean ice cream. ⊠ *1987 N.W. Kearney St., 97205* ☎ *503/295–6487* ⊙ *Closed Sun. and Mon.* ⊟ *AE, MC, V.*

★ Fodor'sChoice ✕**Paley's Place.** This charming bistro serves
$$–$$$ French cuisine Pacific Northwest–style. Among the entrées
are dishes with duck, New York steak, chicken, pork ten-
derloin, and halibut. A vegetarian selection is also available. There are two dining rooms and a classy bar. In
warmer months there's outdoor seating on the front porch
and back patio. ✉*1204 N.W. 21st Ave., Nob Hill 97209*
☎*503/243–2403* ⊟*AE, MC, V* ⊘*No lunch.*

INDIAN

$$–$$$ ✕**Plainfield's Mayur.** Portland's finest Indian cuisine is served
in an elegant Victorian house. The tomato-coconut soup
with fried curry leaves and the vegetarian and vegan dishes
are highlights. Appetizers include the authentic Bombay
bhel salad with tamarind dressing and the *dahi wadi* (crispy
fried lentil croquettes in a spicy yogurt sauce). Meat and
seafood specialties include lobster in brown onion sauce
and tandoori lamb. ✉*852 S.W. 21st Ave., one block south
of Burnside, close to Nob Hill 97205* ☎*503/223–2995*
⊟*AE, D, DC, MC, V* ⊘*No lunch.*

ITALIAN

$–$$ ✕**Bastas.** In a converted Tastee-Freez, this arty bistro serves
dishes from all over Italy. The walls are painted with Italian
earth tones, and a small side garden provides alfresco dining in good weather. The menu includes scaloppine, grilled
lamb, and creative seafood and pasta dishes. ✉*410 N.W.
21st Ave., Nob Hill 97209* ☎*503/274–1572* ⊟*AE, MC,
V* ⊘*No lunch.*

¢ ✕**Pastini.** It's hard to go wrong with anything at this classy
Italian bistro, which has more than two dozen pasta dishes
under $10. Rigatoni *zuccati* comes in a light cream sauce
with butternut squash, wild mushrooms, and spinach; *lin-
guini misto mare* is a seafood linguine in white wine. It also
has panini sandwiches, antipasti, and dinner salads. Open
for lunch and dinner, Pastini is part of a local chain. There's
often a crowd, but from this location you can browse the
shops while waiting for a table. ✉*1506 N.W. 23rd Ave.,
97210* ☎*503/595–1205* ⌂*Reservations not accepted* ⊟*AE,
DC, MC, V* ⊘*No lunch Sun.*

KOREAN

$–$$ ✕**BeWon.** Named for the favorite secret garden of ancient Korean royalty, BeWon prepares a tasty Korean feast. An array of traditional Korean side dishes, presented in an elegant assembly of little white bowls, accompanies such entrées as stir-fried seafood, simmered meat and fish, rice and soup dishes, and fermented vegetables (kimchi). To really experience a dynasty there's *han jung shik,* a traditional seven-course prix-fixe dinner available with or without wine pairings. ✉*1203 N.W. 23rd Ave., 97210* ☎*503/464–9222* ▤*AE, D, MC, V* ⊙*No lunch weekends.*

EAST OF THE WILLAMETTE

A whole new food movement is sprouting up east of the river, just outside downtown Portland. As restaurants become more progressive, daring, and inventive, they are also finding more unique locations to peddle their culinary wares. One benefit of dining outside of downtown is that parking is less expensive and easier to find. Getting from place to place takes more time as these establishments are not necessarily concentrated in any one area. But with some of Portland's most sought after dining spots—such as Rocket, Pok Pok, Lovely Hula Hands, and Fife—on the eastside, a little research will go a long way toward uncovering amazing new flavors.

AMERICAN/CASUAL

$–$$$ ✕**The Country Cat.** Bacon lovers beware: you've found hog heaven. Slow cooked, smoked country ham and samplers of pork shoulders, belly, and head await you. Menu items entail a whole 'lotta South mixed in with a Northwest twist. Chowder potpie, hickory-smoked duck leg, and fried chicken coated with a Tabasco vinaigrette are favorites. There's also a bar; brunch is served on Saturdays and Sundays. ✉*7937 S.E. Stark St., 97215* ☎*503/408–1414* ▤*AE, MC, V.*

$–$$$ ✕**Perry's on Fremont.** This diner, still famous for burgers, chicken potpies, and fish-and-chips, has gone a bit more upscale with the addition of pricier menu items such as steak and salmon. Eat outside on the large patio among the flowers, and don't pass up one of the desserts. ✉*2401*

A Chef's Paradise

The quest for the most eco-friendly, farm-supporting methods has become an obsession among chefs who flock from all over the world to take advantage of the area's local abundance. Portland is perfectly poised to take the cooking universe by storm. First, compared to major metropolitan cities like New York, Chicago, and Los Angeles, real estate is still somewhat affordable, which makes setting up shop a more obtainable reality for aspiring chefs.

Second, because of the urban growth boundary, city sprawl is kept to a minimum. Farm land is within miles, and therefore everyday deliveries of a broad spectrum of fruits and vegetables are achievable. Most chefs in Portland try to adhere to delivery from a distributor within a 100-mile radius. Not only does this make the menu offerings exciting and ever-changing, it requires chefs to come up with creative new dishes based on what's available for that month, that week, or even that day. Many chefs

indicate that it's the artistic challenge and constant change of ingredients that makes Portland seductive.

Also within the 100-mile proximity of Portland are lush forests and the Pacific Ocean, where regional specialty ingredients, such as chanterelle mushrooms and wild caught salmon, are in fresh supply. Walk into any one of Portland's most notable restaurants, and you'll find entire menus serving dishes exclusively made from regional ingredients. For desserts you're bound to discover the amazing selection of local fruits—Anjou pears, peaches, and blackberries—imbued into pies, pastries, toppings, and cakes.

Exploration of creative cuisine infused by local ingredients isn't only reserved for fine dining. Scores of local bakeries (such as Ken's Artisan Bakery), pizzerias (Hot Lips Pizza), and vegetarian establishments (Veganopolis) have built their businesses around locally harvested, organic-based menu items as well.

N.E. Fremont St., 97212 ☎*503/287–3655* ⊟*AE, D, MC, V* ⊙*Closed Sun. and Mon. No lunch weekdays.*

¢–$$ ✕**Alameda Brewhouse.** A spacious dining room and bar in a high-ceiling room with light wood and stainless steel gives this brewhouse a feeling of urban chic while still managing to remain friendly and casual. Many people come for the excellent microbrews made on premises, but the food must not be overlooked; this is no pub grub. With creative pasta dishes such as mushroom-artichoke linguine, salmon gyros, ahi tacos, and delicious burgers, it is clear that this restaurant has as much thought going into its menu and ingredients as it does into its brewing. ⊠*4675 N.E. Fremont St., Alameda 97213* ☎*503/460–9025* ▭*AE, DC, MC, V.*

¢–$$ ✕**Bread and Ink.** The old-fashioned elegance will strike you as soon as you walk in, but the high-ceiling dining room, done in cream and forest green, is not trendy in any way, and it is partly this earnest dedication to quality food that has helped it gain its name as a neighborhood landmark. Breakfast is a specialty and might include brioche French toast, smoked fish, and legendary blintzes. Lunch and dinner yield good choices, including burgers, poached salmon, and crab cakes. ⊠*3610 S.E. Hawthorne Blvd., Hawthorne District 97214* ☎*503/239–4756* ▭*AE, D, MC, V.*

$ ✕**Savoy.** Diners have their choice of sitting in either the dark and cozy tavern or the bright and open bistro. The macaroni and Wisconsin white cheddar cheese, buttery-rich garlic bread, and crispy roasted chicken are served without fanfare. Reasonably priced, seasonal menu items and a world-class tiramisu make this a solid choice for no-fuss dining. ⊠*2500 S.E. Clinton 97202* ☎*503/808–9999* ⊘*No lunch* ▭*MC, V.*

¢–$ ✕**McMenamins Kennedy School Courtyard Restaurant.** Whether you are coming to the Kennedy School to stay overnight at the hotel, to watch a movie, or just to enjoy dinner and drinks, the Courtyard Restaurant can add to your evening. The food, ranging from burgers, salads, and pizzas to fish-and-chips, pasta, prime rib, and beef stew, can satisfy most any appetite. Several standard McMenamins microbrews are always available, in addition to seasonal specialty brews. ⊠*5736 N.E. 33rd Ave., near Alberta District 97215* ☎*503/288–2192* ▭*AE, D, MC, V.*

ASIAN

$–$$ ✕**Siam Society.** Oversize red shutter doors, a beautiful outdoor patio surrounded by full plants and flowers, and a lush upstairs lounge create an inviting atmosphere that mirrors the diverse dining experience. Expect large portions of menu highlights such as chargrilled steak with a red wine reduction sauce and sweet potato fries lightly sprinkled with white truffle oil. The banana roasted pork is made by slow-cooking pork shoulder for five days while

Where to Eat
East of the
Willamette River

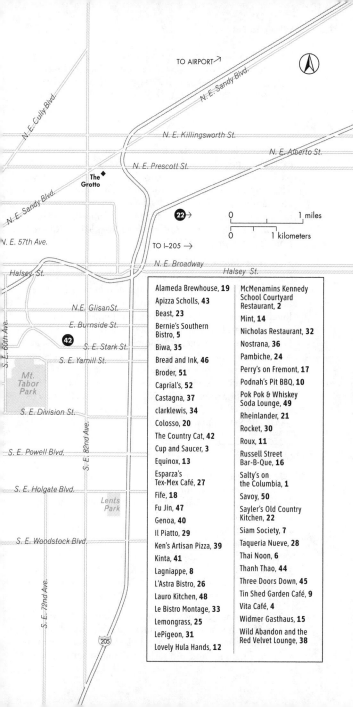

TO AIRPORT ↗

N. E. Sandy Blvd.

N. E. Cully Blvd.

N. E. Killingsworth St.

N. E. Alberta St.

N. E. Prescott St.

The Grotto

N. E. Sandy Blvd.

22 →

0   1 miles

0   1 kilometers

N. E. 57th Ave.

TO I-205 →

N. E. Broadway

Halsey St.

Halsey St.

N.E. Glisan St.

E. Burnside St.

42

S. E. Stark St.

S. E. Yamhill St.

N. E. 60th Ave.

Mt. Tabor Park

S. E. Division St.

S. E. 82nd Ave.

S. E. Powell Blvd.

S. E. Holgate Blvd.

Lents Park

S. E. Woodstock Blvd.

S. E. 72nd Ave.

205

Alameda Brewhouse, **19**

Apizza Scholls, **43**

Beast, **23**

Bernie's Southern Bistro, **5**

Biwa, **35**

Bread and Ink, **46**

Broder, **51**

Caprial's, **52**

Castagna, **37**

clarklewis, **34**

Colosso, **20**

The Country Cat, **42**

Cup and Saucer, **3**

Equinox, **13**

Esparza's Tex-Mex Café, **27**

Fife, **18**

Fu Jin, **47**

Genoa, **40**

Il Piatto, **29**

Ken's Artisan Pizza, **39**

Kinta, **41**

Lagniappe, **8**

L'Astra Bistro, **26**

Lauro Kitchen, **48**

Le Bistro Montage, **33**

Lemongrass, **25**

LePigeon, **31**

Lovely Hula Hands, **12**

McMenamins Kennedy School Courtyard Restaurant, **2**

Mint, **14**

Nicholas Restaurant, **32**

Nostrana, **36**

Pambiche, **24**

Perry's on Fremont, **17**

Podnah's Pit BBQ, **10**

Pok Pok & Whiskey Soda Lounge, **49**

Rheinlander, **21**

Rocket, **30**

Roux, **11**

Russell Street Bar-B-Que, **16**

Salty's on the Columbia, **1**

Savoy, **50**

Sayler's Old Country Kitchen, **22**

Siam Society, **7**

Taqueria Nueve, **28**

Thai Noon, **6**

Thanh Thao, **44**

Three Doors Down, **45**

Tin Shed Garden Café, **9**

Vita Café, **4**

Widmer Gasthaus, **15**

Wild Abandon and the Red Velvet Lounge, **38**

wrapped in banana leaves; it's served with grilled pineapple. Drinks not to be missed are gingerlime Cosmo and jalapeño-pear kamikaze. ⊠ *2703 N.E. Alberta St., 97211* ☎ *503/922–3675* ⊟ *MC, V* ⊙ *Closed Mon.*

CAFÉS

¢ ×**Cup and Saucer.** This casual diner-style restaurant is extremely popular with hip young locals and is always packed on weekends, especially for breakfast and lunch. The long menu includes all-day-breakfast, quiches, burgers, sandwiches, soups, and salads, with plenty of vegetarian and vegan options. ⊠ *3566 S.E. Hawthorne Blvd., Hawthorne District 97214* ☎ *503/236–6001* ⊉ *Reservations not accepted* ⊟ *MC, V.*

¢ ×**Tin Shed Garden Cafe.** This small restaurant is a popular breakfast spot, known for its shredded potato cakes, biscuits and gravy, sweet-potato cinnamon French toast, creative egg and tofu scrambles, and breakfast burritos. The lunch and dinner menu has creative items like a creamy artichoke sandwich, and a chicken sandwich with bacon, Gorgonzola, and apple, in addition to burgers, salads, and soups. A comfortable outdoor patio doubles as a beer garden on warm spring and summer evenings, and the adjacent community garden rounds off the property with a peaceful sitting area. ⊠ *1438 N.E. Alberta St., Alberta District 97211* ☎ *503/288–6966* ⊉ *Reservations not accepted* ⊟ *MC, V* ⊙ *No dinner Mon.–Tues.*

CAJUN/CREOLE

$$$ ×**Roux.** Close your eyes and you'd never know you're in a former drapery factory that was converted into a large, jovial Cajun joint, with large booths, a sizable bar area, and an adjacent deli by day. Add some spice to your life by trying some down-home favorites like roasted rabbit with cornbread-andouille stuffing and mustard sauce and hickory-smoked pork baby back ribs. Bartenders are known for their excellent southern cocktails. Don't miss the New Orleans–style Sunday brunch. ⊠ *1700 N. Killingsworth St., 97217* ☎ *503/285–1200* ⊟ *AE, D, MC, V.*

¢–$ ×**Le Bistro Montage.** Spicy Cajun is the jumping-off point for the chef at this sassy bistro under the Morrison Bridge on Portland's east side. Jambalayas, blackened pork, chicken, catfish, linguine, and old-fashioned macaroni dishes are served up from around noon until the wee hours in a spot that's loud, crowded, and casually hip. The wine list includes more than 100 varieties. ⊠*301 S.E. Morrison St., off Martin Luther King Jr. Blvd. beneath the Morrison Bridge 97214* ☏*503/234–1324* ⚞*Reservations not accepted* ⊟*No credit cards* ⊘*No lunch weekends.*

CHINESE

ȼ ✕**Fu Jin.** Although the place looks a bit tattered, this family-run neighborhood restaurant consistently serves good wok-cooked favorites at reasonable prices. The fried tofu dishes and sesame-crusted shrimp are tasty. ⊠*3549 S.E. Hawthorne Blvd., Hawthorne District 97214* ☏*503/231–3753* ⊟*D, MC, V* ⊘*Closed Thurs.*

CONTINENTAL

$$$$ ✕**Beast.** This restaurant is a quintessential example of Portland's creative cuisine. An unidentified red building houses two large communal tables, seating eight and 16, respectively, and an open kitchen. Diners have the option of constantly changing three- or five-course prix-fixe menus. Courses live up to the restaurant's namesake with dishes such as chicken and duck liver mousse, wine and truffle-braised beef, and steak tartare with quail egg toast. (That said, vegetarians may find it a bit of a struggle to eat here.) ⊠*5425 N.E. 30th Ave., 97211* ☏*503/841–6968* ⊟*MC, V.*

$$$ ✕**Castagna.** Enjoy the bouillabaisse or one of the inventive Mediterranean seafood entrées at this tranquil Hawthorne restaurant. The pan-seared scallops with mushrooms are the signature dish. Next door is the more casual **Cafe Castagna** (☏*503/231–9959*), a bistro and bar open nightly serving pizzas and other slightly less expensive, lighter fare. ⊠*1752 S.E. Hawthorne Blvd., Hawthorne District 97214* ☏*503/231–7373* ⊟*AE, D, DC, MC, V* ⊘*Closed Mon.– Tues. No lunch*

$$$ ✕**Rocket.** Invention, not convention, rules this restaurant's roost. If the contemporary, posh dining room and the rooftop garden from where herbs and lettuces are plucked don't leave an impression, then entrées such as the carrot and quinoa crepe surely will. Try the "Q Kompressor" cocktail, which has cucumber vodka and compressed cucumber blended with salt and pepper. ⊠*1111 E. Burn-*

side St., 97214 ☎*503/236–1110* ⊘*Closed Sun. and Mon. No lunch.* ▭*MC, V.*

$$–$$$ ✕**Caprial's.** PBS cooking-show star Caprial Pence serves Northwest-inspired creations at her bustling, brightly lit bistro with an open kitchen, full bar, and velvet armchairs. The dinner menu changes monthly and is limited to four or five choices, which have included pan-roasted salmon as well as smoked and grilled pork loin chop. The wine "wall" (you pick the bottle) has more than 200 varieties. ✉*7015 S.E. Milwaukie Ave., Sellwood 97202* ☎*503/236–6457* ▭*AE, MC, V* ⊘*Closed Sun. and Mon.*

$$–$$$ ✕**Fife.** To really appreciate how good food gets made, visit welcoming and comfortable Fife. The open kitchen allows diners to capture glimpses of sizzling chef Marco Shaw in action, cooking up whatever seasonal ingredients dictate. Whether it's smoked chili-rubbed cast iron chicken with potatoes and wilted greens, or lamb rack chops with black lentils, carrots, and pecan-mint purée, menu items are prepared to perfection. Don't miss the coconut cream pie with bittersweet chocolate sauce for dessert. ✉*4440 N.E. Fremont St., 97213* ☎ *971/222–3433* ⊘*Closed Sun. and Mon. No lunch* ▭*MC, V.*

$$–$$$ ✕**Lovely Hula Hands.** Two sisters and co-owners have spent a great deal of effort to create a warm, contemporary environment. The menu changes daily: in winter, expect a stew of roasted vegetables, served with saffron rice and minted yogurt. In summer, try a creamy soufflé made with chanterelles, sweet corn, spinach, and cippolini onions. Year-round you can count on one of the best burgers in town, as well as authentic 1920s cocktails. Seating here is limited and they don't take reservations, so aside from the romantic ambience, expect a wait. ✉*4057 N. Mississippi Ave., 97227* ☎*503/445–9910* ▭*MC, V* ⌂*Reservations not accepted.*

$–$$$ ✕**clarklewis.** This cutting-edge restaurant, aka "darklewis" for impractical lighting, is making big waves for inventive farm-fresh meals served inside a converted warehouse loading dock. Regional vegetables, seafood, and meat cultivated from local suppliers appear on a daily changing menu of pastas, entrées, and sides. Diners can order small, large, and family-style sizes, or let the chef decide with the fixed-price meal. Although the food is flawless, a lack of signage and proper reception can make your first visit feel a little like arriving to a party uninvited. ✉*1001 S.E. Water*

Ave., Produce Row 97214 ☎*503/235–2294* ⊘*Closed Sun. No lunch weekends* ☰*AE, MC, V.*

$–$$$ ✕**Equinox.** Locally grown organic produce, free-range meats, wild seafood, and cage-free chickens come to the table as many world cuisines at this eclectic neighborhood restaurant on North Mississippi Street. Renovated-garage chic and a pleasant outdoor patio create a casual atmosphere for enjoying an unusual combination of ingredients. Spicy *togorashi* chicken is roasted with sesame seeds, chilies, and orange peel, and topped with a ginger demi-glace. Vegetarian entrées might be tofu, spinach, and coconut-tomato-basil curry. An almond flan dessert is served in a towering martini glass. ✉ *830 N. Shaver St., at N. Mississippi St., Albina 97227* ☎*503/460–3333* ⊘*Closed Mon. No dinner Sunday.*

$–$$$ ✕**Mint.** The owner of this cool, romantic restaurant happens also to be a top-notch bartender. Drinks made with maple syrup, nutmeg, and avocados are commonplace—and just as her drinks selections are hard to categorize, so too are the menu items. Global flavors influence an evolving choice of interesting items like opah poached in coconut lemongrass sake and sautéed rabbit loin with garlic mashed potatoes and wild boar bacon. When you're done, slip next door to 820, the sister lounge to this suave establishment. ✉ *816 N. Russell St., 97227* ☎*503/284–5518* ☰*AE, MC, V* ⊘*Closed Sun. No lunch.*

¢–$$ ✕**Wild Abandon and the Red Velvet Lounge.** Inside this small, bohemian-looking building, owner Michael Cox creates an inventive Mediterranean-influenced menu that includes fresh seafood, pork, beef, and pasta entrées. Vegetarian selections might be ziti, panfried tofu, or polenta lasagna made with roasted eggplant, squash, and spinach. The popular Sunday brunch includes omelets, Benedict dishes, breakfast burritos, and vegan French toast. ✉ *2411 S.E. Belmont St., near Hawthorne District 97214* ☎*503/232–4458* ☰*AE, D, DC, MC, V* ⊘*Closed Tues. No lunch weekdays.*

¢–$ ✕**L'Astra Bistro.** Come as you are to this no-frills restaurant for a simple selection of Italian and French dishes: gnocchi with spinach, garlic sausage with lentils, and roasted duck are some unassuming favorites. Ice cream lovers will appreciate special flavors which change daily. Ask for them if they're not on the menu. ✉ *22 N.E. 7th Ave., 97214* ☎*503/236–3896* ⊘*Closed Sun. No lunch.* ☰*MC, V.*

CUBAN

¢–$ ✕**Pambiche.** Locals know that you can drive by Pambiche
★ any night of the week and find it packed. With traditional
Cuban fare including plantains, roast pork, mojitos, and
Cuban espresso, it is no surprise why. If you have some
time to wait for a table, you should stop by and make an
evening of it at this hopping neighborhood hot spot. Don't
miss out on the incredible dessert here; it is the sole reason
why some people make the trip. ✉*2811 N.E. Glisan St.,
near Laurelhurst 97232* ☎*503/233–0511* ⚑*Reservations
not accepted* ▭*D, MC, V.*

FRENCH

$$$ ✕**LePigeon.** With exposed brick, bar seating, and an open
kitchen, the atmosphere at this 42-seat restaurant is trendy,
yet casual. And yes, pigeon—cooked in red wine and
served with liver crostini—is served as an entrée. Hardcore
meat lovers might also appreciate the veal tongue appetizer.
Aside from a changing menu, there are a few pasta and
salad dishes as well. The wine menu is extensive and they
are open late. ✉*738 E. Burnside St., 97214* ☎*503/546–
8796* ⚑*Reservations essential* ▭*MC, V* ⊗*No lunch.*

GERMAN

$–$$ ✕**Rheinlander.** A strolling accordionist and singing servers
entertain as patrons dine on authentic traditional German
food, including sauerbraten, hasenpfeffer, schnitzel, sausage, and rotisserie chicken. **Gustav's,** the adjoining pub and
grill, serves slightly less expensive entrées, including sausages, cabbage rolls, and German meatballs, in an equally
festive, if slightly more raucous, environment. ✉*5035 N.E.
Sandy Blvd., 97213* ☎*503/288–5503* ▭*AE, MC, V.*

¢–$ ✕**Widmer Gasthaus.** This Old World–style brewpub, part of
the adjacent Widmer Brothers Brewery, is just steps away
from the MAX light rail station on North Interstate Avenue. Ale-dunked sausages, schnitzel, and sauerbraten are
well matched to the signature hefeweizen and other German-style beers, tapped from the handsome hardwood-
and-brass bar. Chicken potpie, steak, pasta, and burgers are
also served, in addition to the Widmer brothers' beloved
beer cheese soup. ✉*955 N. Russell St., at N. Interstate*

Ave., Albina 97227 ☎*503/281–3333* ⌖*Reservations not accepted* ⊟*AE, D, MC, V.*

ITALIAN

$$$$ ✕**Genoa.** Widely regarded as the finest restaurant in Port-
★   land, Genoa serves a seven-course prix-fixe menu focusing
on authentic Italian cuisine, that changes every two weeks.
Although the dining room is a bit drab, seating is limited to
a few dozen diners, so service is excellent. Smoking is per-
mitted in a separate sitting room. ⊠*2822 S.E. Belmont St.,
near Hawthorne District 97214* ☎*503/238–1464* ⌖*Reservations essential* ⊟*AE, D, DC, MC, V* ⊘*No lunch.*

$$–$$$ ✕**Three Doors Down.** Down a side street in the busy Haw-
★   thorne shopping district, this small Italian restaurant is
known for quality Italian food, with exquisite seafood
dishes, skillful pasta concoctions, and decadent desserts.
The intimate restaurant's reputation brings people coming
back again and again, even though they might have to wait
on the sidewalk for close to an hour. ⊠*1429 S.E. 37th
Ave., Hawthorne District 97214* ☎*503/236–6886* ⊟*AE,
D, MC, V* ⊘*Closed Mon. No lunch.*

$–$$ ✕**Apizza Scholls.** You will pay more for this pizza, but the
crispy yet chewy crust—the end result of 24-hour fermentation—is worth it. Slow fermentation with a minimum of
yeast produces acidity, which gives it creamy, textured flavor. Dough is made daily then topped by whole fresh cheeses
and minimal meats to spotlight the richness of the crust
and sauce flavorings. ⊠*4741 S.E. Hawthorne Blvd., 97215*
☎*503/233–1286* ⊟*MC, V* ⊘*Closed Sun. and Mon.*

$–$$ ✕**Il Piatto.** On a quiet residential street, this laid-back tratto-
ria and espresso house turns out inventive dishes and clas-
sic Italian favorites. A tasty sun-dried-tomato–pesto spread
instead of butter accompanies the bread. Entrées include
smoked salmon ravioli in a lemon cream sauce with capers
and leeks. The vegetarian lasagna with grilled eggplant and
zucchini, topped with pine nuts, is rich and satisfying. The
extensive wine selection focuses on varieties from Tuscany.
⊠*2348 Ankeny St., near Laurelhurst 97214* ☎*503/236–
4997* ⊟*DC, MC, V* ⊘*No lunch Sat.–Mon.*

$–$$ ✕**Ken's Artisan Pizza.** Old wine barrels and hungry crowds
surround the pizza prep area here, a glowing, 700-degree
wood-fired oven. Ken, also of Ken's Artisan Bakery &
Café, prides himself on the use of fresh, seasonal, organic

ingredients for the dough, sauces, and toppings. Fans rave about the margherita style pizza with arugula. Another favorite is the handpressed sausage and onion. Although there are some fun appetizers and salads here, pizza is the star. ⊠ *304 S.E. 28th Ave., 97214* ☎ *503/517–9951* ⊟ *MC, V* ⊘ *Closed Sun. and Mon.*

$–$$ ✕ **Nostrana.** Named *The Oregonian's* 2006 Restaurant of the Year, this restaurant delivers delicious pizzas and wood-grilled specialties (even desserts) from their signature oven. Between pies topped with roasted squash and smoked mozzarella to those sprinkled with radicchio and pancetta, the pizzas here would make mamma mia proud. Other tempting entrées are the fresh prawns and Satsuma oranges with white bean purée and the Tuscan pork ribs with smashed celery root and spicy onion relish. ⊠ *1401 S.E. Morrison St., 97214* ☎ *503/234–2427* ⊟ *MC, V.*

JAPANESE

$ ✕ **Biwa.** Taking ramen to whole new heights is what this bustling, industrial restaurant with its open kitchen does best. Homemade noodles are the focal point of aromatic, flavorful soups mixed in with accompaniments such as sliced pork and grilled chicken. Also try the thicker udon noodles served in a soup made from dried fish and seaweed. Top off a filling, authentic meal with one of the many choices in sake. ⊠ *215 S.E. 9th Ave., 97214* ☎ *503/239–8830* ⊟ *MC, DC, V* ⊘ *Closed Sun. No lunch.*

LEBANESE

¢ ✕ **Nicholas Restaurant.** In a small streetfront along an unim-
★ pressive stretch of Grand Avenue, this hidden gem serves some of the best Lebanese food in Portland, for prices that can't be beat. Everything from the fresh homemade pita to the hummus, falafel, baba ghanoush, and kebabs is delicious and comes in enormous portions. No alcohol is served here. ⊠ *318 S.E. Grand Ave., near Burnside Bridge 97214* ☎ *503/235–5123* ⊟ *No credit cards.*

MEDITERRANEAN

$$ ✕**Lauro Kitchen.** The wide, inviting space, large windows, and exposed wooden beams set the mood for enjoying the action from an open kitchen—though the real action takes place once dishes like the seafood paella or the Greek-style braised pork shoulder land in front of you. Complete your meal with an exquisite glass of scotch or brandy, or warm cherry bread pudding with pistachio caramel sauce. Since this place is usually busy, expect to wait for a table. ⊠ *3377 S.E. Division St., 97202* ☎ *503/239–7000* ▭ *AE, DC, MC, V.*

MEXICAN

¢–$ ✕**Taqueria Nueve.** If you have a South of the border sense of adventure—and a healthy appetite—then order a a full plate of wild boar enchiladas or a *nopales* salad: cactus leaves with red onions and cilantro. Generous portions, a colorful wait staff, and a constantly bustling dining room make this a lively choice to try a new take on old favorites and sip a "Bloody Maria." Reservations are accepted only for parties of six or more. ⊠ *28 N.E. 28th Ave., 97232* ☎ *503/236–6195* ▭ *MC, V.*

PAN-ASIAN

$ ✕**Kinta.** Organic seasonal vegetables, such as eggplant, shiitake mushrooms, and bok choy, accompanied by a selection of noodles, are cooked into a variety of Malaysian dishes. Soups are flavorful and aromatic and can have spice-marinated meat or shrimp added upon request. Be sure to try anything curry, especially the potato and mushroom puffs. ⊠ *3450 S.E. Belmont St., 97214* ☎ *503/234–2623* ▭ *AE, MC, V.*

¢–$ ✕**Pok Pok & Whiskey Soda Lounge.** There's no shortage here of culinary adventure here. Food here resembles what street vendors in Thailand would make: charcoal-grilled game hen stuffed with lemongrass or shredded chicken and house-pressed coconut milk. Diners have options of sitting outside by heated lamps under tents, or down below in the dark, funky cave of the Whiskey Soda Lounge. Foods are unique blends of flavors and spices, such as the coconut and jackfruit ice cream served on a sweet bun with sticky rice, condensed milk, chocolate syrup, and peanuts.

✉ *3226 S.E. Division St., 97202* ☎ *503/232–1387* ▭ *MC, V* ☾ *Closed Sun.*

SEAFOOD

$$–$$$$ ✕ **Salty's on the Columbia.** Pacific Northwest salmon (choose blackened or grilled, a half or full pound) is what this comfortable restaurant overlooking the Columbia River is known for. Blackberry-barbecue-glazed salmon highlights local ingredients. Loaded with prawns, oysters, crab, mussels, and clams, the seafood platter offers plenty of variety. The menu also includes chicken and steak. There are both a heated, covered deck and an uncovered deck for open-air dining. ✉ *3839 N.E. Marine Dr., 97211* ☎ *503/288–4444* ▭ *AE, D, DC, MC, V.*

SOUTHERN

$–$$$ ✕ **Bernie's Southern Bistro.** You definitely won't find finer soul food in Portland. At first glance, Bernie's may seem fairly expensive for the cuisine, but then, this food is in a different realm from that of your garden variety fried chicken. Restaurant specialties include crisp fried green tomatoes, crawfish, and catfish, in addition to delectable fried chicken, collard greens, and black-eyed peas. The inside of the restaurant is painted in warm oranges, and the lush outdoor patio is a Portland favorite. ✉ *2904 N.E. Alberta St., 97211* ☎ *503/282–9864* ▭ *AE, D, MC, V* ☾ *Closed Sun. and Mon. No lunch.*

$ ✕ **Podnah's Pit BBQ.** This nondescript little storefront diner hardly even declares itself with outdoor signage—but don't be fooled. Like any true Southern dish worth its sauce, the Texas- and Carolina-style dishes at Podnah's are the stuff big boy barbecues are made of. Melt-in-your-mouth pulled pork, ribs, chicken, and lamb are all slow-smoked on hardwood and served up in a sassy vinegar-based sauce. ✉ *1469 N.E. Prescott St., 97211* ☎ *503/281–3700* ▭ *MC, V.*

¢ ✕ **Lagniappe.** Catfish, oysters, shrimp, and crawfish trails are served up as jambalaya and po'boys at this New Orleans–style soul-food diner. Lagniappe (pronounced "lan-yap") also makes sandwiches from smoked pulled pork and beef brisket. Black-eyed peas, hush puppies, and collard greens round out the menu of sides. Dining is informal and extends to an outside patio in good weather. ✉ *1934 N.E. Alberta St., Alberta District 97211* ☎ *503/249–7675*

⚘*Reservations not accepted* ▭*AE, D, MC, V* ⊘*Closed Mon and Tues.*

¢ ✕**Russell St. Bar-B-Que.** Pig bric-a-brac inside this redbrick building tips you off to the specialty here. Pork is the star of the deliciously messy barbecue served by this casual neighborhood joint off Martin Luther King Jr. Boulevard, which also has beef, poultry, seafood, and smoked tofu. A saucy pulled pork sandwich and collard greens washes down nicely with a strawberry soda. ✉*325 N.E. Russell St., off N.E. Martin Luther King Jr. Blvd., 97212* ☎*503/528–8224* ▭*AE, MC, V.*

SOUTHWESTERN

¢–$ ✕**Esparza's Tex-Mex Cafe.** Be prepared for south-of-the-border craziness at this beloved local eatery. Wild West kitsch festoons the walls, but it isn't any wilder than some of the entrées that emerge from chef-owner Joe Esparza's kitchen. Look for such creations as lean smoked-sirloin tacos—Esparza's is renowned for its smoked meats—and, for the truly adventurous diner, ostrich enchiladas. ✉*2725 S.E. Ankeny St., at S.E. 28th Ave., near Laurelhurst 97214* ☎*503/234–7909* ⚘*Reservations not accepted* ▭*AE, D, MC, V* ⊘*Closed Sun.*

SPANISH

¢–$ ✕**Colosso.** A dimly lit tapas bar and restaurant, casual Colosso is one of the most romantic places to dine in northeast Portland. The best way to get the full experience of the place is to order a pitcher of sangria and split a few of the small tapas plates between you and your companions. In the evening the restaurant is usually crowded with folks drinking cocktails late into the night. ✉*1932 N.E. Broadway, Broadway District 97232* ☎*503/288–3333* ▭*D, MC, V* ⊘*No lunch.*

STEAK

$–$$$ ✕**Sayler's Old Country Kitchen.** Home of the massive 72-ounce steak (free if you can eat it in an hour—and some do), Sayler's complements its steak-focused menu with a few seafood and chicken dinners. With no pretense of being trendy or hip, this large family-style restaurant and lounge near Gresham has been around since 1946 and relies today on the same old-fashioned menu and quality it did back then. ✉*10519 S.E. Stark St., 97216* ☎*503/252–4171* ▱*AE, D, MC, V* ☻*No lunch.*

SWEDISH

¢ ✕**Broder.** Smells of freshly brewed coffee and wonderful breads greet you as you walk in. Broder is known for its perfectly translated takes on breakfast: if you can't decide between the many tasty, home-cooked options on the menu, go with the Swedish Breakfast Bord. For only ten bucks, you get the best of what's offered which, depending on the day, could include walnut toasts, smoked trout, ham, seasonal fruit, yogurt and honey, a soft boiled egg, and some sort of brilliant cheese. The coffee cakes, pastries, and breads are delectable. Lunch includes a variety of sandwiches and salads—and yes, they serve meatballs. ✉*2508 S.E. Clinton St.* ☎*503/736–3333* ▱*MC, V* ☻*No dinner.*

THAI

★ Fodor'sChoice ✕**Lemongrass.** Set in an old house, this lovely,
$ intimate establishment consistently serves tantalizing Pad Thai and a garlic basil chicken with sauce so delicious you wish you had a straw. Fresh flowers adorn the white linen tables. Dishes are cooked to order and just about everything is delectable, including the chicken chili paste and peanut curry. This restaurant only accepts cash and checks. ✉*1705 N.E. Couch St., 97232* ☎*503/231–5780* ⌂*Reservations not accepted.*

¢–$ ✕**Thai Noon.** Thai Noon is a popular spot that serves excellent traditional dishes including red, green, and yellow curry; stir fries; and noodle dishes in a vibrant orange dining room with only about 12 tables. You can choose the spiciness of your meal, but beware that although "medium" may be milder than "hot," it is still quite spicy. Thai iced tea is also available as a boozy cocktail from the adjoining bar and lounge. Try the fried banana split or the mango ice cream for dessert. ✉*2635 N.E. Alberta St., Alberta District 97211* ☎*503/282–2021* ▱*MC, V.*

VEGETARIAN

¢ ✕**Vita Cafe.** Vegan mac and cheese and vegetarian biscuits and gravy are but a few of the old favorites with a new spin. This hip restaurant along Alberta Street has a large menu with American, Mexican, Asian, and Middle Eastern–inspired entrées, and both herbivores and carnivores are sure to find something. There is plenty of free-range, organic meat to go around, in addition to the vegan and vegetarian options. Finish off your meal with a piece of decadent German chocolate cake or a peanut-butter fudge bar. ✉*3024 N.E. Alberta St., Alberta District 97211* ☎*503/335–8233* ▭*MC, V.*

VIETNAMESE

¢–$ ✕**Thanh Thao.** This busy Asian diner in the heart of Portland's bohemian Hawthorne neighborhood has an extensive menu of Vietnamese stir-fries, noodles, soups, and Thai favorites. Be prepared to wait for *and* at your table: the place is often packed, and service is famously slow. But the food and generous portions are worth the wait. ✉*4005 S.E. Hawthorne Blvd., Hawthorne District 97214* ☎*503/238–6232* ▭*D, MC, V* ☺*Closed Tues.*

Where to Stay

WORD OF MOUTH

"[The Hotel] Monaco and most other downtown hotels are within walking (or streetcar) distance of a fair share of Portland's attractions. Others to consider: Lucia, Vintage Plaza. Even Inn at Nortrup Station would work, though it's more on the fringe."

—beachbum

Updated
by Janna
Mock-
Lopez

WHEN IT COMES TO LODGING, Portland has the best of all worlds: modern to historical, fancy to basic, innovative to conventional. Reputable, large chains offer both ends of the spectrum in terms of price and amenities; luxury boutique hotels emphasize service and splendor; convenient options abound for destinations like the convention center and airport; and, sprinkled throughout the city in the midst of all these choices, one-of-a-kind bed-and-breakfast establishments offer travelers a glimpse of authentic Portland living.

Aside from price point, the main thing to consider is where in the city you want to be. Many of the elegant hotels near the city center and on the riverfront appeal because of their proximity to Portland's attractions. MAX light rail is within easy walking distance of most properties. Additional accommodations clustered near the Convention Center and the airport are almost exclusively chain hotels and tend to be slightly less expensive than those found downtown. On the other hand, a lot of downtown hotels cater to business travelers and offer special discounts on weekends.

An alternative to the standard city hotel scene is to stay at one of the several beautiful B&Bs spread throughout residential neighborhoods in the northwest and northeast. These are usually lovely homes, with unique and luxurious guest rooms, deluxe home-cooked breakfasts, and friendly and knowledgeable innkeepers.

HOTEL PRICES

Portland's hotels will please visitors used to big-city lodging prices. Even most the more luxurious hotels can be booked for under $250 per night, and there are a lot of options for around $169 per night or less. If you are willing to stay outside of the downtown area (though this is the most convenient place to stay), you can easily find a room in a suburban chain hotel for well under $100 per night. Unlike in some cities, you will not see quite as many weekend discounts (some of the top hotels catering more to business travelers do offer these, however, but the trade-off is that prices are more reasonable all the time.

Before booking your stay, visit ⊕*www.travelportland.com* to check out "Big Deal" packaged specials, which usually include double-occupancy accommodation, free nightly parking, complimentary Continental breakfast for two, and visitor vouchers for savings on dining, tax-free shopping, and more.

WHAT IT COSTS				
HOTELS				
¢	$	$$	$$$	$$$$
under $60	$61–$100	$101–$140	$141–$180	over $180

Hotel prices are for a double room excluding room tax, which varies from 6%–9½% depending on location

DOWNTOWN

From large chains to boutique properties, staying downtown ensures you'll have immediate access to just about everything Portland offers: events, restaurants, cultural venues, shops, movie theaters, and more. Transportation options are abundant thanks to the MAX, bus lines, and taxis; many hotels offer shuttle service. Portland has clean streets and, overall, is considered relatively safe.

★ Fodor's Choice ⊡**Avalon Hotel & Spa.** On the edge of Portland's
$$$$ progressive South Waterfront District, just a few minutes from downtown, this boutique property is nestled within the trees and tranquillity along the meandering Willamette River. Rooms range in size and are tastefully decorated with simple yet warm furnishings; most have a balcony. There are a full service spa and extensive fitness facility on-site. Aquariva, an Italian restaurant and wine bar on the premises, serves wonderful tapas and drinks. **Pros:** Great river views, nearby trails for walking and jogging, breakfast served on each hotel floor. **Cons:** Not in the heart of downtown, spa tubs in the fitness facility are not coed, steep overnight parking fee. ⊠*0455 S.W. Hamilton Ct., Downtown, 97239* ☎*503/802–5800 or 888/556–4402* ⊟*503/802–5820* ⊕*www.avalonhotelandspa.com* ⇩*99 rooms* ⌂*In-room: refrigerator (some), Wi-Fi. In-hotel: restaurant, room service, bar, gym, concierge, laundry service, public Wi-Fi, parking (fee), no-smoking rooms* ⊟*AE, MC, V* ⊺◯*CP.*

★ Fodor's Choice ⊡**Heathman Hotel.** The Heathman more than
$$$$ deserves its reputation for quality. From the teak-paneled lobby hung with Warhol prints to the rosewood elevators and marble fireplaces, this hotel exudes refinement. The guest rooms provide the latest in customized comfort: a bed menu allows you to choose from orthopedic, European pillowtop, or European featherbed mattresses, and the

bathrooms have plenty of marble and mirrors. The second-floor mezzanine—with a small art gallery (works change every several weeks) and a small library (primarily filled with the works of notable Heathman guests)—overlooks the high-ceiling Tea Court, a popular gathering spot in the evening. **Pros:** Superior service, central location adjoining the Performing Arts Center, renowned on-site restaurant. **Cons:** Small rooms, expensive parking. ⊠ *1001 S.W. Broadway, Downtown, 97205* ☎ *503/241–4100 or 800/551–0011* ⊟ *503/790–7110* ⊕ *www.heathmanhotel.com* ⤶ *117 rooms, 33 suites* ⌂ *In-room: refrigerator, ethernet, dial-up. In-hotel: restaurant, room service, bar, gym, concierge, laundry service, public Wi-Fi, parking (fee), some pets allowed, no-smoking rooms* ⊟ *AE, D, DC, MC, V.*

$$$–$$$$ ▧**Embassy Suites.** The grand lobby welcomes you at this property in the historic Multnomah Hotel building. The spacious, two-room suites have large windows, sofa beds, and wet bars. The indoor pool curves around the lower level of the hotel. A complimentary shuttle will take you within a 2-mi radius, based on availability. A cooked-to-order full breakfast and cocktail reception with light snacks are included in the rate. **Pros:** Beautiful historic building, free shuttle service, excellent location. **Cons:** Snack reception is popcorn and nachos, no in-and-out privileges in self-park garage across the street. ⊠ *319 S.W. Pine St., Downtown, 97204* ☎ *503/279–9000 or 800/642–7892* ⊟ *503/497–9051* ⊕ *www.embassyportland.com* ⤶ *276 suites* ⌂ *In-room: refrigerator, Wi-Fi. In-hotel: restaurant, bar, pool, gym, spa, concierge, laundry service, public Wi-Fi, parking (fee)* ⊟ *AE, D, DC, MC, V* ⊚ *BP.*

$$$–$$$$ ▧**Governor Hotel.** With its mahogany walls and mural of Pacific Northwest Indians fishing in Celilo Falls, the clubby lobby of the distinctive Governor sets the overall tone for the hotel's 1920s Arts and Crafts style. Painted in soothing earth tones, the tastefully appointed guest rooms have large windows, honor bars, and bathrobes. Some have whirlpool tubs, fireplaces, and balconies. Jake's Grill is on the property, the streetcar runs right out front, and the hotel is one block from MAX. **Pros:** Large rooms, beautiful historic property, excellent restaurant. **Cons:** Some rooms in need of updates, no late-night room service. ⊠ *614 S.W. 10th Ave., Downtown, 97205* ☎ *503/224–3400 or 800/554–3456* ⊟ *503/241–2122* ⊕ *www.govhotel.com* ⤶ *68 rooms, 32 suites* ⌂ *In-room: refrigerator, dial-up. In-hotel: restau-*

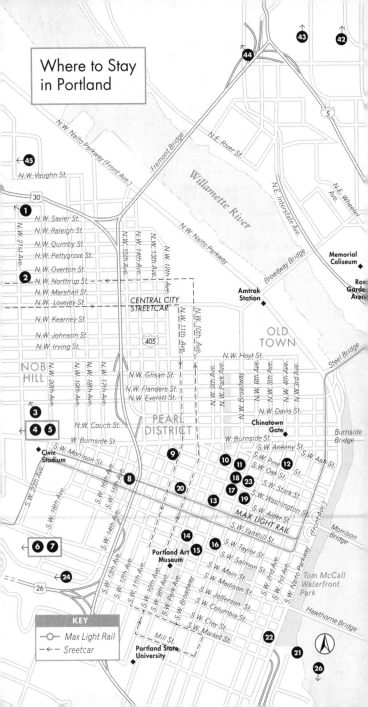

Where to Stay in Portland

N.W. Naito Parkway (Front Ave.)

Fremont Bridge

N.E. River St.

Willamette River

N.E. Interstate Ave.

N.E. Wheeler Ave.

N.W. Vaughn St.

45

N.W. Naito Parkway

Broadway Bridge

Memorial Coliseum

30

1

N.W. Savier St.
N.W. Raleigh St.
N.W. Quimby St.
N.W. Pettygrove St.
N.W. Overton St.

Ros Garde Aren

N.W. 21st Ave.

N.W. 15th Ave.
N.W. 14th Ave.
N.W. 13th Ave.
N.W. 12th Ave.

2

N.W. Northrup St.
N.W. Marshall St.
N.W. Lovejoy St.

CENTRAL CITY STREETCAR

Amtrak Station

N.W. Kearney St.
N.W. Johnson St.
N.W. Irving St.

405

N.W. 11th Ave.

N.W. 10th Ave.

OLD TOWN

Steel Bridge

NOB HILL

N.W. 20th Ave.
N.W. 19th Ave.
N.W. 18th Ave.
N.W. 17th Ave.

N.W. Glisan St.
N.W. Flanders St.
N.W. Everett St.

N.W. Hoyt St.

N.W. 9th Ave.
N.W. Park Ave.
N.W. Broadway
N.W. 6th Ave.
N.W. 5th Ave.
N.W. 4th Ave.
N.W. 3rd Ave.

N.W. Davis St.

3

N.W. Couch St.

PEARL DISTRICT

Chinatown Gate

Burnside Bridge

4 **5**

W. Burnside St.

W. Burnside St.

S.W. Ankeny St.   S.W. Ash St.

Civic Stadium

S.W. Morrison St.

9

10 **11**

S.W. Pine St.
S.W. Oak St.

12

St.

S.W. 20th Ave.
S.W. 18th Ave.
S.W. 16th Ave.
S.W. 14th Ave.

8

18 **23**

S.W. Stark St.

20

17

S.W. Washington St.

13

19

S.W. Alder St.

MAX LIGHT RAIL

S.W. Yamhill St.

Morrison Bridge

6 **7**

S.W. 18th Ave.

14

S.W. Taylor St.

Portland Art Museum

15 **16**

S.W. Salmon St.

24

26

S.W. 12th Ave.
S.W. 11th Ave.
S.W. 10th Ave.
S.W. 9th Ave.
S.W. Park Ave.
S.W. Broadway

S.W. Main St.
S.W. Madison St.
S.W. Jefferson St.
S.W. Columbia St.
S.W. Clay St.
S.W. Market St.

S.W. 5th Ave.
S.W. 4th Ave.
S.W. 3rd Ave.
S.W. 2nd Ave.
S.W. 1st Ave.
S.W. Naito Parkway (Front Ave.)

Tom McCall Waterfront Park

Hawthorne Bridge

Mill St.

22

Portland State University

21

26

KEY
—O— Max Light Rail
– ← – Sreetcar

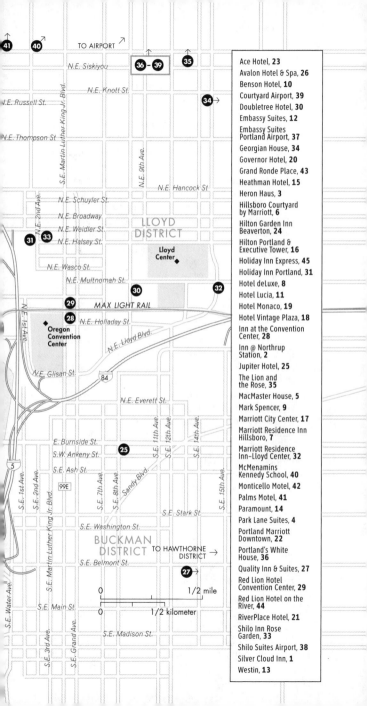

TO AIRPORT

N.E. Siskiyou
36 – 39   35
N.E. Knott St.
34

N.E. Russell St.
N.E. Thompson St.

N.E. Hancock St.

N.E. Schuyler St.
N.E. Broadway
LLOYD
DISTRICT
N.E. Weidler St.
N.E. Halsey St.
31   33

Lloyd
Center
N.E. Wasco St.
N.E. Multnomah St.
30   32

29   MAX LIGHT RAIL
28   N.E. Holladay St.
Oregon
Convention
Center
N.E. Lloyd Blvd.
N.E. Glisan St.
84

N.E. Everett St.
N.E. Everett St.

E. Burnside St.
25
S.W. Ankeny St.
S.E. Ash St.
99E

S.E. Stark St.

S.E. Washington St.
BUCKMAN
DISTRICT   TO HAWTHORNE
DISTRICT
S.E. Belmont St.
27
0   1/2 mile

S.E. Main St.
0   1/2 kilometer
S.E. Madison St.

Ace Hotel, 23
Avalon Hotel & Spa, 26
Benson Hotel, 10
Courtyard Airport, 39
Doubletree Hotel, 30
Embassy Suites, 12
Embassy Suites Portland Airport, 37
Georgian House, 34
Governor Hotel, 20
Grand Ronde Place, 43
Heathman Hotel, 15
Heron Haus, 3
Hillsboro Courtyard by Marriott, 6
Hilton Garden Inn Beaverton, 24
Hilton Portland & Executive Tower, 16
Holiday Inn Express, 45
Holiday Inn Portland, 31
Hotel deluxe, 8
Hotel Lucia, 11
Hotel Monaco, 19
Hotel Vintage Plaza, 18
Inn at the Convention Center, 28
Inn @ Northrup Station, 2
Jupiter Hotel, 25
The Lion and the Rose, 35
MacMaster House, 5
Mark Spencer, 9
Marriott City Center, 17
Marriott Residence Inn Hillsboro, 7
Marriott Residence Inn–Lloyd Center, 32
McMenamins Kennedy School, 40
Monticello Motel, 42
Palms Motel, 41
Paramount, 14
Park Lane Suites, 4
Portland Marriott Downtown, 22
Portland's White House, 36
Quality Inn & Suites, 27
Red Lion Hotel Convention Center, 29
Red Lion Hotel on the River, 44
RiverPlace Hotel, 21
Shilo Inn Rose Garden, 33
Shilo Suites Airport, 38
Silver Cloud Inn, 1
Westin, 13

TOP 5 PORTLAND LODGING TIPS

■ Vintage glamour meets the future at the Hotel deLuxe, where 1940s decor and black-and-white photographs coexist with flat-screen HDTVs and iPod docking stations in each room.

■ Make yourself at home at the Lion and the Rose, a 1906 Queen Anne–style mansion that is the city's only Victorian B&B.

■ Experience the funky, eclectic flair of the McMenamins Kennedy School, a renovated elementary school where guests can sleep in former classrooms and hang out at the Honor Bar or the Detention Bar.

■ See the city without having to leave your room: take in gorgeous river, marina, and skyline views at the River-Place Hotel.

■ Some hotels offer a pillow menu; the Heathman Hotel offers a bed menu—and plenty of refinement to spare.

rant, room service, bar, concierge, laundry service, parking (fee), no-smoking rooms ⊟*AE, D, DC, MC, V.*

$$$–$$$$ 🖫**Hotel Lucia.** Modern track lighting, black-and-white David Kennerly celebrity photos, and comfy leather chairs adorn this eight-story boutique hotel in the heart of downtown—within walking distance to Nordstrom, Powell's, and the MAX line. The hotel's goal to "deliver calm" is accomplished in part through seven choices in pillows, stored customer profiles (so you automatically receive that same pillow next time), and Aveda soaps and lotions. The Pet Package caters to the small, furry members of your family with a special bed, set of dishes, treats, and even Fiji water. **Pros:** Prime location, luxurious amenities, consistently good service. **Cons:** Small rooms, limited shelf and storage space in the bathrooms, those with allergies should request a pet-free room. ⊠*400 S.W. Broadway St., Downtown, 97205* ☎*503/225–1717 or 877/225–1717* 🖷*503/225–1919* ⊕*www.hotellucia.com* ⤶*127 rooms, 33 suites* ⌂*In-room: Wi-Fi. In-hotel: restaurant, room service, gym, concierge, laundry service, parking (fee), no-smoking rooms, some pets allowed* ⊟*AE, D, DC, MC, V.*

$$$–$$$$ 🖫**Hotel Monaco.** Constructed in 1912, this building originally served as Lipman Wolfe, an upscale downtown department store. In 1996 the historic building reopened as a 221-suite luxury boutique hotel, and in 2007 new ownership completed a $4 million upgrade to the property. A tall vestibule

4

with a marble mosaic floor leads to the art-filled lobby, where guests gather by the fireplace for an early-evening glass of wine or a morning cup of coffee. Upholstered chairs, fringed ottomans, and other appointments in the sitting areas will make you feel right at home (or wish you had one like this). Downstairs in the lobby is the Dosha Spa. **Pros:** Bathrooms stocked with every amenity, historic building, free Starbucks coffee in the morning. **Cons:** Can get chilly at night because of drafty windows, rooms on lower floors tend to be noisier. ⊠*506 S.W. Washington St., Downtown, 97204* ☎*503/222–0001 or 888/207–2201* ≞*503/222–0004* ⊕*www.portland-monaco.com* ⊸*82 rooms, 137 suites* ⬠*In-room: refrigerator, dial-up, Wi-Fi. In-hotel: restaurant, room service, gym, laundry service, public Wi-Fi, parking (fee), no-smoking rooms, some pets allowed* ⊟*AE, D, DC, MC, V.*

\$\$\$–\$\$\$\$ ▥**Hotel Vintage Plaza.** This historic landmark takes its theme from the area's vineyards. Guests can fall asleep counting stars in top-floor rooms, where skylights and wall-to-wall conservatory-style windows rate highly among the special details. Hospitality suites have extra-large rooms with a full living area, and the deluxe rooms have a bar. All are appointed in warm colors and have cherrywood furnishings; some rooms have hot tubs. Complimentary wine is served in the evening, and an extensive collection of Oregon vintages is displayed in the tasting room. Two-story town house suites are named after local wineries. **Pros:** Beautiful decor, nice complimentary wine selections, pet-friendly. **Cons:** Those with allergies should ask for pet-free rooms, some street noise on the lower levels on the Washington side of the hotel. ⊠*422 S.W. Broadway, Downtown, 97205* ☎*503/228–1212 or 800/243–0555* ≞*503/228–3598* ⊕*www.vintageplaza.com* ⊸*107 rooms, 21 suites* ⬠*In-room: refrigerator, dial-up, Wi-Fi. In-hotel: restaurant, room service, bar, gym, concierge, public Wi-Fi, parking (fee), some pets allowed* ⊟*AE, D, DC, MC, V.*

\$\$\$–\$\$\$\$ ▥**Paramount.** Inside this 15-story boutique-style property—
★ two blocks from Pioneer Square, MAX, and the Portland Art Museum—earth tones, plush dark-wood furnishings, and dried flowers adorn the cozy rooms. Some have outdoor balconies and whirlpool tubs. The grand suites also have wet bars and gas fireplaces. Dragonfish, an excellent Pan-Asian restaurant, is on the premises. **Pros:** Beautiful granite bathrooms, in-room honor bars. **Cons:** Small fitness facilities, near ongoing downtown construction. ⊠*808*

S.W. Taylor St., Downtown, 97205 ☎*503/223–9900* 🖶*503/223–7900 or 800/663–1144* ⊕*www.portlandpara-mount.com* ⟿*154 rooms* ⚐*In-room: refrigerator, dial-up, Wi-Fi. In-hotel: restaurant, room service, gym, concierge, laundry service, parking (fee), no-smoking rooms* ⊟*AE, D, DC, MC, V.*

$$$–$$$$ 🖵**Portland Marriott Downtown.** The large rooms at Marriott's 16-floor corporate-focused waterfront property are decorated in off-whites; the best ones face east with a view of the Willamette and the Cascades. All rooms have work desks, high-speed Internet access, and voice mail. Champions Lounge, filled with sports memorabilia, is a singles' hot spot on weekends. **Pros:** Excellent waterfront location, six blocks from MAX light rail. **Cons:** No refrigerators or minibars, can get crowded. ⊠*1401 S.W. Naito Pkwy., Downtown, 97201* ☎*503/226–7600 or 800/228–9290* 🖶*503/221–1789* ⊕*www.marriott.com* ⟿*503 rooms, 6 suites* ⚐*In-room: dial-up. In-hotel: restaurant, room service, bar, pool, gym, concierge, laundry facilities, laundry service, airport shuttle (fee), parking (fee), no-smoking rooms* ⊟*AE, D, DC, MC, V.*

$$$–$$$$ 🖵**RiverPlace Hotel.** This hotel is adorned with muted color schemes, Craftsman-style desks, and ergonomic chairs in all guest rooms. Over a quarter of the rooms have the best views in Portland—overlooking the river, marina, and skyline, as well as a landscaped courtyard. Extras include bathrobes, afternoon tea and cookies, and rooms stocked with Starbucks coffee and Tazo tea. **Pros:** Great location, wide selection of room options, great beds. **Cons:** No pool. ⊠*1510 S.W. Harbor Way, Downtown, 97201* ☎*503/228–3233 or 800/227–1333* 🖶*503/295–6161* ⊕*www.riverplacehotel.com* ⟿*39 rooms, 45 suites* ⚐*In-room: DVD, dial-up, Wi-Fi. In-hotel: restaurant, room service, concierge, parking (fee), no-smoking rooms* ⊟*AE, D, DC, MC, V.*

$$$–$$$$ 🖵**Westin.** This European-style boutique property combines luxury with convenience. Its tastefully appointed rooms include entertainment-center armoires, work desks, plush beds covered with layers of down, and granite bathrooms with separate showers and tubs. Pioneer Square and MAX are two blocks away. The Daily Grill features traditional American fare in an upscale, casual atmosphere. **Pros:** Prime downtown location, comfortable beds, well-equipped fitness center. **Cons:** No spa or sauna, limited

room service menu. ✉*750 S.W. Alder St., Downtown, 97205* ☎*503/294–9000 or 888/625–5144* 🖷*503/241–9565* ⊕*www.westin.com* ⇗*205 rooms* ⌂*In-room: safe, refrigerator, dial-up, Wi-Fi. In-hotel: restaurant, room service, bar, gym, concierge, laundry service, parking (fee)* ▤*AE, D, DC, MC, V.*

$$–$$$$ 🖩**Benson Hotel.** Portland's grandest hotel was built in 1912.
★ The hand-carved Russian Circassian walnut paneling and the Italian white-marble staircase are among the noteworthy design touches in the public areas. In the guest rooms expect to find small crystal chandeliers and inlaid mahogany doors. Some even have the original ceilings. Extra touches include fully stocked private bars and bathrobes in every room. **Pros:** Beautiful lobby, excellent location. **Cons:** Hallways could use updating. ✉*309 S.W. Broadway, Downtown, 97205* ☎*503/228–2000 or 888/523–6766* 🖷*503/471–3920* ⊕*www.bensonhotel.com* ⇗*287 rooms* ⌂*In-room: refrigerator (some), dial-up, Wi-Fi. In-hotel: 2 restaurants, room service, bar, gym, concierge, laundry service, public Wi-Fi, parking (fee)* ▤*AE, D, DC, MC, V.*

$$–$$$$ 🖩**Hotel deLuxe.** If you long to be transported back to the
★ era of 1940s of Hollywood glamour, this vintage hotel is perfect for your time travel itinerary. More than 400 black-and-white photographs adorning corridor walls on eight floors are cast into cinematic themes (Music Masters, Rebels, Exiles, and Immigrants). If the standard King James Bible in the drawer doesn't ignite your spiritual flame, than choose from a selection of other texts, including Buddhist, Taoist, Catholic, and even Scientologist offerings. **Pros:** "Pillow menu" and other extra touches lend air of luxury, artistic vibe. **Cons:** Older windows in building can feel drafty at night, cold bathroom floors. ✉*729 S.W. 15th Ave., Downtown, 97205* ☎*503/219–2094 or 866/895–2094* 🖷*503/219–2095* ⊕*www.hoteldeluxeportland.com* ⇗*130 rooms* ⌂*In-room: refrigerator, Wi-Fi. In-hotel: restaurant, room service, bar, public Wi-Fi, parking (fee), no-smoking rooms, some pets allowed* ▤*AE, D, DC, MC, V* ⦾*CP.*

$–$$$$ 🖩**Ace Hotel.** Designed to appeal to a younger set of budget-minded travelers who crave quality, this funky, bohemian property emulates the creativity and class Portland offers. Each room is uniquely adorned by original hand-painted wall art; in a handful you can find retro accessories like turntables with record collections and bathrooms with

4

cast-iron tubs. In case you forgot your camera, there's even a photo booth in the lobby to capture your stay. Clyde Common, a great restaurant, is downstairs. **Pros:** Unique lodging experience, original artwork in each room, city bicycles available for rent. **Cons:** Poor water pressure, poor noise insulation. ⊠ *1022 S.W. Stark St., Downtown, 97205* ☎ *503/228–2277* ⊕ *www.acehotel.com* ⤏ *79 rooms* ⌂ *In-room: refrigerator, Wi-Fi. In-hotel: restaurant, laundry service, public Wi-Fi, parking (fee), no-smoking rooms, some pets allowed* ▤ *AE, D, DC, MC, V.*

$$$ **Hilton Portland & Executive Tower.** Together, two buildings comprise a gargantuan complex of luxuriously contemporary bedrooms, meeting rooms, restaurants, and athletic facilities, including two indoor swimming pools. The property is within walking distance of the Performing Arts Center, Pioneer Courthouse Square, the Portland Art Museum, and MAX light rail. **Pros:** Nice workout facilities and indoor pools, prime downtown location near attractions and restaurants. **Cons:** Downtown construction could mean noise and traffic, not for those looking for homier lodging. ⊠ *921 S.W. 6th Ave., Downtown, 97204* ☎ *503/226–1611 or 800/445–8667* ⊠ *503/220–2565* ⊕ *www.hilton.com* ⤏ *773 rooms, 9 suites* ⌂ *In-room: dial-up, ethernet. In-hotel: 2 restaurants, bars, pools, gym, parking (fee), no-smoking rooms* ▤ *AE, D, DC, MC, V.*

$$$ **Marriott City Center.** The lobby of this 20-story boutique property, in the heart of the downtown arts and dining area, is accented with a grand staircase, maple paneling, and marble floors. The plush rooms have voice mail, large work desks, and coffeemakers. The MAX light rail is two blocks away. **Pros:** Work-friendly rooms, great location. **Cons:** Refrigerators available upon request only, no in-room safes. ⊠ *520 S.W. Broadway, Downtown, 97205* ☎ *503/226–6300 or 800/228–9290* ⊠ *503/227–7515* ⊕ *www.marriott.com* ⤏ *249 rooms, 10 suites* ⌂ *In-room: dial-up. In-hotel: restaurant, room service, bar, gym, concierge, laundry service, public Wi-Fi, parking (fee)* ▤ *AE, D, DC, MC, V.*

$$–$$$ **Silver Cloud Inn.** Staying at the Silver Cloud, adjacent to the lively Northwest 23rd Avenue, is a great alternative to being right downtown. There's a broad selection of spacious, contemporary rooms—kings, suites, and Jacuzzi suites—with 42" hi-definition plasma TVs. During the week local area van shuttle is available. **Pros:** Free parking, town car service available, spacious rooms. **Cons:** No pool, no in-room safes. ✉ *2426 N.W. Vaughn St., Downtown, 97210* ☎ *503/242–2400 or 800/205–6939* 🖷 *503/242–1770* ⊕ *www.silvercloud.com* 🛏 *82 rooms* ⚴ *In-room: refrigerator, kitchen, Wi-Fi. In-hotel: laundry facilities, laundry service, no-smoking rooms* ⊟ *AE, D, DC, MC, V* ⦿ *CP.*

$–$$$ 🖵 **Mark Spencer.** The Mark Spencer, near Portland's gay-bar district and Powell's City of Books, is one of the best values in town. The rooms are clean and comfortable, and all have full kitchens. The hotel is a major supporter of local arts and offers special packages that include theater tickets to performances by the Artists Repertory Theatre, Portland Opera, and Center Stage. **Pros:** Afternoon tea and cookies is included, rooftop garden deck open to all guests. **Cons:** Some rooms could use updating, those with allergies should request a pet-free room. ✉ *409 S.W. 11th Ave., Downtown, 97205* ☎ *503/224–3293 or 800/548–3934* 🖷 *503/223–7848* ⊕ *www.markspencer.com* 🛏 *102 rooms* ⚴ *In-room: kitchen, Wi-Fi. In-hotel: laundry facilities, laundry service, public Wi-Fi, no-smoking rooms, pets allowed* ⊟ *AE, D, DC, MC, V* ⦿ *CP.*

$–$$$ 🖵 **Park Lane Suites.** Located just blocks from Washington Park, Nob Hill, and downtown, this all-suites property has spacious, work-friendly living areas. The kitchens have plenty of cabinet space, and come stocked with decent dishware, full-size refrigerator, stovetop, microwave, and dishwasher. **Pros:** Proximity to several of Portland's most prominent neighborhoods, expanded kitchen capacity. **Cons:** Parking is free but limited, not enough noise insulation. ✉ *809 S.W. King Ave., Downtown, 97205* ☎ *503/226–6288* 🖷 *503/274–0038* ⊕ *www.parklanesuites. com* 🛏 *44 rooms* ⚴ *In-room: refrigerator, kitchen, ethernet. In-hotel: laundry facilities, laundry service, no-smoking rooms, some pets allowed* ⊟ *AE, D, DC, MC, V.*

EAST OF THE WILLAMETTE

The area east of the Willamette is not nearly as condensed as downtown Portland, which means getting around here is less convenient—though, because of MAX and excellent bus service, still doable. Properties tend to be older, with lower prices than downtown and greater availability. The majority of chain hotels are clustered around the convention center; nearby is Lloyd Center Mall, which has an ice-skating rink, movie theaters, and several levels of shops and restaurants. There are also a number of B&Bs on this side of town, tucked away in historical neighborhoods like Irvington.

$$$-$$$$ ⊞**Grand Ronde Place.** For a unique view of the city, try seeing it from the Columbia River and staying on Portland's only "yacht & breakfast." This beautiful 34-foot yacht has two well-equipped staterooms, a microwave, cable TV, a bathroom with shower, and even Wi-Fi access. Once on board, you'll be greeted by a fresh fruit and cheese platter and nice selection of Oregon wine; you can also have a catered dinner brought on board to enjoy while cruising down the river. **Pros:** Unique travel experience, fresh-brewed coffee and pastries in the morning. **Cons:** Kids aren't allowed, smaller than usual quarters compared with standard hotel rooms. ⊠*250 N.E. Tomahawk Island Dr., Slip H-3, Hayden Island, 97217* ☎*503/901–9802 or 866/330–7245* 🖷*503/285–1596* ⊕*www.thegrandronde-place.com* ⬧*2 staterooms* ⌂*In-room: Wi-Fi. In-hotel: no kids under 18, no-smoking rooms* ⊟*AE, MC, V.*

$$$-$$$$ ⊞**Portland's White House.** Hardwood floors with Oriental
★ rugs, chandeliers, antiques, and fountains create a warm and romantic mood at this elegant B&B in the historic Irvington District. The Greek Revival mansion was built in 1911 and is on the National Register of Historic Landmarks. Rooms have private baths, flat-screen TVs, and mahogany canopy or four-poster queen- and king-size beds. A full breakfast is included in the room rate, and the owners offer vegetarian or vegan options. Smoking and pets are not permitted. **Pros:** Romantic, authentic historical Portland experience, excellent service. **Cons:** Located in residential neighborhood, shops and restaurants several blocks away. ⊠*1914 N.E. 22nd Ave., Irvington, 97212* ☎*503/287–7131 or 800/272–7131* 🖷*503/249–1641* ⊕*www.portlandswhitehouse.com* ⬧*8 suites* ⌂*In-room: dial-up, Wi-Fi. In-hotel: no elevator, parking (no fee), no-smoking rooms* ⊟*AE, D, MC, V* ⏃*BP.*

$$-$$$$ ⊞**Doubletree Hotel.** This bustling, business-oriented hotel maintains a huge traffic in meetings and special events. The public areas are a tasteful mix of marble, rose-and-green carpet, and antique-style furnishings. The large rooms, many with balconies, have views of the mountains or the city center. Lloyd Center and the MAX light-rail

line are across the street; the Oregon Convention Center is a five-minute walk away. **Pros:** Convenient location, nice views, access to shops. **Cons:** Pool is outdoors, can be crowded. ⊠*1000 N.E. Multnomah St., Lloyd District, 97232* ☎*503/281–6111 or 800/222–8733* ☏*503/284–8553* ⊕*www.doubletree.com* ➘*476 rooms* ⚭*In-room: dial-up, ethernet. In-hotel: 2 restaurants, room service, bar, pool, gym, concierge, laundry service, public Wi-Fi, parking (fee)* ☰*AE, D, DC, MC, V.*

★ **Fodor'sChoice** ▨ **Lion and the Rose.** Oak and mahogany floors,
$$–$$$$ original light fixtures, antique silver, and the coffered dining-room ceiling set a tone of formal elegance, while the wonderfully friendly, accommodating, and knowledgeable innkeepers make sure that you feel perfectly at home. A two-course breakfast and evening snacks are served daily. In a beautiful residential neighborhood, you're a block from the shops and restaurants that fill northeast Broadway and within an easy walk of a free MAX ride downtown. **Pros:** Gorgeous home, top-notch service, afternoon tea available upon request. **Cons:** Kids under 10 not allowed, books up quickly (particularly in summer). ⊠*1810 N.E. 15th Ave., Irvington, 97212* ☎*503/287–9245 or 800/955–1647* ☏*503/287–9247* ⊕*www.lionrose.com* ➘*7 rooms* ⚭*In-room: dial-up, Wi-Fi. In-hotel: no elevator, parking (no fee), no kids under 7, no-smoking rooms* ☰*AE, D, DC, MC, V.*

$$–$$$$ ▨**Marriott Residence Inn—Lloyd Center.** With large, fully equipped suites and a short walk both to the Lloyd Center and a MAX stop within Fareless Square, this three-level apartment-style complex is perfect for extended-stay visitors or for tourists. Rooms come equipped with full kitchens and ample seating space, and many have wood-burning fireplaces. There's a large complimentary breakfast buffet each morning, and an hors d'oeuvres reception on weekday evenings. **Pros:** Full kitchens, accessible location. **Cons:** Pool is outdoors and closed during winter. ⊠*1710 N.E. Multnomah St., Lloyd District, 97232* ☎*503/288–1400 or 800/331–3131* ☏*503/288–0241* ⊕*www.marriott.com* ➘*168 rooms* ⚭*In-room: kitchen, Wi-Fi. In-hotel: bar, pool, gym, laundry facilities, public Wi-Fi, parking (no fee), no-smoking rooms, some pets allowed* ❉*BP.*

$$–$$$$ ▨ **Shilo Inn Rose Garden.** This family-friendly hotel pro-
☾ vides respectable accommodations and great service. Some rooms have sofas, and furnishings and amenities are up-

to-date. It's a five-minute walk to the MAX transit center, which has direct service to the airport. **Pros:** Recently remodeled property, spa and sauna on-site. **Cons:** No shuttle service, off the beaten path from shops and restaurants. ⊠*1506 N.E. 2nd Ave., Lloyd District, 97232* ☎*503/736–6300 or 800/222–2244* 🖷*503/736–6316* ⊕*www.shiloinns.com* ⇨*44 rooms* ⌂*In-room: refrigerator, Wi-Fi. In-hotel: spa, no elevator, laundry service, public Wi-Fi, parking, some pets allowed, no-smoking rooms* ⊟*AE, D, DC, MC, V* ⦿*CP.*

$$ ▥**Holiday Inn Express.** You'll find spacious, updated rooms at this chain hotel right on the edge of Portland's trendy N.W. 23rd Avenue neighborhood. On-site is an indoor pool and you're offered a generous complimentary breakfast buffet. **Pros:** Indoor pool, friendly service. **Cons:** Located right near a highway. ⊠*2333 N.W. Vaughn Ave., N.W. 23rd Avenue, 97210* ☎*503/484–1100 or 800/718–8466* 🖷*503/484–1101* ⊕*www.holidayinnwashington oregon.com* ⇨*90 rooms* ⌂*In-room: refrigerator, ethernet. In-hotel: laundry facilities, laundry service, no-smoking rooms* ⊟*AE, D, DC, MC, V* ⦿*CP.*

$$ ▥**Holiday Inn Portland.** This sleek, modern hotel is close to the Rose Quarter, the Coliseum, and the convention center, and is within easy walking distance of Lloyd Center, the MAX line, and the Broadway Bridge leading to downtown. Between its attractive rooms and its ample facilities, it provides a reliable and convenient option for both business travelers and tourists. **Pros:** Indoor pool, convenient location. **Cons:** In-room refrigerators are based upon request and not guaranteed. ⊠*1441 N.E. 2nd Ave., Lloyd District/ Convention Center, 97232* ☎*503/233–2401 or 877/777–2704* 🖷*503/238–7016* ⊕*www.hiportland.com* ⇨*240 rooms* ⌂*In-room: refrigerator (some), Wi-Fi. In-hotel: restaurant, bar, pool, gym* ⊟*AE, D, DC, MC, V.*

$–$$ ▥**Georgian House.** This redbrick Georgian Colonial–style house with neoclassical columns is on a quiet, tree-lined street in the Irvington neighborhood. The gardens in back can be enjoyed from one of the guest verandas or from the gazebo. The largest and sunniest of the guest rooms is the Lovejoy Suite, with a tile fireplace and brass canopy bed. **Pros:** Warm hospitality, intimate environment. **Cons:** Located in residential neighborhood, some rooms have shared bathrooms. ⊠*1828 N.E. Siskiyou St., Irvington, 97212* ☎*503/281–2250 or 888/282–2250* 🖷*503/281–*

3301 ⊕*www.thegeorgianhouse.com* ⟋*2 rooms with shared bath, 2 suites* ♿*In-room: no phone, no TV (some). In-hotel: no elevator, no-smoking rooms* ⊟*MC, V* ⟋O⟍*BP.*

$–$$ ⬚**Inn at the Convention Center.** Convenience is the main asset of this no-frills, independently run hotel: it's directly across the street from the convention center, four blocks from Lloyd Center, and right along the MAX line. Rooms at this six-story inn are simple and comfortable. **Pros:** Right next to convention center, walking distance to Lloyd Center Mall. **Cons:** Not wheelchair friendly, could use updates. ✉*420 N.E. Holladay St., Lloyd District/Convention Center, 97232* ☎*503/233–6331* 🖷*503/233–2677* ⊕*www.innatcc.com* ⟋*97 rooms* ♿*In-room: refrigerator (some), dial-up, Wi-Fi. In-hotel: laundry facilities, laundry service, public Wi-Fi, parking (no fee), no-smoking rooms* ⊟*AE, D, DC, MC, V.*

$–$$ ⬚**The Jupiter Hotel.** The hip and adventurous, looking for a place to dock their iPods for the night, flock to this contemporary hotel, which provides easy access to downtown. Rooms feature iPod docking stations, modern furniture, down comforters and colorful shag pillows, and chalkboard doors. Also on-site are a hair salon, a tattoo parlor, a clothing and gift boutique, and the Doug Fir rock club. **Pros:** Easy access to downtown, funky lodging, built-in nightlife. **Cons:** Not for everyone's taste, not immediately near a lot of shops or restaurants, near loud hot spot. ✉*800 E. Burnside, Near Downtown, 97214* ☎*503/230–9200 or 877/800–0004* 🖷*503/230–9300* ⊕*www.jupiter hotel.com* ⟋*78 rooms, 1 suite* ♿*In-room: DVD, Wi-Fi. In-hotel: restaurant, room service, bar, spa, public Wi-Fi, parking (fee), no-smoking rooms, some pets allowed* ⊟*AE, D, DC, MC, V.*

$–$$ ⬚**McMenamins Kennedy School.** In a renovated elementary
★ school in northeast Portland, the Kennedy School may well be one of the most unusual hotels you'll ever encounter. With all of the guest rooms occupying former classrooms, complete with the original chalkboards and cloakrooms, the McMenamins brothers have created a multi-use facility that is both luxurious and fantastical. Go to the Detention Bar for cigars and one of the only two TVs on-site; visit the Honors Bar for classical music and cocktails. **Pros:** Funky and authentic Portland experience, room rates include movie admission and use of the outdoor soaking pool. **Cons:** No bathtubs (shower stalls only) in bathrooms, no

TVs in rooms. ✉*5736 N.E. 33rd Ave., Near Alberta District, 97211* ☎*503/249–3983* ⊕*www.kennedyschool.com* ⤴*35 rooms* ♿*In-room: no TV, Wi-Fi. In-hotel: restaurant, bars, no elevator, public Wi-Fi, parking (no fee), no-smoking rooms* ▭*AE, D, DC, MC, V* ❍|*BP.*

$–$$ ▦**Red Lion Hotel Convention Center.** Across the street from the convention Center and adjacent to the MAX, this hotel is as convenient as can be for both business travelers and tourists. It provides a few more on-site amenities than some of the other hotels right by the convention center, which is reflected in its slightly higher rates. They do accept pets so be sure to ask for a no-pet room if you're allergic. **Pros:** Right next to convention center, walking distance to Lloyd Center Mall. **Cons:** Pet-friendly, can be crowded. ✉*1021 N.E. Grand Ave., Lloyd District/Convention Center, 97232* ☎*503/235–2100 or 800/343–1822* ▤*503/238–0132* ⊕*www.redlion.com* ⤴*174 rooms* ♿*In-room: refrigerator, Wi-Fi. In-hotel: restaurant, room service, bar, gym, public Wi-Fi, parking (fee), no-smoking rooms, some pets allowed.*

$ ▦**Monticello Motel.** This is a smaller property with several accommodation options. One- and two-bedroom kitchen suites have cooking ranges with an oven, refrigerator, and microwave oven. Decor is standard motel fare with floral bedspreads and dark wood tables and chairs. It's close to freeway access, the MAX line, and buses. **Pros:** Kitchen suites are well equipped. **Cons:** Not immediately near shops and restaurants, little character. ✉*4801 N. Interstate Ave., North Interstate, 97217* ☎*503/285–6641* ▤*503/289–9778* ⊕*www.monticellomotel.com* ⤴*10 rooms* ♿*In-room: refrigerator. In-hotel: no elevator, public Wi-Fi, no-smoking rooms.*

¢ ▦**Palms Motel.** Clean, simple, and accessible to downtown, this property offers an affordable option to some of the larger chains. It's close to freeway access, the MAX line, and buses. Rooms have recently been renovated and are equipped with microwaves and refrigerators. **Pros:** Affordability, friendly and eager staff. **Cons:** No-frills, not immediately near shops and restaurants. ✉*3801 N. Interstate Ave., North Interstate, 97232* ☎*503/287–5788 or 800/620–9652* ▤*503/249–0751* ⊕*www.palmsmotel.com* ⤴*55 rooms* ♿*In-room: refrigerator. In-hotel: no elevator, public Wi-Fi, parking (fee), no-smoking rooms.*

WEST OF DOWNTOWN

Once you start heading west, beyond Nob Hill and the West Hills, Portland begins to blur into the suburbs of Beaverton and Hillsboro. Several larger companies—such as Nike and Intel—are headquartered here, so there are lots of lodging options, mostly larger chains. As such, weekdays tend to be busier, with lower rates on weekends.

Getting to and from the city from these outlying areas requires a drive on Highway 26, which is heavily congested during commute times. A great alternative to driving is taking the MAX. There are numerous stations throughout Hillsboro and Beaverton, and travel time is less than 30 minutes to downtown by MAX.

$$–$$$$ ⬚**Heron Haus.** This lovely, bright B&B is inside a stately, 100-year-old three-floor Tudor-style mansion near Forest Park. Special features include a tulip-shaped bathtub in one room and a tiled, seven-head antique shower in another. You can enjoy a relaxing afternoon in the secluded sitting garden. All rooms have phones, work desks, and fireplaces. **Pros:** Modern amenities, fancy Continental breakfast included, plenty of room to roam on huge property. **Cons:** Located in a residential neighborhood, not immediately near public transportation. ⊠*2545 N.W. Westover Rd., Nob Hill, 97210* ☎*503/274–1846* 🖷*503/248–4055* ⊕*www.heronhaus.com* ⬚*6 rooms* &*In-room: Wi-Fi. In-hotel: no elevator, public Wi-Fi, parking (no fee), no-smoking rooms* ⊟*MC, V* ⬚*CP.*

$$–$$$ ⬚**Hillsboro Courtyard by Marriott.** This hotel provides easy access to shopping and restaurants in Hillsboro, as well as access onto U.S. 26 toward Portland. With large, comfortable rooms, it's perfect for business travelers, or for tourists who don't mind being several miles from downtown Portland. **Pros:** Nice indoor pool, free shuttle service to downtown Portland (roughly 20 minutes without traffic). **Cons:** A distance from downtown. ⊠*3050 N.W. Stucki Pl., Hillsboro, 97124* ☎*503/690–1800 or 800/321–2211* 🖷*503/690–0236* ⊕*www.marriott.com* ⬚*149 rooms, 6 suites* &*In-room: Wi-Fi. In-hotel: restaurant, room service, bar, pool, gym, laundry facilities, laundry service, public Wi-Fi, no-smoking rooms* ⊟*AE, D, DC, MC, V.*

$$–$$$ 🖼**Inn @ Northrup Station.** Bright colors, original artwork,
★ retro designs, and extremely luxurious suites fill this hotel
in Nob Hill. Just moments from the shopping and dining on
Northwest 21st Avenue, the inn looks like a stylish apart-
ment building from the outside, with patios or balconies
adjoining most of the suites, and a garden terrace for all
guests to use. The striking colors and bold patterns found
on bedspreads, armchairs, pillows, and throughout the
halls and lobby manage to be charming, elegant, and fun,
never falling into the kitsch that plagues many places that
strive for "retro" decor. All rooms have full kitchens, two
TVs, three phones, and large sitting areas. **Pros:** Roomy
suites feel like home, great location. **Cons:** Past guests
have commented on the lack of noise insulation. ⊠*2025
N.W. Northrup St., Nob Hill, 97209* ☎*503/224–0543 or
800/224–1180* 🖷*503/273–2102* ⊕*www.northrupstation.
com* ⌷*70 suites* ⚬*In-room: kitchen. In-hotel: public Wi-
Fi, parking (no fee), no-smoking rooms* ⊟*AE, D, DC, MC,
V* ⦿*CP.*

$–$$$ 🖼**Hilton Garden Inn Beaverton.** This four-level Hilton in
suburban Beaverton brings a much-needed lodging option
to Portland's west side. The property offers bright rooms
with plush carpeting, work desks, and microwaves. It's
right off U.S. 26. **Pros:** Value for money, nice indoor pool
and whirlpool. **Cons:** Not immediately near public trans-
portation, far from shopping and restaurants. ⊠*15520
N.W. Gateway Ct., Beaverton, 97006* ☎*503/439–1717 or
800/445–8667* 🖷*503/439–1818* ⊕*www.hilton.com* ⌷*150
rooms* ⚬*In-room: refrigerator. In-hotel: restaurant, room
service, bar, pool, public Wi-Fi, parking (no fee), no-smok-
ing rooms* ⊟*AE, D, DC, MC, V.*

$–$$$ 🖼**MacMaster House.** On King's Hill, next to Washington
Park's Japanese and rose gardens, this 17-room Colonial
Revival mansion built in the 1890s is comfortable and fascinating. A hybrid assortment of Victorian furniture and
antiques fills the parlors, and the guest rooms on the second and third floors are charming without being too cute.
The two suites with large, private, old-fashioned baths
are the ones to choose, especially the spacious Artist's
Studio, tucked garretlike under the dormers, with a high
brass bed and fireplace. **Pros:** Wonderful decor and ambi-
ence, full breakfast included, complimentary drink in the
evening. **Cons:** Not family-friendly, two-night minimum
stay required on the weekends. ⊠*1041 S.W. Vista Ave.,
Near Nob Hill, 97205* ☎*503/223–7362 or 800/774–9523*

&503/224–8808 ⊕*www.macmaster.com* ↬*5 rooms with shared bath, 2 suites* &*In-room: VCR. In-hotel: no elevator, public Wi-Fi, no kids under 14* ⊟*AE, MC, V* ⊙|*BP.*

$–$$$ ⊞**Marriott Residence Inn Hillsboro.** Near the west side's many high-tech offices and fabrication plants, this all-suites hotel is popular with people relocating to Portland and perfect for extended stays. It's within walking distance of several restaurants, a shopping center, and a multiplex theater. The homey suites, some with fireplaces, have full kitchens. **Pros:** Full kitchens, free Internet access, on-site market open 24 hours. **Cons:** A distance from downtown Portland. ✉*18855 N.W. Tanasbourne Dr., Hillsboro, 97124* ☎*503/531–3200 or 800/331–3131* &*503/645– 1581* ⊕*www.marriott.com* ↬*122 suites* &*In-room: VCR (some), kitchen, Wi-Fi. In-hotel: tennis court, pool, gym, no elevator, laundry facilities, laundry service, public Wi-Fi, parking (no fee), no-smoking rooms, some pets allowed* ⊟*AE, D, DC, MC, V* ⊙|*BP.*

PORTLAND INTERNATIONAL AIRPORT AREA

If you're flying in and out for a quick business trip, then staying by the airport may be a good idea. The lodging options here are only the larger chains. The airport is about a 20- to 25-minute drive away from downtown Portland.

Generally speaking, there's not much here in terms of noteworthy beauty, culture, restaurants, shops, or attractions— with the possible exception of Cascade Station, a new mixed-use development for retail, lodging, and commercial office space. IKEA and Best Buy opened in 2007 and, at this writing, there are plans for three new hotels (Aloft, Marriott Residence Inn, and Hyatt Place) to follow in the next few years. Cascade Station will also have a handful of restaurants, a movie theater, and some smaller retailers.

$$–$$$$ ⊞**Embassy Suites Portland Airport.** Suites in this eight-story atrium hotel have beige walls and blond-wood furnishings. The lobby has a waterfall and koi pond. All suites come with separate bedrooms and living areas with sleeper sofas. It's on the MAX airport light-rail line. **Pros:** Spacious suites, full breakfast included, free cocktails at happy hour. **Cons:** Airport location. ✉*7900 N.E. 82nd Ave., Airport, 97220* ☎*503/460–3000* &*503/460–3030* ⊕*www.portlandairport.*

embassysuites.com ⌨*251 suites* ♿*In-room: refrigerator. In-hotel: restaurant, room service, pool, gym, concierge, laundry service, airport shuttle, public Wi-Fi, parking (no fee)* ☰*AE, D, DC, MC, V* ⎰*BP.*

$$$ ▦**Shilo Suites Airport.** Each room in this large, four-level all-suites inn is bright, with floral-print bedspreads and drapes, and has a microwave, wet bar, and two oversize beds. The indoor pool and hot tub are open 24 hours. **Pros:** Large indoor pool, spacious rooms, free local calls. **Cons:** Airport location. ✉*11707 N.E. Airport Way, Airport, 97220* ☎*503/252–7500 or 800/222–2244* 🖷*503/254–0794* ⊕*www.shiloinns.com* ⌨*200 rooms* ♿*In-room: refrigerator. In-hotel: restaurant, room service, bar, pool, gym, laundry facilities, laundry service, airport shuttle, public Wi-Fi, parking (no fee), no-smoking rooms* ☰*AE, D, DC, MC, V* ⎰*CP.*

$$–$$$ ▦**Red Lion Hotel on the River.** The rooms in this four-story hotel, on the Columbia River, have balconies and good views of the river and Vancouver, Washington. Public areas glitter with brass and bright lights that accentuate the greenery and the burgundy, green, and rose color scheme. **Pros:** River location, views from room balconies, proximity to the Jantzen Beach shopping center. **Cons:** Pool is outdoors. ✉*909 N. Hayden Island Dr., east of I–5's Jantzen Beach exit, Jantzen Beach, 97217* ☎*503/283–4466 or 800/733–5466* 🖷*503/283–4743* ⊕*www.redlion.com* ⌨*320 rooms* ♿*In-room: Wi-Fi. In-hotel: 2 restaurants, room service, bar, tennis court, pool, gym, laundry facilities, laundry service, public Wi-Fi, parking (no fee), no-smoking rooms* ☰*AE, D, DC, MC, V.*

$–$$$ ▦**Courtyard Airport.** This six-story Marriott inn is designed for business travelers. Rooms are brightly decorated in royal blue and gold tones and have sitting areas and work desks. It's ¾ mi east of I–205 and 3 mi east of the airport. **Pros:** Reliable service and amenities, work-friendly. **Cons:** Airport location. ✉*11550 N.E. Airport Way, Airport, 97220* ☎*503/252–3200 or 800/321–2211* 🖷*503/252–8921* ⊕*www.courtyard.com* ⌨*150 rooms, 10 suites* ♿*In-room: Wi-Fi. In-hotel: restaurant, room service, bar, pool, gym, laundry facilities, laundry service, public Wi-Fi, parking (no fee), no-smoking rooms* ☰*AE, D, DC, MC, V.*

$–$$ ▦**Quality Inn and Suites.** Although it's in Gresham, this hotel's proximity to I–205 makes for easy access to downtown, and it's just a short ride from the airport. Rooms are spacious and comfortable, and much of the hotel's interior has a woodsy flair that distinguishes it from many other chain hotels. **Pros:** Suites include kitchenettes, hot breakfast buffet offered every morning, value for money. **Cons:** A distance from downtown Portland. ✉*2323 N.E. 181st Ave., Gresham 97230* ☎*503/492–4000 or 877/424–6423* 📠*503/492–3271* ⊕*www.choicehotels.com/hotel/or160* ↪*70 rooms, 23 suites* &*In-room: kitchen (some), dialup, Wi-Fi. In-hotel: pool, gym, laundry facilities, public Wi-Fi, parking (no fee), no-smoking rooms, some pets allowed* ⊟*AE, D, DC, MC, V* ⫶Ⓘ*BP.*

4

Nightlife & the Arts

5

WORD OF MOUTH

"In downtown, Henry's [12th Street Tavern] is a lot of fun. Over 100 beers on tap, with an ice trough in the bar. Upstairs is a billiards room with another bar in there. The restaurant takes up most of the space...Southpark is another place that has really good food, as well as good drinks. And outdoor seating in the summer, which on a nice day is heaven."

—mms

Updated by Janna Mock-Lopez

PORTLAND HAS BECOME KNOWN FOR BEING QUITE the creative mecca. Performances from top-ranked dance, theater, and musical talent take the stage somewhere in the city every night. Expect to find never-ending choices for things to do, from taking in true independent works of film, performance art, and plays, to checking out some of the northwest's (and the country's) hottest musical groups at one of the city's many nightclubs.

As for the fine art scene, galleries abound in all four corners of Portland, and if you take the time and do a little research, you'll discover extraordinarily creative blends of artistic techniques. Painted, recycled, photographed, fired, fused, welded, or collaged—such a scope and selection of art is one of the most notable attributes of what makes this city so metropolitan and alive.

PUBLICATIONS

"A&E, The Arts and Entertainment Guide," published each Friday in the *Oregonian,* contains listings of performers, productions, events, and club entertainment. *Willamette Week,* published free each Wednesday and widely available throughout the metropolitan area, contains similar, but hipper, listings. *Portland Family Magazine* is a free monthly publication that has an excellent calendar of events for recreational and educational opportunities for families. The *Portland Mercury* is another free entertainment publication distributed each Wednesday. *Just Out,* the city's gay and lesbian newspaper, is published bimonthly.

NIGHTLIFE

Portland's flourishing music scene encompasses everything from classical concerts to the latest permutations of rock and roll and hip-hop. The city has become something of a base for young rock bands, which perform in dance clubs scattered throughout the metropolitan area. Good jazz groups perform nightly in clubs and bars. Top-name musicians and performers in every genre regularly appear at the city's larger venues.

BARS & LOUNGES

From chic to cheap, cool to cult-ish, Portland's diverse bars and lounges blanket the town. The best way to experience some of the city's hottest spots is to check out happy hour menus, which can be found at almost all of Portland's bars and offer excellent deals on both food and drinks.

DOWNTOWN

Many of the best bars and lounges in Portland are found in its restaurants.

At the elegant **Heathman Hotel** (⊠*1001 S.W. Broadway* ☎*503/241–4100*) you can sit in the marble bar or the wood-paneled Tea Court. **Huber's Cafe** (⊠*411 S.W. 3rd Ave.* ☎*503/228–5686*), the city's oldest restaurant, is noted for its Spanish coffee and old-fashioned feel. The young and eclectic crowd at the **Lotus Cardroom and Cafe** (⊠*932 S.W. 3rd Ave.* ☎*503/227–6185*) comes to drink and play pool or foosball. The **Rialto** (⊠*529 S.W. 4th Ave.* ☎*503/228–7605*) is a large, dark bar with several pool tables and enthusiastic pool players as well as some of the best Bloody Marys in town. **Saucebox** (⊠*214 S.W. Broadway* ☎*503/241–3393*) attracts a sophisticated crowd that enjoys colorful cocktails and trendy DJ music Wednesday–Saturday evenings. With over 120 choices, **Southpark** (⊠*901 S.W. Salmon St.* ☎*503/326–1300*) is a perfect spot for a post-symphony glass of wine. At **Veritable Quandary** (⊠*1220 S.W. 1st Ave.* ☎*503/227–7342*), along the river, you can sit on the cozy tree-filled outdoor patio or in the glass atrium.

NORTHWEST

The modern bar at **Bluehour** (⊠*250 N.W. 13th Ave., Pearl District* ☎*503/226–3394*) draws a chic crowd for specialty cocktails such as the Bluehour Breeze (house-infused grapefruit vodka with a splash of cranberry). Close to the trendy restaurants and shops of Northwest 21st and 23rd Streets, the **Brazen Bean** (⊠*2075 N.W. Glisan St., Pearl District* ☎*503/294–0636*) is a house-turned-cocktail-and-cigar-bar that has wraparound porch seating where you can enjoy one of two-dozen-odd specialty martinis. Boisterous **Gypsy** (⊠*625 N.W. 21st Ave., Nob Hill* ☎*503/796–1859*) has 1950s-like furnishings. **Henry's 12th Street Tavern** (⊠*10 N.W. 12th Ave., Pearl District* ☎*503/227–5320*) has 100 beers and hard ciders on draft, plasma-screen TVs, and a billiards room in a historic building, formerly the brewery of Henry Weinhard's. Young hipsters pack **Muu-Muus** (⊠*612 N.W. 21st Ave., Nob Hill* ☎*503/223–8169*) on weekend nights.

CLOSE UP

Classic Cocktails

Classic cocktails are back with a vengeance chic enough to make James Bond proud, and they have a new twist: being infused with anything flavorful that grows under the sun. Throughout the northwest, emphasis on freshness and sustainability has spilled over into the mixers, shakers, and blenders of creative mixologists. Avocados, cucumbers, chilies, green peppers, cilantro, nutmeg, rhubarb, and beets are some of the luminaries infusing tangy hints and boldness into rums, vodkas, and whiskeys. Regionally, drink swanky-ness and sophistication have reached soaring heights; there's even an entire book called *Hip Sips,* by Portland Mint/820 bartender and restaurateur Lucy Brennan, dedicated to the topic with over 60 imaginative recipes to choose from.

5

At **Oba!** (⌧*555 N.W. 12th Ave., Pearl District* ☎*503/228–6161*), plush tans and reds with lime-green backlit walls set a backdrop for South American salsa. **21st Avenue Bar & Grill** (⌧*721 N.W. 21st Ave., Nob Hill* ☎*503/222–4121*) is open until 2:30 AM and has a patio and outdoor bar. The upscale martini set chills at **Wildwood** (⌧*1221 N.W. 21st Ave., Nob Hill* ☎*503/248–9663*).

EAST PORTLAND

An artsy, hip, east-side crowd, not to be mistaken for the downtown jet-setters, hangs and drinks martinis and wine at the minimalist **Aalto Lounge** (⌧*3356 S.E. Belmont St.* ☎*503/235–6041*). One of few bars on northeast Alberta Street, **Bink's** (⌧*2715 N.E. Alberta St.* ☎*503/493–4430*) is a small, friendly neighborhood spot with cozy seats around a fireplace, a pool table, and a good jukebox. It serves only beer and wine. **Colosso** (⌧*1932 N.E. Broadway* ☎*503/288–3333*), a popular tapas bar, draws a cocktail-sipping crowd of hipsters at night. Green lanterns glow on the curvy bar as hip patrons sip Mojitos or other mixed drinks at the no-smoking hot spot **820** (⌧*820 N. Russell St.* ☎*503/460–0820*). A laid-back beer-drinking crowd fills the **Horse Brass Pub** (⌧*4534 S.E. Belmont St.* ☎*503/232–2202*), as good an English-style pub as you will find this side of the Atlantic, with more than 50 beers on tap and air thick with smoke. The open, airy **Imbibe** (⌧*2229 S.E. Hawthorne Blvd.* ☎*503/239–4002*) serves up creative cocktails, such as its namesake, the Imbibe Infusion—a

PORTLAND TOP 5 NIGHTLIFE TIPS

■ Become immersed in an Oregon Symphony classical or pops concert at the Arlene Schnitzer Concert Hall; enjoy a post-symphony glass of wine at a nearby restaurant bar afterwards.

■ Spend a day strolling around the galleries at the Portland Art Museum and exploring the contemporary and Native American exhibits.

■ Catch an internationally known jazz band or discover a new blues group at one of Portland's many live music venues.

■ Go to a First Thursday event in the Pearl District or a Last Thursday showing in Alberta and soak up the local visual arts scene.

■ Sip a designer artisan cocktail made with fresh ingredients—from run-of-the-mill juices and mixers to chilies, nutmeg, and even rhubarb—at any one of the trendy downtown bars.

thyme-and-ginger-infused vodka and strawberry martini with a touch of lemon. **Noble Rot** (⊠*2724 S.E. Ankeny St.* ☎*503/233–1999*) is a chic east-side wine bar with excellent food and red leather booths.

BREWPUBS, BREW THEATERS & MICROBREWERIES

Dozens of small breweries operating in the metropolitan area produce pale ales, bitters, bocks, barley wines, and stouts. Some have attached pub operations, where you can sample a foaming pint of house ale. "Brew theaters," former neighborhood movie houses whose patrons enjoy food, suds, and recent theatrical releases, are part of the microbrewery phenomenon.

The **Bagdad Theatre and Pub** (⊠*3702 S.E. Hawthorne Blvd., Hawthorne District* ☎*503/236–9234*) screens recent Hollywood films and serves McMenamin's ales and Pizzacato Pizza.

The first McMenamins brewpub, the **Barley Mill Pub** (⊠*1629 S.E. Hawthorne Blvd., Hawthorne District* ☎*503/231–1492*), is filled with Grateful Dead memorabilia and concert posters and is a fun place for families. **BridgePort BrewPub & Restaurant** (⊠*1313 N.W. Marshall St., Pearl District* ☎*503/241–7179*), Portland's oldest microbrewery, prepares hand-tossed pizza *(⇨ Where to Eat)* to accompany its ales. Inside an old warehouse with high ceilings and rustic wood tables, the **Lucky Labrador Brew Pub** (✉915 S.E. Hawthorne Blvd. ☎503/236–3555) serves handcrafted ales and pub food both in the brewery and on the patio, where your four-legged friends are welcome to join you.

The **Mission Theatre** (✉1624 N.W. Glisan St., Nob Hill ☎503/223–4527) was the first brew theater to show recent Hollywood offerings and serve locally brewed McMenamins ales.

In an old church, the **St. John's Pub** (✉8203 N. Ivanhoe, St. John's ☎503/283–8520) is another McMenamins brewpub and includes a beer garden and a movie theater.

Tugboat Brewery (✉711 S.W. Ankeny St., Downtown ☎503/226–2508) is a small, cozy brewpub with books and games, picnic tables, and experimental jazz several nights a week.

The McMenamins chain of microbreweries includes some pubs in restored historic buildings. **Ringlers** (✉1332 W. Burnside St., Downtown ☎503/225–0627) occupies the first floor of the building that houses the famous Crystal Ballroom (⇨Dancing). **Ringlers Annex** (✉1223 S.W. Stark St., Downtown ☎503/525–0520), one block away from Ringlers, is a pie-shaped corner pub where you can puff a cigar while drinking beer, port, or a single-malt scotch. **Widmer Brewing and Gasthaus** (✉955 N. Russell St., North Portland, near Fremont Bridge ☎503/281–3333) brews German-style beers and has a full menu; you can tour the adjacent brewery Fridays and Saturdays.

COFFEEHOUSES & TEAHOUSES

Coffee is to Portland as tea is to England. For Portlanders, sipping a cup of coffee (or tea) is a right, a ritual, and a pasttime that occurs no matter the time of day or night. From Starbucks to the more localized Stumptown, there's no shortage of places to park and read, reflect, or rejuvenate for the long day or night of exploration ahead.

DOWNTOWN

Quite possibly the best coffee around, **Stumptown Coffee Roasters** (✉128 S.W. 3rd Ave., Downtown ☎503/295–6144) has three local cafés, where its beans are roasted daily on vintage cast-iron equipment for a consistent, fresh flavor. **Three Lions Bakery** (✉1138 S.W. Morrison St., Down-

town ☎*503/224–3429*) turns out excellent pastries as well as strong java; sandwiches, fresh-made quiches, and salads are also served.

NOB HILL & VICINITY

Anna Bannanas (✉*1214 N.W. 21st Ave., Nob Hill* ☎*503/274–2559*) serves great espresso and coffee, veggie sandwiches, soup, and smoothies; there's outdoor seating out front. One of the newer additions to the Portland coffee scene, **World Cup Coffee and Tea** (✉*1740 N.W. Glisan St.* ☎*503/228–4152*), sells excellent organic coffee and espresso in Nob Hill, as well as at its store in the Pearl District at the Ecotrust building and at Powell's City of Books on Burnside.

EAST PORTLAND

Common Grounds (✉*4321 S.E. Hawthorne Blvd., East Portland* ☎*503/236–4835*) has plush couches and serves desserts plus sandwiches and soup. **Palio Coffee and Dessert House** (✉*1996 S.E. Ladd St., Ladd's Addition, near Hawthorne District* ☎*503/232–9412*), in the middle of peaceful residential Ladd's Addition, has delicious desserts and espresso, and is open later than many coffee shops in the area. Twentysomething sippers lounge on sofas and overstuffed chairs at **Pied Cow** (✉*3244 S.E. Belmont St., East Portland* ☎*503/230–4866*), a laid-back alternative to the more yuppified establishments. **Stumptown Coffee Roasters** (✉*4525 S.E. Division St.* ☎*503/230–7702* ✉*3356 S.E. Belmont St.* ☎*503/232–8889*) has two cafés on the East Side: the original site, where organic beans are still roasted daily, and the newest site, next door to the Stumptown Annex, where patrons can participate in "cuppings" (tastings) daily at 3 PM. **Rimsky Korsakoffee House** (✉*707 S.E. 12th Ave., East Portland* ☎*503/232–2640*), one of the city's first coffeehouses, is still one of the best, especially when it comes to desserts. With soft music and the sound of running water in the background, the **Tao of Tea** (✉*3430 S.E. Belmont St., East Portland* ☎*503/736–0119*) serves vegetarian snacks and sweets as well as more than 80 loose-leaf teas.

DANCING

A couple of cocktails and some good music are all that's needed to shake your groove thing at Portland's hot spots for dancing. Clubs feature both live bands and DJs spinning the latest in dance floor favorites.

Part 1950s diner, part log cabin, the **Doug Fir** (✉*830 E. Burnside St., Downtown* ☎*503/231–9663*) hosts DJs and live rock shows from up-and-coming bands seven nights a week. Tuesday through Saturday, the **Fez Ballroom** (✉*316 S.W. 11th St., Downtown* ☎*503/221–7262*) draws a dancing crowd at this funky, Moroccan-style space. **McMenamins Crystal Ballroom** (✉*1332 W. Burnside St., Downtown* ☎*503/225–0047*) is a famous Portland dance hall that dates from 1914. Rudolph Valentino danced the tango here in 1923, and you may feel like doing the same once you step out onto the 7,500-square-foot "elastic" floor (it's built on ball bearings) and feel it bouncing beneath your feet. Bands perform everything from swing to hillbilly rock nightly except Monday.

GAY & LESBIAN CLUBS

Portland's gay community has a decent selection of places to go mingle, dance, and drink; several of these night spots are open into the wee hours.

Part of the same disco-bar-restaurant complex as the Fez Ballroom, **Boxxes** (✉*1035 S.W. Stark St., Downtown* ☎*503/226–4171*) has multiple video screens that display everything from music to messages from would-be dates. **C.C. Slaughters** (✉*219 N.W. Davis Ave., Old Town* ☎*503/248–9135*) is a male-oriented bar with a restaurant and a dance floor that's crowded on weekend nights; weeknights yield karaoke and country dancing.

Egyptian Room (✉*3701 S.E. Division St., south of Hawthorne District* ☎*503/236–8689*), Portland's lesbian bar-disco, has pool tables, video poker, and a medium-size dance floor.

Open till 4 AM, **Embers** (✉*11 N.W. Broadway Ave., Old Town* ☎*503/222–3082*) is a popular after-hours place to dance; the club hosts occasional drag shows and theme nights. **Fox and Hounds** (✉*217 N.W. 2nd Ave., Old Town* ☎*503/243–5530*) is popular with gay men and lesbians. A full menu is served in the evenings, and the place is packed for Sunday brunch.

Scandals (✉*1125 S.W. Stark St., Downtown* ☎*503/227–5887*) is low-key and has plate-glass windows with a view of Stark Street and the city's streetcars. The new location, as of December 2005, has a small dance floor, video poker, and a pool table, and the bar serves light food noon to close.

5

LIVE MUSIC

Perhaps one of Portland's greatest attributes is its quality selection of live music—especially jazz and blues—that's available seven nights a week. Clubs are full most nights with faithful followers who go to see and hear some of the most talented musicians take the stage and command the crowds with awesome performances.

BLUES, FOLK & ROCK

The **Aladdin Theater** (✉3017 S.E. Milwaukie Ave. ☎503/233–1994), in an old movie theater, is one of the best music venues in town and serves microbrews and pizza.

Berbati's Pan (✉10 S.W. 3rd Ave., Old Town ☎503/226–2122), on the edge of Old Town, has dancing and presents live music, everything from big band and swing to acid jazz, rock, and R&B.

Candlelight Room (✉2032 S.W. 5th Ave., Downtown ☎503/222–3378) presents blues nightly.

Dublin Pub (✉6821 S.W. Beaverton–Hillsdale Hwy., Beaverton ☎503/297–2889), on the west side, pours more than 50 beers on tap and hosts Irish bands and rock groups.

Kell's Irish Restaurant & Pub (✉112 S.W. 2nd Ave., Old Town ☎503/227–4057) serves terrific Irish food and presents Celtic music nightly. Locals crowd the **Laurelthirst Public House** (✉2958 N.E. Glisan St., Laurelhurst ☎503/232–1504) to eat tasty food, sit in cozy red booths, and listen to folk, jazz, country, or bluegrass music on its tiny stage. There are pool tables in an adjoining room. **Produce Row Cafe** (✉204 S.E. Oak St., east side, near Burnside Bridge and I–5 ☎503/232–8355) has a huge beer list, a great beer garden, a down-to-earth flavor, and live bluegrass, folk, and acoustic music most nights of the week.

The Bite of Oregon (✉Waterfront Park, Downtown ☎503/248–0600) features the best in the local food and wine scene with eclectic choices in live entertainment. Recent performers included Steppenwolf, the Violent Femmes, and the Decemberists.

The second largest blues festival in the country, the **Waterfront Blues Festival** (☎503/973–3378), has been drawing big names in blues and big crowds for a four-day music mecca over Fourth of July weekend since 1987. Past performers include Keb' Mo', Susan Tedeschi, and Guitar Shorty.

COUNTRY & WESTERN

Duke's (✉ *14601 S.E. Division St.* ☎ *503/760–1400*) books occasional country and country-rock performers and hosts nightly DJ dancing to country music. Not your ordinary truck stop, the Ponderosa Lounge at **Jubitz Truck Stop** (✉ *10210 N. Vancouver Way* ☎ *503/283–1111*) presents live country music and dancing Thursdays through Saturdays.

JAZZ

Upstairs at the **Blue Monk** (✉ *3341 S.E. Belmont St., East Portland* ☎ *503/595–0575*) local artists' works are on display and patrons nosh on large plates of pasta and salads; the live-jazz venue downstairs displays jazz memorabilia and photos. Dubbed one of the world's Top 100 Places to Hear Jazz by *DownBeat*, **Jimmy Mak's** (✉ *300 S.W. 10th, Pearl District* ☎ *503/295–6542*) also serves Greek and Middle Eastern dishes and has a basement lounge outfitted with two pool tables and an Internet jukebox.

Since 1982 the **Mt. Hood Jazz Festival** (✉ *26000 S.E. Stark St., Gresham* ☎ *503/224–4400* ⊕ *www.mthoodjazz.com*) has drawn big names as well as new talent to this three-day event in August. Past years have seen appearances by Ella Fitzgerald, Sarah Vaughan, and George Benson. The festival is held on the campus of Mount Hood Community College in suburban Gresham. Take MAX light rail to Gresham Transit Center and transfer to Bus 26.

THE ARTS

The conundrum of delving into Portland's art scene won't be *if* you can find something to do—it will be *what* to do when you discover there's almost too much to choose from. For a city of this size, there is truly an impressive—and accessible—scope of talent from visual artists, performance artists, and musicians. The arts are alive from outdoor sculptural works strewn around the city, ongoing festivals, and premieres of traveling Broadway shows. Top-named international acts, such as Bruce Springsteen, Rolling Stones, Paul McCartney, and Billy Joel, regularly include Portland in their worldwide stops.

TICKETS

Most Portland-based performing arts groups have their own box-office numbers; *see individual listings.*

For tickets to most events, call **Ticketmaster** (☎*503/224–4400* ⊕*www.ticketmaster.com*).

TicketsWest (☎*503/224–8499* ⊕*www.ticketswest.com*).

During the summer half-price tickets for almost any event are available the day of the show at Ticket Central in the **Visitor Information and Services Center** (✉*Pioneer Courthouse Sq., Downtown* ☎*503/275–8358 after 10* AM), open Monday–Saturday 9–4:30. This is an outlet for tickets from Ticketmaster and TicketsWest. Credit cards are accepted, but you must buy tickets in person.

PERFORMANCE VENUES

The 2,776-seat **Arlene Schnitzer Concert Hall** (✉*Portland Center for the Performing Arts, S.W. Broadway and Main St., Downtown* ☎*503/274–6560*), built in 1928 in Italian rococo revival style, hosts rock stars, choral groups, lectures, and concerts by the Oregon Symphony and others.

With 3,000 seats and outstanding acoustics, **Keller Auditorium** (✉*222 S.W. Clay St., Downtown* ☎*503/274–6560*) hosts performances by the Portland Opera and Portland Ballet as well as country and rock concerts and touring shows.

Memorial Coliseum (✉*1 Center Ct., Rose Quarter, Lloyd Center District* ☎*503/235–8771* ⊕*www.rosequarter.com*), a 12,000-seat venue on the MAX light-rail line, books rock groups, touring shows, the Ringling Brothers circus, ice-skating extravaganzas, and sporting events.

PGE Park (✉*1844 S.W. Morrison St., Downtown/Nob Hill* ☎*503/553–5400* ⊕*www.pgepark.com*) is home to the Portland Beavers Triple-A baseball team and the Portland Timbers soccer team. The 20,000-seat stadium also hosts concerts and other sporting events. No parking is available at the park; MAX light rail is the most convenient option. Your game ticket entitles you to a free round-trip.

Portland Center for the Performing Arts (✉*1111 S.W. Broadway, Downtown* ☎*503/274–6560* ⊕*www.pcpa.com*) hosts opera, ballet, rock shows, symphony performances, lectures, and Broadway musicals in its three venues (⇨*Downtown in Exploring Portland*).

The 21,000-seat **Rose Garden** (✉*1 Center Ct., Broadway and N. Interstate Ave., Lloyd Center District* ☎*503/235–8771* ⊕*www.rosequarter.com*) is home to the Portland Trail Blazers basketball team and the site of other sporting events and rock concerts. The arena is on the MAX light-rail line.

The **Roseland Theater** (⊠*8 N.W. 6th Ave., Old Town/Chinatown* ☎*503/224–2038*), which holds 1,400 people, primarily stages rock and blues shows.

CLASSICAL MUSIC

The Oregon Symphony was established over 100 years ago in 1896, and is Portland's largest classical group—and one of the largest orchestras in the country. Its season officially starts in September and ends in May, but throughout the summer the orchestra and its smaller ensembles can be seen at Waterfront Park, Washington Park, and other large festivals.

CHAMBER MUSIC

Chamber Music Northwest (⊠*522 S.W. 5th Ave., Suite 725, Downtown* ☎*503/294–6400* ⊕*www.cnmw.org*) presents some of the most sought-after soloists, chamber musicians, and recording artists from the Portland area and abroad for a five-week summer concert series; performances take place at Reed College and Catlin Gabel School.

OPERA

Portland Opera (⊠*222 S.W. Clay St.* ☎*503/241–1802 or 866/739–6737* ⊕*www.portlandopera.org*) and its orchestra and chorus stage five productions annually at the Keller Auditorium.

ORCHESTRAS

The **Oregon Symphony** (⊠*923 S.W. Washington* ☎*503/228–1353 or 800/228–7343* ⊕*www.orsymphony.org*) presents more than 40 classical, pop, children's, and family concerts each year at the Arlene Schnitzer Concert Hall.

☾ The **Metropolitan Youth Symphony** (⊠*1133 S.W. Market St., Suite 210* ☎*503/239–4566* ⊕*www.metroyouthsymphony. org*) a talented collective of youth musicians perform family-friendly concerts throughout the year at various Portland venues including the Arlene Schnitzer Concert Hall.

The **Portland Baroque Orchestra** (☎*503/222–6000* ⊕*www. pbo.org*) performs works on period instruments in a season that runs October–April. Performances are held at **Reed College's Kaul Auditorium** (⊠*3203 S.E. Woodstock Blvd., Reed/Woodstock*), the **Agnes Flanagan Chapel at Lewis & Clark College** (⊠*615 S.W. Palatine Hill Rd., Southwest*

Portland), and downtown at **First Baptist Church** (⊠*1425 S.W. 20th Ave., Downtown*).

DANCE

Portland has a wonderful variety of both progressive and traditional dance companies. As part of their productions, many of these companies bring in international talent for choreography and guest performances.

Body Vox (☎*503/229–0627* ⊕*www.bodyvox.com*) performs energetic contemporary dance–theater works at several locations in Portland.

Do Jump! Extremely Physical Theatre (⊠*1515 S.E. 37th Ave.* ☎*503/231–1232* ⊕*www.dojump.org*) showcases its creative acrobatic work at the Echo Theatre near Hawthorne.

Oregon Ballet Theatre (⊠*818 S.E. 6th Ave.* ☎*503/222–5538 or 888/922–5538* ⊕*www.obt.org*) produces five classical and contemporary works a year, including a much-loved holiday *Nutcracker.* Most performances are at Keller Auditorium.

Since its founding in 1997, **White Bird Dance** (⊠*5620 S.W. Edgemont Pl.* ☎*503/245–1600* ⊕*www.whitebird.org*) has been dedicated to bringing exciting dance performances to Portland from around the world.

FILM

If you're a film buff, be sure to check out the Northwest Film Center's calendar of events for special screenings and film festivals, including international, gay, animated, and others genres, which occur throughout the year.

Cinema 21 (⊠*616 N.W. 21st Ave., Nob Hill* ☎*503/223–4515*) is an art-movie house in Nob Hill; it is also a host of the annual gay and lesbian film festival.

Cinemagic (⊠*2021 S.E. Hawthorne Blvd., Hawthorne District* ☎*503/231–7919*) shows progressive and cult films.

A 70-year-old landmark, and another host of the annual gay and lesbian film festival, the **Hollywood Theatre** (⊠*4122 N.E. Sandy Blvd., Hollywood District* ☎*503/281–4215*) shows everything from obscure foreign art films to old American classics and second-run Hollywood hits.

The **Laurelhurst Theatre** (✉*2735 E. Burnside* ☎*503/232–5511*) is a beautiful theater and pub showing excellent second-run features and cult classics for only $3.

Not-to-be-missed Portland landmarks when it comes to movie-viewing, the **McMenamins theaters and brewpubs** offer beer, pizza, and inexpensive tickets to second-run blockbusters in uniquely renovated buildings that avoid any hint of corporate streamlining. Local favorites include the **Bagdad Theatre** (✉*3702 S.E. Hawthorne Blvd.* ☎*503/236–9234*), the **Mission Theatre** (✉*1624 N.W. Glisan* ☎*503/223–4527*), and the **Kennedy School** (✉*5736 N.E. 33rd St.* ☎*503/249–3983*), found in a renovated elementary school along with a bed-and-breakfast and a restaurant.

The **Northwest Film Center** (✉*1219 S.W. Park Ave., Downtown* ☎*503/221–1156* ⊕*www.nwfilm.org*), a branch of the Portland Art Museum, screens all manner of art films, documentaries, and independent features and presents the three-week Portland International Film Festival in February and March. Films are shown at the Whitsell Auditorium, next to the museum, and at the **Guild Theatre** (✉*879 S.W. Park Ave.*).

THEATER

From the largest of productions to the smallest of venues, theater comes to life in Portland year-round. Comedy, puppetry, tragedy, and artistry can be found at any of these theater company performances.

Artists Repertory Theatre (✉*1516 S.W. Alder St., Downtown* ☎*503/241–1278* ⊕*www.artistsrep.org*) stages seven productions a year—regional premieres, occasional commissioned works, and selected classics.

Imago Theatre (✉*17 S.E. 8th Ave.* ☎*503/231–9581* ⊕*www.imagotheatre.com*) is considered by some to be Portland's most outstanding innovative theater company, specializing in movement-based work for both young and old.

☾ **Oregon Children's Theatre** (☎*503/228–9571* ⊕*www.octc.org*) puts on three or four shows a year at major venues throughout the city for school groups and families.

☾ **Tear of Joy Puppet Theater** (☎*503/248–0557* ⊕*www.tojt.org*) stages five children's productions a year at different locations in town.

Portland Center Stage (⊠*The Gerding Theater at the Armory is located at 128 NW Eleventh Ave, Downtown* ☎*503/274–6588* ⊕*www.pcs.org*) produces six contemporary and classical works between October and April in the 800-seat Newmark Theater.

Sports & the Outdoors

6

WORD OF MOUTH

"You can rent bikes in [Portland], Fat [Tire Farm] is good. There is Forest Park, a huge forest right in the middle of the city of Portland [with] trails and views, [offering] great hiking for any age or ability."
—Scarlett

Updated
by Janna
Mock-
Lopez

PORTLANDERS DEFINITELY GRAVITATE TO THE OUT-DOORS and are, therefore, well acclimated to the elements year-round—including winter's wind, rain, and cold. However, once the sun starts to shine in spring and into summer, the city fills with hikers, joggers, and mountain bikers, who flock to Portland's hundreds of miles of parks, paths, and trails. The Willamette and Columbia rivers are used for boating and water sports—though it's not easy to rent any kind of boat for casual use. Locals also have access to a playground for fishing, camping, skiing, and snowboarding all the way through June, thanks to the proximity of Mt. Hood.

As for competitive sports, Portland is home to several minor league teams, including the Winterhawks (hockey), Beavers (baseball), Timbers (soccer), and Lumberjax (lacrosse). Big-sports fervor is reserved for Trail Blazer basketball games, held at the Rose Quarter arena on the east side of the river. The Portland/Oregon Visitors Association (⇨ *Visitor Information in Portland Essentials*) provides information on sports events and outdoor activities in the city.

PARTICIPANT SPORTS

If there's something recreational to be done outdoors, Portlanders will find a way to do it. Because of the many parks, rivers, streams, mountains, and beaches within reach of the city, this region is a playground for all manner of sports enthusiasts.

BICYCLING

Bicycling has become a cultural phenomenon in Portland—possibly the most beloved mode of transportation in the city. *Bicycling* magazine has named Portland the number one cycling city in the United States. Aside from the sheer numbers of cyclists you see on every road and pathway, notable bike-friendly aspects of this city include well-marked bike lanes on many major streets, bike paths meandering through parks and along the shoreline of the Willamette River, street signs reminding motorists to yield to cyclists at many intersections, and bike racks on the front of Tri-Met buses.

Despite the occasionally daunting hills and frequent wintertime rain, cycling remains one of the best ways to see what Portland offers. Bike paths on both the east and west sides

PORTLAND TOP 5 OUTDOOR TIPS

■ Cheer on the Portland Trail Blazers when they're home playing a basketball game at the Rose Garden.

■ Skidown a Mt. Hood Meadows slope on a crisp, clear, early spring morning—less than an hour's drive away from the city.

■ Rent a bicycle and pedal down Portland's many bike-friendly roads and pathways, or on the Esplanade alongside the Willamette River, in what has been called the number one cycling city in the U.S.

■ Hike up and around Mt. Tabor and be rewarded with an awesome view of downtown Portland.

■ Hang out at PGE Park on a warm summer night, hot dog and beer in hand, and watch a Portland Beavers baseball game.

of the Willamette River continue south of downtown, and you can easily make a several-mile loop by crossing bridges to get from one side to the other. (Most bridges, including the Broadway Bridge, the Steel Bridge, the Hawthorne Bridge, and the Sellwood Bridge, are accessible to cyclists.)

Forest Park's Leif Erikson Drive is an 11-mi ride through Northwest Portland's Forest Park, accessible from the west end of Northwest Thurman Street. Parts of this ride and other Forest Park trails are recommended only for mountain bikes. Bicycling on Sauvie Island is a rare treat, with a 12-mi loop around the island with plenty of spots for exploring. To get to Sauvie Island from Portland, you can brave the 10-mi ride in the bike lane of U.S. 30, or you can shuttle your bike there via Tri-Met Bus 17. The Springwater Corridor, when combined with the Esplanade ride on the east side of the Willamette, can take you all the way from downtown to the far reaches of southeast Portland along a former railroad line. The trail heads east beginning near Sellwood, close to Johnson Creek Boulevard.

For more information on bike routes and resources in and around Portland, visit the **Department of Transportation** (*www.portlandonline.com/transportation*) Web page. Here you can download maps, or order "Bike There," a glossy detailed bicycle map of the metropolitan area. Bikes can be rented at several places in the city. Rentals can run from $20 to $50 per day and commonly are available for cheaper weekly rates, running from $75 to $150 per week. Bike helmets are generally included in the cost of rental.

Good hybrid bikes for city riding are available at **CityBikes Workers Cooperative** (✉*734 S.E. Ankeny St., Near Burnside and Martin Luther King Blvd.* ☎*503/239–6951*) on the east side. For treks in Forest Park, mountain bikes can be rented at **Fat Tire Farm** (✉*2714 N.W. Thurman St., Near Forest Park* ☎*503/222–3276*). For jaunts along the Willamette, try **Waterfront Bicycle Rentals** (✉*315 S.W. Montgomery St., Suite 3, Downtown* ☎*503/227–1719*).

FISHING

The Columbia and Willamette rivers are major sportfishing streams with opportunities for angling virtually year-round. Though salmon can still be caught here, runs have been greatly reduced in both rivers in recent years, and the Willamette River is still plagued by pollution. Nevertheless, the Willamette still offers prime fishing for bass, channel catfish, sturgeon, crappies, perch, panfish, and crayfish. It's also a good winter steelhead stream. June is the top shad month, with some of the best fishing occurring below Willamette Falls at Oregon City. The Columbia River is known for its salmon, sturgeon, walleye, and smelt. The Sandy and Clackamas rivers, near Mt. Hood, are smaller waterways popular with local anglers.

OUTFITTERS

Outfitters throughout Portland operate guide services. Few outfitters rent equipment, so bring your own or be prepared to buy. **Countrysport Limited** (✉*126 S.W. 1st Ave., Old Town* ☎*503/221–3964*) specializes in all things fly-fishing, including tackle, rentals, and guided outings.

G.I. Joe's (✉*9600 S.E. 82nd Ave., Near Powell Blvd.* ☎*503/943–6180*) sells rods, reels, tackle, accessories, and fishing licenses. You can find a broad selection of fishing gear, including rods, reels, and fishing licenses, at **Stewart Fly Shop** (✉*23830 N.E. Halsey St., Near Troutdale* ☎*503/666–2471*).

REGULATIONS

Local sport shops are the best sources of information on current fishing hot spots, which change from year to year. Detailed fishing regulations are available from the **Oregon Department of Fish and Wildlife** (✉*17330 S.E. Evelyn St., Clackamas 97015* ☎*503/943–6180* ⊕*www.dfw.state.or.us*).

GOLF

There are several public and top-class golf courses within Portland and just outside the city where you can practice your putt or test your swing. Even in the wet months, Portlanders still golf—and you can bet the first clear day after a wet spell will mean courses fill up with those who have so faithfully waited for the sun. Depending upon the time of year, it's not a bad idea to call ahead and verify wait times.

Broadmoor Golf Course (✉ *3509 N.E. Columbia Blvd., Near airport, 97211* ☎ *503/281–1337*) is an 18-hole, par-72 course where the green fee runs $22 and an optional cart costs $22.

At the 18-hole, par-72 **Colwood National Golf Club** (✉ *7313 N.E. Columbia Blvd., Near Airport, 97218* ☎ *503/254–5515*), the green fee is $20–$24, plus $26 for an optional cart.

Eastmoreland Golf Course (✉ *2425 S.E. Bybee Blvd., Sellwood, 97202* ☎ *503/775–2900*) has a highly regarded 18-hole, 72-par course close to the Rhododendron Gardens, Crystal Springs Lake, and Reed College. The green fee is $15–$32 plus $28 for an optional cart.

Glendoveer Golf Course (✉ *14015 N.E. Glisan St., Near Gresham, 97230* ☎ *503/253–7507*) has two 18-hole courses, one par-71 and one par-73, and a covered driving range. The green fee runs $16–$30; carts are $13 for 9 holes, $26 for 18 holes.

Heron Lakes Golf Course (✉ *3500 N. Victory Blvd., west of airport, off N. Marine Dr., 97217* ☎ *503/289–1818*) consists of two 18-hole, par-72 courses: the less-challenging Greenback and the Great Blue, generally acknowledged to be the most difficult links in the greater Portland area. The green fee at the Green, as it's locally known, is $26–$30, while the fee at the Blue runs $37–$40. An optional cart at either course costs $26.

Pumpkin Ridge Golf Club (✉ *12930 N.W. Old Pumpkin Ridge Rd., North Plains 97133* ☎ *503/647–4747 or 888/594–4653* ⊕ *www.pumpkinridge.com*) has 36 holes, with the 18-hole Ghost Creek par-71 course open to the public. According to *Golf Digest,* Ghost Creek is one of the best public courses in the nation. Pumpkin Ridge hosted the U.S. Women's Open in 1997 and in 2003. The green fee is $135; the cart fee is $15.

Rose City Golf Course (✉2200 N.E. 71st Ave., *East of Hollywood District, 97213* ☎503/253–4744) has one 18-hole, par-72 course. Green fees are $28–$32; carts are $26 for 18 holes.

ICE-SKATING

Ice-skating is the recreational activity of choice for Portlanders in good health and of all ages. Lloyd Center has a large rink right in the middle of the mall, which rents skates and other needed equipment by the hour; lessons are available as well.

Ice Chalet at Lloyd Center (✉*Multnomah St. and N.E. 9th Ave., Lloyd District* ☎503/288–6073) has open skating and skate rentals ($7.50 admission includes skate rental). The indoor rinks are open year-round.

SKIING

With fairly easy access to decent skiing nearly eight months out of the year, it's no wonder that skiers love Portland. There are several ski resorts on Mt. Hood, less than an hour's drive away, including Ski Bowl, Mt. Hood Meadows, and Timberline Lodge.

Mountain Shop (✉628 N.E. Broadway, Lloyd District/ Irvington ☎503/288–6768) rents skis and equipment. **REI** (✉1405 N.W. Johnson St., Pearl District ☎503/221–1938) can fill all your ski-equipment rental needs.

SWIMMING & SUNBATHING

Swimming and sunbathing season in Portland is brief: in summer temperatures are never too hot for too long, while most of the waters—including lakes, rivers, and the Pacific Ocean—remain cold. On those few hot and sunny days, though, locals and visitors flock to these watering holes to cool off and splash around.

Blue Lake Regional Park (✉20500 N.E. Marine Dr., Troutdale ☎503/797–1850) has a swimming beach that's packed on hot summer days. You can also fish and rent small boats here. This is a great place for a hike on the surrounding trails or for a picnic.

If you feel like tanning au naturel, drive about a half hour northwest of downtown to **Sauvie Island,** a wildlife refuge with a secluded beachfront that's popular with (and legal for) nude sunbathers. If the sky is clear, you'll get a spectacular view from the riverbank of three Cascade mountains—Hood, St. Helens, and Adams. Huge oceangoing vessels cruise by on their way to and from the Port of Portland. To get here, take U.S. 30 north to Sauvie Island bridge, turn right, and follow Reeder Road until you hit gravel. Look for the Collins Beach signs. There's plenty of parking, but a permit is required. You can buy it ($3.50 for a one-day permit, $11 for an annual permit) at the Cracker Barrel country store just over the bridge on the left side of the road.

TENNIS

If tennis is your racquet, then you'll have the opportunity to try your hand at it on both indoor and outdoor courts. The Portland Parks and Recreation Department is an excellent resource for discovering where the nearest courts are located. For more information, visit ⊕*www.portlandonline.com/parks*.

Lake Oswego Indoor Tennis Center (⊠*2900 S.W. Diane Dr., Lake Oswego* ☎*503/635–5550*) has four indoor tennis courts. **Portland Parks and Recreation** (☎*503/823–7529*) operates more than 100 outdoor tennis courts (many with night lighting) at Washington Park, Grant Park, and many other locations. The courts are open on a first-come, first-served basis year-round, but you can reserve one, starting in March, for play May–September. The **Portland Tennis Center** (⊠*324 N.E. 12th Ave., just south of I–84* ☎*503/823–3189*) operates four indoor courts and eight lighted outdoor courts. The **St. John's Racquet Center** (⊠*7519 N. Burlington Ave., St. John's* ☎*503/823–3629*) has three indoor courts.

SPECTATOR SPORTS

Since Portland isn't home to a large national football or baseball team, fans tend to show a lot of support for their city's only true professional team, the NBA's Portland Trail Blazers. Fans are also loyal in cheering on their minor league teams: hockey, auto racing, baseball, and soccer events are well-attended by lively crowds.

AUTO RACING

Portland International Raceway (⊠ *West Delta Park, 1940 N. Victory Blvd., west of I–5, along Columbia Slough* ☎ *503/823–7223*) presents bicycle and drag racing and motocross on weeknights and sports-car, motorcycle, and go-kart racing on weekends April–September.

BASEBALL

The **Portland Beavers** (☎ *503/553–5555*), Portland's Triple-A team, play at the downtown **PGE Park** (⊠ *1844 S.W. Morrison St., Downtown* ☎ *503/553–5400*) April–September.

BASKETBALL

The **Portland Trail Blazers** (⊠ *1 Center Ct., Rose Quarter* ☎ *503/797–9617*) of the National Basketball Association play in the Rose Garden.

HORSE RACING

Thoroughbred and quarter horses race, rain or shine October–May, at **Portland Meadows** (⊠ *1001 N. Schmeer Rd., between I–5 and Martin Luther King Blvd., Along Columbia Slough* ☎ *503/285–9144 or 800/944–3127*).

ICE HOCKEY

The **Portland Winter Hawks** (☎ *503/236–4295*) of the Western Hockey League play home games September–March at **Memorial Coliseum** (⊠ *300 N. Winning Way, Rose Quarter*) and at the **Rose Garden** (⊠ *1 Center Ct., Rose Quarter*).

SOCCER

The **Portland Timbers** (☎ *503/553–5400*), Portland's United Soccer League First Division team, play at the downtown **PGE Park** (⊠ *1844 S.W. Morrison St., Downtown* ☎ *503/553–5400*) April–September.

Shopping

WORD OF MOUTH

"You don't even need to open your wallet to enjoy soaking in the sights and sounds of [Portland Saturday Market,] the largest outdoor crafts market in North America. Absolutely THE place to go to find that unique gift for that hard to please Parent/Friend. Plan on grabbing lunch and enjoying some of the best street performers you'll ever see."

—Ryan

Updated
by Janna
Mock-
Lopez

ONE OF PORTLAND'S GREATEST ATTRIBUTES IS its diversity of neighborhoods and the dynamic spectrum of retail and specialty shops within them. The Pearl District is known for chic interior design and high-end clothing boutique shops. Trek over to the Hawthorne area and you'll discover wonderful stores for handmade jewelry, clothing, and books. The Northwest has some funky shops for housewares, clothing, and jewelry, while in the Northeast there are fabulous galleries and crafts. Downtown has a blend of it all, including the large Pioneer Place mall and department stores such as Nordstrom's and Macy's.

Of course, no Portland shopping experience would be complete without a visit to the nation's largest open-air market, Saturday Market (which, as it were, is also open Sunday), where an array of talented artists converge to peddle handcrafted wares beyond your wildest do-it-yourself dreams.

Portland merchants are generally open Monday–Saturday between 9 or 10 AM and 6 PM, and on Sunday noon–6. Most shops in downtown's Pioneer Place, the east side's Lloyd Center, and the outlying malls are open until 9 PM Monday–Saturday and until 6 PM on Sunday.

SHOPPING AREAS

Portland's main shopping area is **downtown,** between Southwest 2nd and 10th avenues and between Southwest Stark and Morrison streets. The major department stores are scattered over several blocks near Pioneer Courthouse Square. Northeast **Broadway** between 10th and 21st avenues is lined with boutiques and specialty shops. **Nob Hill,** north of downtown along Northwest 21st and 23rd avenues, is home to eclectic clothing, gift, book, and food shops. Most of the city's fine-art galleries are concentrated in the booming **Pearl District,** north from Burnside Street to Marshall Street between Northwest 8th and 15th avenues, along with furniture and design stores. **Sellwood,** 5 mi from the city center, south on Naito Parkway and east across the Sellwood Bridge, has more than 50 antiques and collectibles shops along southeast 13th Avenue, plus specialty shops and outlet stores for sporting goods. You can find the larger antiques stores near the intersection of Milwaukie Avenue and Bybee. **Hawthorne Boulevard** between 30th and 42nd avenues has an often countercultural grouping of bookstores, coffeehouses, antiques stores, and boutiques.

PORTLAND TOP 5 SHOPPING TIPS

■ Munch on a fresh-out-of-the-fryer elephant ear pastry while perusing aisles of handmade wares at Portland's Saturday Market.

■ Scout for something totally fun and funky at one of Northwest 23rd Avenue's boutique gift shops.

■ Leisurely rifle through racks of clothes at some of Portland's more notable secondhand stores, such as Buffalo Exchange downtown and Red Light in Hawthorne.

■ Visit Columbia Sportswear downtown to see just how surprisingly fashionable clothing options for every type of outdoor condition can be.

■ Saunter through the rare books section at Powell's City of Books and dream about actually purchasing a rare first edition.

FLEA MARKETS

★ FodorsChoice The open-air **Portland Saturday Market** (⊠*Burnside Bridge, underneath west end, Old Town* ☎*503/222–6072*), open on weekends (including Sunday, despite the name), is a favorite place to experience the people of Portland and also find one-of-a-kind, unique handcrafted home, garden, and gift items. *(See* ⇨*Old Town/Chinatown in Exploring Portland.)*

MALLS & DEPARTMENT STORES

DOWNTOWN/CITY CENTER

Shopping downtown is not only fun, it's also easy, thanks to easy transportation access and its proximity to many of Portland's hotels. Do visit locally based favorites Nike and Columbia Sportswear, both of which have major stores downtown, as well as REI, which is in the Pearl District.

Macy's at Meier & Frank Square (⊠*621 S.W. 5th Ave., Downtown* ☎*503/223–0512*), a Portland department store that dates from 1857, has five floors of general merchandise at its main location downtown.

Seattle-based **Nordstrom** (⊠*701 S.W. Broadway, Downtown* ☎*503/224–6666*) sells fine-quality apparel and accessories and has a large footwear department. Bargain lovers should head for the **Nordstrom Rack** (⊠*245 S.W. Morrison*

St., Downtown ☎*503/299–1815*) outlet across from Pioneer Place mall.

Pioneer Place (✉*700 S.W. 5th Ave., Downtown* ☎*503/228–5800*) has more than 80 upscale specialty shops (including April Cornell, Coach, J. Crew, Godiva, and Fossil) in a three-story, glass-roof atrium setting. You can find good, inexpensive ethnic foods from more than a dozen vendors in the Cascades Food Court in the basement.

Saks Fifth Avenue (✉*850 S.W. 5th Ave., Downtown* ☎*503/226–3200*) has two floors of men's and women's clothing, jewelry, and other merchandise.

BEYOND DOWNTOWN

Once you venture outside of downtown, you can find several major malls and outlets in all directions to shop 'til you drop. Both Woodburn (30 mi south of Portland) and Troutdale (20 mi east of Portland) have outlet malls with dozens of discount name-brand clothing stores.

NORTHEAST PORTLAND

Lloyd Center (✉*N.E. Multnomah St. at N.E. 9th Ave., Northeast Portland* ☎*503/282–2511*), which is on the MAX light-rail line, has more than 170 shops (including Nordstrom, Sears Roebuck, and Macy's), an international food court, a multiscreen cinema, and an ice-skating pavilion. The mall is within walking distance of Northeast Broadway, which has many specialty shops, boutiques, and restaurants.

SOUTHEAST PORTLAND

Clackamas Town Center (✉*Sunnyside Rd. at I–205 Exit 14, Southeast Portland* ☎*503/653–6913*) has four major department stores, including Nordstrom and Macy's as well as more than 180 shops. Discount stores are nearby.

SOUTHWEST PORTLAND

Washington Square (✉*9585 S.W. Washington Square Rd., at S.W. Hall Blvd. and Hwy. 217, Tigard* ☎*503/639–8860*) contains five major department stores, including Macy's and Sears Roebuck; a food court; and more than 140 specialty shops. Discount and electronics stores are nearby. A little farther south of Portland, the **Streets of Tanasbourne** (✉*N.W. 194th at Cornell Rd., off U.S. 26, Hillsboro* ☎*503/533–0561*) has 52 choices of high-end specialty shops, including Clogs 'n' More, Abercrombie & Fitch, and White House/Black Market.

The **Water Tower** (✉ *5331 S.W. MacAdam Ave., Southwest Portland*), in the John's Landing neighborhood on the Willamette River, is a pleasant mall, with Pier 1 Imports and several restaurants.

SPECIALTY STORES

Portland's specialty stores are as varied and authentic as the city itself. Residents applaud and encourage locally made quirky goods, so stores offering these creative wares are abundant. Discover all the innovative approaches to household items, art, jewelry, and clothing for a fun afternoon.

ANTIQUES

Moreland House (✉ *826 N.W. 23rd Ave., Nob Hill* ☎ *503/222–0197*) has eclectic antiques and gifts, with a notable selection of dog collectibles, old printing-press type, and fresco tiles.

Shogun's Gallery (✉ *206 N.W. 23rd Ave., Nob Hill* ☎ *503/224–0328*) specializes in Japanese and Chinese furniture, especially the lightweight wooden Japanese cabinets known as *tansu*. Also here are chairs, tea tables, altar tables, armoires, ikebana baskets, and Chinese wooden picnic boxes, all of them at least 100 years old and at extremely reasonable prices.

Stars Antique Mall (✉ *7027 S.E. Milwaukie Ave., Sellwood-Moreland* ☎ *503/239–0346*), Portland's largest antiques mall, with three stores in the Sellwood-Moreland neighborhood, rents its space to 300 antiques dealers; you might find anything from low-end 1950s kitsch to high-end treasures. The stores are within walking distance of each other.

ART DEALERS & GALLERIES

Portland's art galleries, once concentrated downtown, are spreading throughout the city to Northeast and Southeast Portland. **First Thursday** gives art appreciators a chance to check out new exhibits while enjoying music and wine. Typically, the galleries are open in the evening but hours vary depending on the gallery. Find out what galleries are participating in First Thursday **Downtown** (☎ *503/295–*

4979 ⊕*www.firstthursdayportland.com*). Many galleries in the **Pearl District** (⊕*www.firstthursday.org*) also host First Thursday events. The Alberta Arts District hosts a **Last Thursday Arts Walk** (☎*503/972–2206* ⊕*www.artonalberta. org*) each month.

Butters Gallery, Ltd. (✉*520 N.W. Davis, Pearl District* ☎*503/248–9378*) has monthly exhibits of the works of nationally known and local artists in its Pearl District space.

The **Laura Russo Gallery** (✉*805 N.W. 21st Ave., Nob Hill* ☎*503/226–2754*) displays contemporary Northwest work of all styles, from landscapes to abstract expressionism.

Photographic Image Gallery (✉*79 S.W. Oak St., Old Town* ☎*503/224–3543*) carries prints by nationally known nature photographers Christopher Burkett and Joseph Holmes, among others, and has a large supply of photography posters.

Pulliam/Deffenbaugh Gallery (✉*929 N.W. Flanders St., Pearl District* ☎*503/228–6665*) generally shows contemporary abstract and expressionistic works by Pacific Northwest artists.

Quintana's Galleries of Native American Art (✉*120 N.W. 9th Ave., Pearl District* ☎*503/223–1729 or 800/321–1729*) focuses on Pacific Northwest coast, Navajo, and Hopi art and jewelry, along with photogravures by Edward Curtis.

Talisman Gallery (✉*1476 N.E. Alberta St., Alberta District* ☎*503/284–8800*) is a cooperative gallery formed in 1999 that showcases two artists each month, including local painters and sculptors.

Twist (✉*30 N.W. 23rd Pl., Nob Hill* ☎*503/224–0334* ✉*Pioneer Pl.* ☎*503/222–3137*) has a huge space in Nob Hill and a smaller shop downtown. In Nob Hill are contemporary American ceramics, glass, furniture, sculpture, and handcrafted jewelry; downtown carries an assortment of objects, often with a pop, whimsical touch.

BOOKS

Annie Bloom's (✉*7834 S.W. Capital Hwy., Multnomah Village* ☎*503/246–0053*), a local favorite, has a friendly, knowledgeable staff and great selections of children's books, remainders, Judaica, and fun greeting cards.

Broadway Books (⌧*1714 N.E. Broadway, Broadway District* ☎*503/284–1726*) is a fabulous independent bookstore with books on all subjects, including the Pacific Northwest and Judaica.

In Other Words (⌧*3734 S.E. Hawthorne Blvd., Hawthorne District* ☎*503/232–6003*) is a nonprofit bookstore that carries feminist literature and hosts feminist events and readings.

New Renaissance Bookshop (⌧*1338 N.W. 23rd Ave., Nob Hill* ☎*503/224–4929*), between Overton and Pettygrove, is dedicated to new-age and metaphysical books and tapes.

★ **Powell's City of Books** (⌧*1005 W. Burnside St., Downtown* ☎*503/228–4651*), the largest retail store of used and new books in the world (with more than 1.5 million volumes), covers an entire city block on the edge of the Pearl District. It also carries rare hard-to-find editions.

Powell's for Cooks and Gardeners (⌧*3747 Hawthorne Blvd., Hawthorne District* ☎*503/235–3802*), on the east side, has a small adjoining grocery. There's also a small store in the Portland International Airport.

Twentythird Ave. Books (⌧*1015 N.W. 23rd Ave., Nob Hill* ☎*503/224–5097*) is a cozy independent bookstore that makes for great browsing if you want to escape the bustle of 23rd Avenue.

CLOTHING

Clogs 'n' More (⌧*717 S.W. Alder St., Downtown* ☎*503/279–9358* ⌧*3439 S.E. Hawthorne, Hawthorne District* ☎*503/232–7007*), with locations both on the west and east sides of the city, carries quality clogs and other shoes.

Eight Women (⌧*3614 S.E. Hawthorne Blvd., Hawthorne District* ☎*503/236–8878*) is a tiny boutique "for mother and child," with baby clothes, women's nightgowns, jewelry, and handbags.

Elizabeth Street and Zelda's Shoe Bar (⌧*635 N.W. 23rd Ave., Nob Hill* ☎*503/243–2456*), two connected boutiques in Nob Hill, carry a sophisticated, highly eclectic line of women's clothes, accessories, and shoes.

Hanna Andersson sells high-quality, comfortable clothing for children and families from their **retail store** (⌧*327 N.W.*

10th Ave. ☎*503/321–5275*), next to the company's corporate office as well as through their **outlet store** (✉*7 Monroe Pkwy., Lake Oswego* ☎*503/697–1953*) in Lake Oswego's Oswego Towne Square, south of Portland.

Imelda's Designer Shoes (✉*3426 S.E. Hawthorne Blvd., Hawthorne District* ☎*503/233–7476*) is an upscale boutique with funky, fun shoes for women with flair.

Mario's (✉*833 S.W. Morrison St., Downtown* ☎*503/227–3477*), Portland's best store for fine men's and women's clothing, carries designer lines by Prada, Dolce & Gabbana, Etro, and Loro Piana—among others.

Mimi and Lena (✉*1914 N.E. Broadway, Broadway District* ☎*503/224–7736*) is a small boutique with expensive but beautifully feminine and unique designer clothing.

Niketown (✉*930 S.W. 6th Ave., Downtown* ☎*503/221–6453*), Nike's flagship retail store, has the latest and greatest in Nike products. **Portland Nike Factory Store** (✉*2650 N.E. Martin Luther King Jr. Blvd., Northeast Portland* ☎*503/281–5901*) sells products that have been on the market six months or more.

Nob Hill Shoes and Repair (✉*921 N.W. 23rd Ave.* ☎*503/224–8682*), a tiny spot, sells men's and women's shoes from Keen and Earth Shoes, as well as Dansko clogs.

Norm Thompson Outfitters (✉*1805 N.W. Thurman St., Nob Hill* ☎*503/221–0764*) carries classic fashions for men and women, innovative footwear, and one-of-a-kind gifts.

Portland Outdoor Store (✉*304 S.W. 3rd Ave., Downtown* ☎*503/222–1051*) stubbornly resists all that is trendy, both in clothes and decor, but if you want authentic Western gear— saddles, Stetsons, boots, or cowboy shirts—head here.

Portland Pendleton Shop (✉*S.W. 4th Ave. and Salmon St., Downtown* ☎*503/242–0037*) stocks clothing by the famous local apparel maker.

Tumbleweed (✉*1804 N.E. Alberta St., Alberta District* ☎*503/335–3100*) carries fun and stylish designer clothing you might describe as "country chic," for the woman who likes to wear flirty feminine dresses with cowboy boots. There's also unique baby and toddler clothing in their children's shop next door.

GIFTS

Babik's (✉738 N.W. 23rd Ave., Nob Hill ☎503/248–1771) carries an enormous selection of handwoven rugs from Turkey, all made from hand-spun wool and all-natural dyes.

The **Backyard Bird Shop** (✉8960 S.E. Sunnyside Rd., Clackamas ☎503/496–0908) has everything for the bird lover: bird feeders, birdhouses, a huge supply of bird seed, and quality bird-theme gifts ranging from wind chimes to stuffed animals.

Christmas at the Zoo (✉118 N.W. 23rd Ave., Nob Hill ☎503/223–4048 or 800/223–5886) is crammed year-round with decorated trees and has Portland's best selection of European hand-blown glass ornaments and plush animals.

Hawthorne Coffee Merchant (✉3564 Hawthorne Blvd., Hawthorne District ☎503/230–1222) will lure you in with its aroma of coffee and candy, and once inside, you can find coffeepots and teapots, coffee and tea blends, espresso makers, and candy.

Heaven and Earth Home and Garden (✉3206 S.E. Hawthorne Blvd., Hawthorne District ☎503/230–7033) is a lovely small store with gifts for home and garden as well as plants and flowers.

La Bottega de Mamma Ro (✉940 N.W. 23rd Ave., Nob Hill ☎503/241–4960) carries Italian tabletop and home accessories, including a colorful line of dishes and cloth for tablecloths and napkins.

Made in Oregon (☎800/828–9673), which sells books, smoked salmon, local wines, Pendleton woolen goods, carvings made of myrtle wood, and other products made in the state, has shops at Portland International Airport, the Lloyd Center, the Galleria, Washington Square, and Clackamas Town Center.

Moonstruck (✉526 N.W. 23rd Ave., Nob Hill ☎503/542–3400), even without its nod from Oprah, is doing well for itself as a chocolatier extraordinaire. Just a couple of the rich confections might sustain you if you're nibbling—water is available for palate cleansing in between treats—but whether you're just grazing or boxing some up for the road, try the Ocumarian Truffle, chocolate laced with chili pepper; the unusual kick of sweetness and warmth is worth experiencing.

7

Pastaworks (⊠*3735 S.E. Hawthorne Blvd., Southeast Portland* ☎*503/232–1010*) sells cookware, fancy deli food, organic produce, beer, wine, and pasta.

At **Stella's on 21st** (⊠*1108 N.W. 21st Ave., Nob Hill* ☎*503/295–5930*), there are eccentric, colorful, and artsy items for the home, including lamps, candles, and decorations, as well as jewelry.

JEWELRY

Carl Greve (⊠*731 S.W. Morrison St., Downtown* ☎*503/223–7121*), in business since 1922, carries exclusive designer lines of fine jewelry, such as Mikimoto pearls, and has the state's only Tiffany boutique. The second floor is reserved for china, stemware, and housewares.

MUSIC

Artichoke Music (⊠*3130 S.E. Hawthorne Blvd., Hawthorne District* ☎*503/232–8845*) is a friendly family-owned business that sells guitars, banjos, mandolins, and other instruments that might come in handy for a bluegrass band. Music lessons are given in two soundproof practice rooms, and music performances and song circles are held in the café in the back.

Classical Millennium (⊠*3144 E. Burnside St., Laurelhurst* ☎*503/231–8909*) has the best selection of classical CDs and tapes in Oregon.

Music Millennium Northwest (⊠*3158 E. Burnside St., Laurelhurst* ☎*503/231–8926*) stocks a huge selection of CDs and tapes in every possible musical category, from local punk to classical.

OUTDOOR SUPPLIES

Andy and Bax (⊠*324 S.E. Grand Ave., Near Morrison Bridge* ☎*503/234–7538*) is an army-navy/outdoors store, with good prices on everything from camo gear to rafting supplies.

Next Adventure Sports (⊠*426 S.E. Grand Ave., Near Morrison Bridge* ☎*503/233–0706*) carries new and used sporting goods, including camping gear, snowboards, kayaks, and mountaineering supplies.

PERFUME

Aveda Lifestyle Store and Spa (✉ *500 S.W. 5th Ave., Downtown* ☎ *503/248–0615*) sells the flower-based Aveda line of scents and skin-care products.

Perfume House (✉ *3328 S.E. Hawthorne Blvd., Hawthorne District* ☎ *503/234–5375*) carries hundreds of brand-name fragrances for women and men.

TOYS

Finnegan's Toys and Gifts (✉ *922 S.W. Yamhill St., Downtown* ☎ *503/221–0306*), downtown Portland's largest toy store, stocks artistic, creative, educational, and other types of toys.

Kids at Heart (✉ *3445 S.E. Hawthorne Blvd., Hawthorne District* ☎ *503/231–2954*) is a small, colorful toy store on Hawthorne with toys, models, and stuffed animals for kids of all ages.

7

Easy Side Trips from Portland

WORD OF MOUTH

"I really think you will like Multnomah Falls. The Historic Highway is wonderful, an old two-lane road past farms and forests...winding past waterfalls. The views are stunning from the Womens Forum, an outlook from where you can see forever, and at Vista House. Take a picnic if it is nice."

—Scarlett

IT'S HARD TO IMAGINE EVER WANTING TO LEAVE PORTLAND. However, for all the beauty and diversity this city offers, so too do outlying areas within immediate to short-distance proximity. Expanding beyond the city bridges is when the scenery gets exciting and there are endless side trips to enhance the Portland experience.

Arguably Oregon's number one tourist destination is Multnomah Falls, 30 mi east of Portland in the scenic Columbia Gorge. Multnomah Falls drops down 620 feet and is the second-tallest year-round waterfall in the nation. There are accessible hiking trails that meander up and around the falls area. On the Oregon side of the Columbia Gorge (Washington is across the river) there nearly 80 waterfalls. The Gorge is 80 mi in length and, depending upon location, some cliffs are up to 4,000 feet high. Wayward winds take advantage of the Cascades' only range break and whip through this steep canyon crevasse. As such, places within the Gorge like Hood River and the Dalles draw world-class windsurfers and kite-boarders for some of the most prime conditions for these sports.

Beyond the Gorge to the east is Mt. Hood National Forest. With more than 60 mi of lakes, streams, and fir-carpeted mountains, the forest encompasses some 1,067,043 acres. Visitors can enjoy Mt. Hood year-round. In summer there's camping, fishing, and hiking; in fall people hunt and mushroom pick; in winter it's a popular place for skiing and snowboarding; and in spring visitors collect wildflowers.

8

Traveling down from the hills to the valleys, just southwest of Portland are Washington and Yamhill counties—sometimes informally referred to as the "Napa of the Northwest." Thanks to a mild climate and soil, air, water, and temperature conditions comparable to the Burgundy region of France, this region is recognized for producing prime pinot noir. More than 100 wineries cultivate grapes on 13,000 acres of vineyards. Many of the vineyards offer behind-the-scenes tours and have quaint wine-tasting rooms where sampling the merchandise in encouraged.

If you're looking to find a fabulous seafood dish to pair with your favorite wine, then travel 1½ hours west of Portland: you'll end up at the shores of the breathtaking Oregon Coast. There are endless beaches where pounding surf collides against dramatic cliffs, and hikes into dense forest only footsteps away. Because of their proximity to Portland, the most frequented destinations are Astoria, Seaside, and Cannon Beach. Though only within a 20-minute drive of one another, each community has its own unique charm and personality.

People love the Oregon Coast because of its tremendous beauty, wonderful selection of restaurants specializing in seafood, bountiful art galleries, and access to unspoiled terrain for picnics, hikes, and camping. Long walks along the shore for seekers of solitude can be had as easily as a less-reclusive evening of small theater performances.

Tourism grows every year, as visitors from all over the world discover the scenic and recreational treasures that so thrill Oregonians themselves. A sophisticated hospitality industry has appeared, making Oregon more accessible than ever before. You'll feel more than welcome here, but when you visit, expect a little ribbing if locals catch you mispronouncing the state's name: it's "Ore-ey-gun" not "Ore-uh-gone."

THE OREGON COAST

Updated by Deston S. Nokes

Oregon has 300 mi of white-sand beaches, not a grain of which is privately owned. U.S. 101, called Highway 101 by most Oregonians, parallels the coast along the length of the state. It winds past sea-tortured rocks, brooding headlands, hidden beaches, historic lighthouses, and tiny ports, with the gleaming gun-metal-gray Pacific Ocean always in view. With its seaside hamlets, outstanding fresh seafood eateries, and small hotels and resorts, the Oregon Coast epitomizes the finest in Pacific Northwest living.

Points of interest can be found on the Northwest Oregon map.

ASTORIA

96 mi northwest of Portland on U.S. 30.

The mighty Columbia River meets the Pacific at Astoria, the oldest city west of the Rockies. In its early days Astoria was a placid amalgamation of small town and hard-working port city. Settlers built sprawling Victorian houses on the flanks of **Coxcomb Hill.** Many of the homes have since been restored and are no less splendid as bed-and-breakfast inns. In recent years, the city itself has awakened with a

Northwest Oregon

WASHINGTON

PACIFIC OCEAN

greater variety of trendy dining and lodging options, staking its claim as a destination resort town.

★ Fodor'sChoice The **Columbia River Maritime Museum,** on the downtown waterfront, explores the maritime history of the Pacific Northwest and is one of the two most interesting man-made tourist attractions on the Oregon coast (Newport's aquarium is the other). Beguiling exhibits include the personal belongings of some of the ill-fated passengers of the 2,000 ships that have foundered here since 1811. Also here are a bridge from the World War II destroyer USS *Knapp* (which can be viewed from the inside), the fully operational U.S. Coast Guard Lightship *Columbia,* and a 44-foot Coast Guard motor lifeboat. ⊠*1792 Marine Dr., at 17th St.* ☎*503/325–2323* ⊕*www.crmm.org* ⊡*$8* ⊙*Daily 9:30–5.*

The **Astoria Column,** a 125-foot monolith atop Coxcomb Hill that was patterned after Trajan's Column in Rome, rewards your 164-step, spiral-stair climb with views over Astoria, the Columbia River, the Coast Range, and the Pacific. Or if you don't want to climb, the column's artwork, depicting important Pacific Northwest historical milestones, is stunning. ⊠*From U.S. 30 downtown take 16th St. south 1 mi to top of Coxcomb Hill* ⊑*Free* ☾*Daily 9–dusk.*

The prim **Flavel House** was built between 1884 and 1886. Its Victorian-era furnishings, including six handcrafted fireplace mantels carved from different hardwoods and accented with tiles imported from Asia and Europe, yield insight into the lifestyle of a wealthy 19th-century shipping tycoon. Visits start in the Carriage House interpretive center. ⊠*441 8th St., at Duane St.* ☎*503/325–2203* ⊕*www.oldoregon.com/ visitor-info/flavel-house-museum* ⊑*$5* ☾*May–Sept., daily 10–5; Oct.–Apr., daily 11–4.*

☾ "Ocean in view! O! The joy!" recorded William Clark,
★ standing on a spit of land south of present-day Astoria in the fall of 1805. **Fort Clatsop National Memorial** is a faithful replica of the log stockade depicted in Clark's journal. Park rangers, who dress in period garb in summer and perform such early-19th-century tasks as making fire with flint and steel, lend an air of authenticity, as does the damp and lonely feel of the fort itself. ⊠*Fort Clatsop Loop Rd. 5 mi south of Astoria; from U.S. 101 cross Youngs Bay Bridge, turn east on Alt. U.S. 101, and follow signs* ☎*503/861– 2471* ⊕*www.nps.gov/focl* ⊑*$3* ☾*Daily 9–5.*

☾ The earthworks of 37-acre **Fort Stevens,** at Oregon's northwestern tip, were mounded up during the Civil War to guard the Columbia against a Confederate attack. No such event occurred, but during World War II, Fort Stevens became the only mainland U.S. military installation to come under enemy (Japanese submarine) fire since the War of 1812. The fort's abandoned gun mounts and eerie subterranean bunkers are a memorable destination. The corroded skeleton of the *Peter Iredale,* a century-old English four-master ship, protrudes from the sand just west of the campground, a stark testament to the temperamental nature of the Pacific. ⊠*Fort Stevens Hwy., from Fort Clatsop, take Alt. U.S. 101 west past U.S. 101, turn north onto Main St.–Fort Stevens Hwy., and follow signs* ☎*503/861– 2000* ⊕*www.visitfortstevens.com* ⊑*$3 per vehicle* ☾*Mid-May–Sept., daily 10–6; Oct.–mid-May, daily 10–4.*

★ One of the Oregon coast's oldest commercial smokehouses, **Josephson's** uses alderwood for all processing and specializes in Pacific Northwest chinook and coho salmon. You can choose mouthwatering selections of fish smoked on the premises, including hot smoked pepper or wine-maple salmon, as well as smoked halibut, sturgeon, tuna, oysters, mussels, scallops and prawns by the pound or in sealed gift packs. ⊠*106 Marine Dr., 97103* ☎*503/325–2190* ⊕*www. josephsons.com* ☞*Free* ⊙*Mon.–Sat. 9–6, Sun. 9–5:30.*

In a 100-year-old Colonial Revival building originally used as the city hall, the **Heritage Museum** has two floors of exhibits detailing the history of the early pioneers, Native Americans, and logging and marine industries of Clatsop County, the oldest American settlement west of the Mississippi. The research library, where you may research local family and building history, is also open to the public. ⊠*1618 Exchange St.* ☎*503/325–2203* ⊕*www.clatsophistorical society.org* ☞*$4* ⊙*May–Labor Day, daily 10–5; Labor Day–Apr., Tues.–Sat. 11–4.*

The **Astoria Riverfront Trolley,** also known as "Old 300," is a beautifully restored 1913 streetcar, which travels for 4 mi along Astoria's historic riverfront. Get a close-up look at the waterfront, from the Port of Astoria to the East Morring Basin; the Columbia River; and points of interest in between; while reliving the past through guided and narrated historical tours. ⊠*1095 Dwayne St.* ☎*503/325–6311* ⊕*homepage.mac.com/cearl/trolley/* ☞*$1 per boarding, $2 all-day pass* ⊙*Memorial Day–Labor Day, Mon.–Thurs. 3–9, Fri.–Sun. noon–9; fall, winter and spring, check trolley shelters.*

WHERE TO EAT

¢–$$$ × **Bridgewater Bistro.** Astoria's new, fine-dining entry has
★ a broad range of selections whether you want meat, fish, or vegetarian fare. Next to the new Columbia Pier Hotel, the restaurant serves inexpensive bistro fare (such as burgers and fish-and-chips) as well as more refined dishes such as Moroccan chicken and duck breast. It also offers a prix-fixe four-course meal and a large selection of fine wines. ⊠*20 Basin St.* ☎*503/325–6777* ⊕*www. bridgewaterbistro.com* ☰*AE, D, MC, V* ⊙*Mon.–Thurs. 11–9, Fri. and Sat. 11–10.*

¢–$$$ × **Cannery Cafe.** Original fir floors, windows, and hardware combine with expansive views of the Columbia River to give this restaurant in a renovated 1879 cannery an authentic, nautical feel. Homemade breakfast fare, often with crab or salmon, comes with potato pancakes and buttermilk biscuits. Fresh salads, large, specialty sandwiches, clam chowder, and crab cakes are lunch staples. The dinner menu emphasizes seafood, including cioppino, an Italian fish stew, and Dungeness crab Alfredo. ⌂ *1 6th St.* ☎ *503/325–8642* ☱ *AE, D, DC, MC, V* ⊘ *Tues.–Sun. 8 AM–9 PM, Mon. 11–9; bar until midnight.*

★ Fodor'sChoice ✕ **Clemente's.** Serving possibly the best seafood
¢–$$ on the Oregon Coast, chefs Gordon and Lisa Clement are making a significant critical and popular splash in Astoria. Grounded in Mediterranean cuisine from Italy and the Adriatic Coast, Clemente's inventive specials feature the freshest catches of that day. From succulent sea bass salad to a hearty sturgeon sandwich—meals are dished up for reasonable prices. Dungeness crab cakes stuffed with crab rather than breading, and wild scallop fish and chips liven up a varied menu. Not interested in fish? Try the spaghetti with homemade meatballs. ⌂ *1335 Marine Dr.* ☎ *503/325–1067* ☱ *AE, D, MC, V* ⊘ *Lunch Tues. 11–6, Wed.–Sun. 11–4; dinner Wed.–Sun. 5:30–9.*

WHERE TO STAY

★ Fodor'sChoice ☖ **Cannery Pier Hotel.** Every room has a gor-
$$$$ geous river view where you can watch tugboats shepherding barges to and fro. Built upon century-old pilings right where the Columbia River meets the Pacific Ocean, the hotel is in the restored Union Fisherman's Cooperative Packing Company building, an integral part of the town's history. The interior, however, is modern and bright with a liberal use of glass and polished wood, including hardwood floors in the rooms. The property sits on the Astoria Riverwalk and on the Trolley Line, and gourmet dining is within walking distance. ⌂ *10 Basin St., 97103* ☎ *503/325–4996 or 888/325–4996* ⊕ *www.cannerypier hotel.com* ⤳ *46 rooms, 8 suites* ⌂ *In-room: No a/c, kitchen, DVD, ethernet. In-hotel: Gym, spa, bicycles, laundry facilities, some pets allowed* ☱ *AE, D, MC, V* ⋈ *CP.*

$$$–$$$$ ☖ **Hotel Elliott.** This upscale, five-story downtown hotel is in
★ the heart of Astoria's historic district. The property retains the elegance of yesteryear updated with modern comforts. On the rooftop, you can relax in the garden and enjoy views of the Columbia River and the Victorian homes dotting the hillside. Warm your feet on the heated stone floors in your bathroom. Downstairs you can sample fine wines in the Cabernet Room or enjoy a cigar in the tucked-away Havana Room. ⌂ *357 12th St., 97103* ☎ *877/378–1924* ⊕ *www.hotelelliott.com* ⤳ *32 rooms* ⌂ *In-room: No a/c, ethernet. No a/c. In-hotel: Bar, some pets allowed* ☱ *AE, D, MC, V.*

$$–$$$ ⊠**Benjamin Young Inn.** On the National Register of Historic Places, this handsome 5,500-square-foot Queen Anne inn is surrounded by century-old gardens. Among the ornate original details are faux graining on frames and molding, shutter-blinds in windows, and Povey stained glass. The spacious guest rooms mix antiques with contemporary pieces and have views of the Columbia River from their tall windows. City tennis courts are right next door. There's a two-night minimum on holiday and July, August, and September weekends. ⊠*3652 Duane St., 97103* ☎*503/325–6172 or 800/201–1286* ⊕*www.benjaminyounginn.com* ⇝*4 rooms, including 1 2-bedroom suite* ⚐*In-room: No a/c. In-hotel: TV, no-smoking rooms, no elevator* ⊟*AE, D, MC, V* ⎧*BP.*

SEASIDE

12 mi south of Astoria on U.S. 101.

Seaside has grown up around the spot where the Lewis and Clark expedition finally reached the Pacific Ocean. A bronze statue of the two explorers commemorates the end of their trail and faces the ocean at the center of Seaside's historic Promenade. The Prom, built in 1908 as a wooden walkway, was extended in 1920 to its current length, 1½ mi, with concrete sidewalks.

As a resort town Seaside has brushed off its former garish, arcade-filled reputation and now supports a bustling tourist trade with hotels, condominiums, and restaurants surrounding a long beach. It still has fun games and noise to appeal to young people, but it has added plenty of classy getaways for adults. Only 90 mi from Portland, Seaside is often crowded, so it's not the place to come if you crave solitude. Peak times include February, during the Trail's End Marathon; mid-March, when hordes of teenagers descend on the town during spring break; and July, when the annual Miss Oregon Pageant is in full swing.

Just south of town, waves draw surfers to the Cove, a spot jealously guarded by locals.

It's a 2½-mi hike from the parking lot of **Saddle Mountain State Park** to the summit of Saddle Mountain. It's much cooler at that elevation. The campground, 14 mi north of Seaside, has 10 primitive sites. ⊠*Off U.S. 26* ☎*800/551–6949* ⊜*$9 for overnight camping, first come, first served. Hiking is free* ⊗*Mar.–Nov., daily dawn to dusk.*

WHERE TO EAT

$-$$$ ✕**Guido & Vito's Italian Eatery.** In a sea of family-oriented
★ fish restaurants sits this pleasant, quiet restaurant cooking
Italian food right. Be it a zesty Caeser, sausage and beef
meatballs, or a belly-warming, mushroom-slathered veal
marsala, diners won't be disappointed. ⊠*604 Broadway*
☎*503/717-1229* ▭*D, MC, V* ⊙*Sun.–Fri. 4:30–9, Sat.
4:30–9:30.*

$-$$$ ✕**Girtle's Seafood & Steaks.** Huge portions at reasonable
prices is the motto of this family-oriented restaurant. Here
you can find juicy steaks, fresh local seafood, and plenty of
home-spun selections for kids. It also lays out a substantial,
classic breakfast spread. ⊠*604 Broadway* ☎*503/738-8417*
⊕*www.girtles.com* ▭*AE, D, MC, V* ⊙*Daily 9–1:30.*

$-$$ ✕**Yummy Wine Bar & Bistro.** Despite the name, this is a warm,
fun wine bar for adults. Owner Corey R. Albert serves
inventive dishes such as paninis and fresh seafood that blend
well with fine Pacific Northwet wines. No children admit-
ted. ⊠*831 Broadway* ☎*503/738-3100* ⊕*www.yummy
winebarbistro.com* ▭*AE, MC, V* ⊙*Sun., Mon., Thurs. 3–
10, Fri. and Sat. 3–midnight; Closed Tues. and Wed.*

WHERE TO STAY

$$$$ ▦**Rivertide Suites.** Seaside's new hotel may not be right on
☾ the beach, but its splendid accommodations are within
★ walking distance of the town's best cuisine, shopping,
and beach activities. Offering one- and two-bedroom
suites and studios, Rivertide gives you different packages
that appeal to golfers, whale-whatchers, or romantic couples. All units have in-suite laundry facilities. Breakfast
is complimentary. If a view isn't a priority, this is a fine
property. ⊠*102 N. Holladay, 97138* ☎*503/436-2241 or
888/777-4047* ⊕*www.rivertidesuites.com* ⤳*45 rooms*
⚲*In-room: No a/c (some), kitchen, DVD. In-hotel: Pool,
gym, public Internet, public Wi-Fi, some pets allowed*
▭*AE, D, MC, V* ⑩*BP.*

¢-$$$ ▦**Hillcrest Inn.** Friendliness, cleanliness, and convenience
are bywords of the Hillcrest, which is one block from both
the beach and the convention center, and three blocks from
the downtown area's restaurants and shops. You're wel-
come to use the picnic tables, lawn chairs, and even the
barbecue on the grounds. ⊠*118 N. Columbia St., 97138*
☎*503/738-6273 or 800/270-7659* ⊕*www.seasidehillcrest.
com* ⤳*19 rooms, 4 suites, 3 2-bedroom cottages, 1 6-bed-*

room house ⟨In-room: No a/c (some), kitchen. In-hotel:
Public Wi-Fi, laundry facilities ═AE, D, MC, V.

¢–$ ⊡**Royale.** This small motel right in the center of downtown
is on the Necanicum River, 3½ blocks from the beach and
walking distance to shopping and restaurants. Some rooms
have river views. There's ample off-street parking. ⊠531
Ave. A, 97138 ☎503/738–9541 ⤴26 rooms ⟨In-room:
No a/c. In-hotel: No elevator ═D, DC, MC, V.

A BRISK 2-MI HIKE FROM U.S. 101 south of Seaside leads to the
1,100-foot-high viewing point atop **Tillamook Head.** The view
from here takes in the Tillamook Rock Light Station, which
stands a mile or so out to sea. The lonely beacon, built in 1881
on a straight-sided rock, towers 41 feet above the surrounding ocean. In 1957 the lighthouse was abandoned; it's now
a columbarium.

Eight miles south of Seaside, U.S. 101 passes the entrance to
Ecola State Park, a playground of sea-sculpted rocks, sandy
shoreline, green headlands, and panoramic views. The park's
main beach can be crowded in summer, but the Indian Beach
area contains an often-deserted cove and explorable tidal pools.
☎503/436–2844 or 800/551–6949 ⊠$3 per vehicle ⊘Daily
dawn–dusk.

8

CANNON BEACH

10 mi south of Seaside on U.S. 101, 80 mi west of Portland
on U.S. 26.

Cannon Beach is a mellow and trendy place to enjoy art,
wine, fine dining, and to take in the sea air. One of the
most charming hamlets on the coast, the town has beachfront homes and hotels, and a weathered-cedar downtown
shopping district. On the downside, the Carmel of the Oregon coast can be more expensive and crowded than other
towns along Highway 101's shoreline.

Towering over the broad, sandy beach is **Haystack Rock,**
a 235-foot-high monolith that is one of the most-photo-
graphed natural wonders on Oregon coast. △**The rock is
temptingly accessible during some low tides, but the coast
guard regularly airlifts stranded climbers from its precipitous
sides, and falls have claimed numerous lives over the years.**

Every May the town hosts the Cannon Beach Sandcastle Contest, for which thousands throng the beach to view imaginative and often startling works in this most transient of art forms.

Shops and galleries selling kites, upscale clothing, local art, wine, coffee, and food line **Hemlock Street,** Cannon Beach's main thoroughfare.

WHERE TO STAY & EAT

$–$$$ ✕**The Bistro.** Flowers, candlelight, and classical music convey romance at this 11-table restaurant. The menu includes imaginative Continental-influenced renditions of local seafood and pasta dishes as well as specialty salads. The signature dish is the fresh seafood stew. ⊠*263 N. Hemlock St.* ☎*503/436–2661* ⊟*MC, V* ⊘*Closed Tues. and Wed. Nov.–Jan. No lunch.*

¢–$ ✕**Sleepy Monk.** In a region famous for its gourmet cof-
★ fee, one small roaster brews a cup more memorable than any chain. Sleepy Monk attracts java aficionados on caffeine pilgrimages from all over the Pacific Northwest; and it's not unusual to see a line outside the door. Its certified organic and fair trade beans are roasted without adding water, which adds unnecessary weight. There's a variety of teas, too. Local, fresh pastries are stacked high and deep. If you're a coffee fan, this is your Shangri-la. ⊠*1235 S. Hemlock, 97110* ☎*503/436–2796* ⊕*www.sleepymonk coffee.com* ⊟*MC, V* ⊘*Fri., Sat., and Sun. 8–5.*

★ **Fodor's**Choice ✕▨**Stephanie Inn.** One of the most beautiful
$$$$ views on the coast deserves one of the most splendid hotels. With a stunning view of Haystack Rock, the Stephanie Inn keeps its focus on romance, superior service, and luxurious rooms. Impeccably maintained, with country-style furnishings, fireplaces, large bathrooms with whirlpool tubs, and balconies, the rooms are so comfortable you may never want to leave—except perhaps to enjoy the four-course prix-fixe dinners of innovative Pacific Northwest cuisine. The restaurant serves the most delectable rack of lamb in the state. Generous country breakfasts are included in the room price, as are evening wine and hors d'oeuvres. ⊠*2740 S. Pacific St., 97110* ☎*503/436–2221 or 800/633–3466* ⊕*www.stephanie-inn.com* ⋗*50 rooms* ⌂*In-room: DVD, refrigerator. In-hotel: Restaurant, no kids under 12, no-smoking rooms* ⊟*AE, D, DC, MC, V* ⊚*BP.*

$$$$ ✉**Ocean Lodge.** To celebrate special occasions, create new
★ memories, or enjoy first-rate service, this is the destination. Designed to capture the feel of a 1940s beach resort,
this lodge is right on the beach. Most of the rooms have
oceanfront views, and all have open wood beams, simple
but sophisticated furnishings, gas fireplaces, and balconies
or decks. The lobby floor is reclaimed spruce wood, while
stairs were fashioned from old stadium bleachers. A massive rock fireplace anchors the lobby, and there's a second
fireplace in the second-floor library with a large selection
of games for the whole family at your disposal. Other
extras include an extensive book collection and complimentary DVDs. Bungalows across the street do not have
ocean views but are large and private. ✉*2864 S. Pacific
St., 97110* ☎*503/436–2241 or 888/777–4047* ⊕*www.
theoceanlodge.com* ⌨*45 rooms* ♿*In-room: No a/c (some),
kitchen, DVD. In-hotel: Public Wi-Fi, some pets allowed,
no-smoking rooms* ▤*AE, D, MC, V.*

EN ROUTE. South of Cannon Beach, U.S. 101 climbs 700 feet above
the Pacific, providing dramatic views and often hair-raising
curves as it winds along the flank of Neahkahnie Mountain.
Cryptic carvings on beach rocks near here and centuries-old
Native American legends of shipwrecked Europeans gave rise
to a tale that the survivors of a sunken Spanish galleon buried
a fortune in doubloons somewhere on the side of the 1,661-
foot-high mountain.

8

OSWALD WEST STATE PARK

10 mi south of Cannon Beach on U.S. 101.

Adventurous travelers will enjoy a sojourn at one of the
best-kept secrets on the Pacific coast, **Oswald West State
Park,** at the base of Neahkahnie Mountain. Park in one of
the two lots on U.S. 101 and use a park-provided wheel-
barrow to trundle your camping gear down a ½-mi trail.
An old-growth forest surrounds the 36 primitive campsites
(reservations not accepted), and the spectacular beach contains caves and tidal pools.

The trail to the summit, on the left about 2 mi south of the
parking lots for Oswald West State Park (marked only by a
HIKERS sign), rewards the intrepid with unobstructed views
over surf, sand, forest, and mountain. Come in December or March and you might spot pods of gray whales.

Campsites are first-come, first-served, with 30 walk-in tent sites. ⊠*Ecola Park Rd.* ☎*503/368–5943 or 800/551–6949* ⊕*www.oregonstateparks.org* ⊡*Day use free, tent site $14* ☉*Day use daily dawn–dusk; camping Mar.–Oct.*

EN ROUTE. After passing through several small fishing, logging, and resort towns, U.S. 101 skirts around **Tillamook Bay,** where the Miami, Kilchis, Wilson, Trask, and Tillamook rivers enter the Pacific. The bay rewards sportfishing enthusiasts with quarry that includes sea-run cutthroat trout, bottom fish, and silver, chinook, and steelhead salmon, along with mussels, oysters, clams, and the delectable Dungeness crab. Charter-fishing services operate out of the **Garibaldi** fishing harbor 10 mi north of Tillamook. For some of the best rock fishing in the state, try Tillamook Bay's North Jetty.

MANZANITA

20 mi south of Cannon Beach on U.S. 101.

Manzanita is a secluded seaside community with a little more than 500 full-time residents. It's on a sandy peninsula peppered with tufts of grass on the northwestern side of Nehalem Bay. It's a tranquil small town, but its restaurants, galleries, and 18-hole golf course have increased its appeal to tourists. Manzanita and Nehalem Bay both have become popular windsurfing destinations.

Established in 1974, **Nehalem Bay Winery** is known for its pinot noir, chardonnay, blackberry, and plum fruit wines. The winery also has a busy schedule of events, with concerts, barbecues, an occasional pig roast, children's activities, performances at the Theatre Au Vin, and a bluegrass festival the third week of August. ⊠*34965 Hwy. 53, Nehalem 97131* ☎*503/368–9463 or 888/368–9463* ⊕*www.nehalembaywinery.com* ☉*Daily 9–6.*

WHERE TO STAY

$$–$$$$ ▥ **Inn at Manzanita.** This 1987 Scandinavian structure, filled with light-color woods, beams, and glass, is half a block from the beach. Shore pines on the property give upper-floor patios a tree-house feel, all rooms have decks, and two have skylights. A nearby café serves breakfast, and area restaurants are nearby. In winter the inn is a great place for storm-watching. There's a two-day minimum stay on weekends. Now there are three child-friendly rooms

and a new penthouse suite. A 20-day cancellation notice is required. ⊠*67 Laneda Ave., Box 243, 97130* ☎*503/368–6754* ⊕*www.innatmanzanita.com* ⊷*13 rooms, 1 penthouse suite* ⌂*In-room: No a/c, no phone (some), kitchen (some), refrigerator (some), DVD, VCR, Wi-Fi. In-hotel: No elevator.* ⊟*AE, D, MC, V.*

TILLAMOOK

30 mi south of Oswald West State Park and Neahkahnie Mountain on U.S. 101.

More than 100 inches of annual rainfall and the confluence of three rivers contribute to the lush green pastures around Tillamook, probably best known for its thriving dairy industry and cheese factory. The Tillamook County Cheese Factory ships about 40 million pounds of cheese around the world every year.

Just south of town is the largest wooden structure in the world, one of two gigantic buildings constructed in 1942 by the U.S. Navy to shelter blimps that patrolled the Pacific Coast during World War II. Hangar A was destroyed by fire in 1992, and Hangar B was subsequently converted to the Tillamook Naval Air Station Museum.

The **Three Capes Loop** over Cape Meares, Cape Lookout, and Cape Kiwanda offers spectacular views of the ocean and coastline. A lighthouse and an old Indian burial Sitka spruce, Octopus Tree, are worth the trip to Cape Meares, while Cape Lookout is one of the Northwest's best whale-watching viewpoints. Along the route from Tillamook's small resort area of Oceanside, take a look at Three Arch Rocks, a National Wildlife Refuge, with hundreds of sea lions and seals and nesting habitat for as many as 200,000 birds.

Ⓒ The **Pioneer Museum** in Tillamook's 1905 county courthouse has an intriguing if old-fashioned hodgepodge of Native American, pioneer, logging, and natural-history exhibits, along with antique vehicles and military artifacts. ⊠*2106 2nd St.* ☎*503/842–4553* ⊠*$3* ☉*Tues.–Sun. 9–5.*

The **Latimer Quilt and Textile Center** is dedicated to the preservation, promotion, creation, and display of the fiber arts. Spinners, weavers, beaders, and quilters can be found working on projects in the Quilting Room and may engage you in hands-on demonstrations. Rotating exhibits range from costumes, cloth dolls, crocheted items from the 1940s and 1950s, exquisite historical quilts dating from the early to mid-1800s, basketry, and weavings. ⊠*2105 Wilson River Loop Rd.* ☎*503/842–8622* ⊕*www.latimerquiltand textile.com* ⊠*$2.50* ⊙*May–Sept., daily 10–5, Oct.–Apr. Tues.–Sat. 10–4.*

More than 750,000 visitors annually journey through the **Tillamook County Creamery,** the largest cheese-making plant on the West Coast. Here the rich milk from the area's thousands of Holstein and brown Swiss cows becomes ice cream, butter, and cheddar and Monterey Jack cheeses. There's a self-guided cheese-making tour and an extensive shop where tasty cheeses and smoked meats can be purchased; and you'll definitely want a waffle cone full of your favorite ice-cream flavor. Try the marionberry. ⊠*4175 U.S. 101 N, 2 mi north of Tillamook* ☎*503/815–1300* ⊕*www. tillamookcheese.com* ⊠*Free* ⊙*Mid-Sept.–May, daily 8–6; June–mid-Sept., daily 8–8.*

☺ The **Blue Heron French Cheese Company** specializes in French-style cheeses—Camembert, Brie, and others. There are a free petting zoo for kids, a sit-down deli, wine and cheese tastings, and a gift shop that carries wines and jams, mustards, and other products from Oregon. ⊠*2001 Blue Heron Dr., watch for signs from U.S. 101* ☎*503/842– 8281* ⊕*www.blueheronoregon.com* ⊠*Free* ⊙*Memorial Day–Labor Day, daily 8–8; Labor Day–Memorial Day, daily 8–6.*

In the world's largest wooden structure, a former blimp hangar south of town, the **Tillamook Naval Air Station Museum** displays one of the finest private collections of vintage aircraft from World War II, including a B-25 Mitchell and an ME-109 Messerschmidt. The 20-story building is big enough to hold half a dozen football fields. ⊠*6030 Hangar Rd., ½ mi south of Tillamook; head east from U.S. 101 on Long Prairie Rd. and follow signs* ☎*503/842–1130* ⊕*www.tillamookair.com* ⊠*$11* ⊙*Daily 9–5.*

WHERE TO STAY & EAT

$–$$$ ✕**Roseanna's.** Nine miles west of Tillamook in Oceanside, Roseanna's is in a rustic 1915 building on the beach opposite Three Arch Rock, so you might be able to watch sea lions and puffins while you eat. The calm of the beach is complemented in the evening by candlelight and fresh flowers. Have halibut or salmon half a dozen ways, or try the poached baked oysters or Gorgonzola seafood pasta.

⌧ *1490 Pacific Ave., Oceanside 97134* ☏ *503/842–7351*
⌲ *Reservations not accepted* ⊟ *MC, V.*

$-$$ ✕**Artspace.** You'll be surrounded by artwork as you enjoy
homemade creations at Artspace in Bay City, 6 mi north
of Tillamook. The menu may include garlic-grilled oysters,
vegetarian dishes, and other specials, all beautifully pre-
sented, often with edible flowers. ⌧ *9120 5th St., Bay City
97107* ☏ *503/377–2782* ⊟ *No credit cards* ⊙ *Closed Mon.*

$$-$$$ ⌸**Sandlake Country Inn.** Tucked into a bower of old roses on 2
acres, this intimate bed-and-breakfast is in a farmhouse built
of timbers that washed ashore from a shipwreck in 1890.
It's listed on the Oregon Historic Registry and filled with
antiques. The Timbers Suite has a massive, king-size wood
canopy bed, wood-burning fireplace, and two-person jetted
tub; the Starlight Suite occupies four rooms on the second
floor and includes a canopy queen bed and double-sided fireplace. Four-course breakfast delivered to the door. ⌧ *8505
Galloway Rd., Pacific City 97112* ☏ *503/965–6745 or
877/726–3525* ⊛ *www.sandlakecountryinn.com* ⌲ *1 room, 2
suites, 1 cottage* ⌕ *In-room: No a/c, no phone (some), kitchen
(some), DVD: In-hotel: No elevator* ⊟ *D, MC, V* ⊙ *BP.*

THREE CAPES LOOP

Starts south of downtown Tillamook off 3rd St.

★ The Three Capes Loop, a 35-mi byway off U.S. 101, is one
of the coast's most thrilling driving experiences. The loop
winds along the coast between Tillamook and Pacific City,
passing three distinctive headlands—Cape Meares, Cape
Lookout, and Cape Kiwanda. Bayocean Road heading
west from Tillamook passes what was the thriving resort
town of Bay Ocean. More than 30 years ago, Bay Ocean
washed into the sea—houses, a bowling alley, everything—
during a raging Pacific storm.

Nine miles west of Tillamook, trails from the parking lot at
the end of Bay Ocean Spit lead through the dunes to a usually uncrowded and highly walkable white-sand beach.

Cape Meares State Park is on the northern tip of the Three
Capes Loop. Cape Meares was named for English naviga-
tor John Meares, who voyaged along this coast in 1788.
The restored **Cape Meares Lighthouse,** built in 1890 and
open to the public May–September, provides a sweeping

8

view over the cliff to the caves and sea-lion rookery on the rocks below. A many-trunked Sitka spruce known as the Octopus Tree grows near the lighthouse parking lot. ⊠ *Three Capes Loop 10 mi west of Tillamook* ☎ *800/551–6949* ⊕ *www.oregonstateparks.org* ⊠ *Free* ⊙ *Park daily dawn–dusk. Lighthouse Apr.–Oct., daily 11–4.*

Cape Lookout State Park lies south of the beach towns of Oceanside and Netarts. A fairly easy 2-mi trail—marked on the highway as WILDLIFE VIEWING AREA—leads through giant spruces, western red cedars, and hemlocks to views of Cascade Head to the south and Cape Meares to the north. Wildflowers, more than 150 species of birds, and migrating whales passing by in early April make this trail a favorite with nature lovers. The park has a picnic area overlooking the sea and a year-round campground. ⊠ *Three Capes Loop 8 mi south of Cape Meares* ☎ *800/551–6949* ⊕ *www. oregonstateparks.org* ⊠ *Day use $3* ⊙ *Daily, dawn–dusk.*

Huge waves pound the jagged sandstone cliffs and caves at **Cape Kiwanda State Natural Area.** The much-photographed, 235-foot-high **Haystack Rock** juts out of Nestucca Bay just south of here. Surfers ride some of the longest waves on the coast, hang gliders soar above the shore, and beachcombers explore tidal pools and take in unparalleled ocean views. ⊠ *Three Capes Loop 15 mi south of Cape Lookout* ☎ *800/551–6949* ⊕ *www.oregonstateparks.org* ⊠ *Free* ⊙ *Daily dawn–dusk.*

THE OREGON COAST ESSENTIALS

BY CAR

U.S. 101 runs the length of the coast, sometimes turning inland for a few miles. The highway enters coastal Oregon from Washington State at Astoria and from California near Brookings. U.S. 30 heads west from Portland to Astoria. U.S. 20 travels west from Corvallis to Newport. Highway 126 winds west to the coast from Eugene. Highway 42 leads west from Roseburg toward Coos Bay.

VISITOR INFORMATION

Contacts **Astoria–Warrenton Area Chamber of Commerce** (⊠ *111 W. Marine Dr., Astoria 97103* ☎ *503/325–6311 or 800/875–6807* ⊕ *www.oldoregon.com*).

Cannon Beach Chamber of Commerce (⊠ *207 N. Spruce St., 97110* ☎ *503/436–2623* ⊕ *www.cannonbeach.org*).

Seaside Visitors Bureau (⊠ *7 N. Roosevelt Ave., 97138* ☎ *503/738–3097 or 888/306–2326* ⊕ *www.seasideor.com*).

Tillamook Chamber of Commerce (⊠ *3705 U.S. 101 N, 97141* ☎ *503/842–7525* ⊕ *www.tillamookchamber.org*).

THE WILLAMETTE VALLEY & WINE COUNTRY

Updated by Deston S. Nokes

During the 1940s and 1950s, researchers at Oregon State University concluded that the Willamette Valley—the wet, temperate trough between the Coast Range to the west and the Cascade Range to the east—had an unsuitable climate for the propagation of varietal wine grapes. Evidently, they were wrong.

The faultiness of the researchers' techniques has been proven by the success of Oregon's burgeoning wine industry. More than 100 wineries dot the Willamette (pronounced "wil-*lam*-it") Valley, with the bulk of them in Yamhill County in the northern part of the state. Their products—mainly cool-climate varietals like pinot noir, chardonnay, and Johannesberg Riesling—have won gold medals in blind tastings against the best wines of California and Europe.

Points of interest can be found on the Willamette Valley & Wine Country map.

8

NEWBERG

25 mi southwest of Portland on Hwy. 99 W.

Fertile fields of the Willamette Valley surround the community of Newberg, named by the first postmaster for his Bavarian hometown, Newburgh. Many of its early settlers were Quakers from the Midwest who founded the school that has become George Fox University, an accredited four-year institution. Newberg's most famous resident, likewise a Quaker, was Herbert Hoover, the 31st president of the United States. For about five years during his adolescence, he lived with an aunt and uncle at the Hoover-Minthorn House, now a museum listed on the National Register of Historic Places. In addition to numerous well-reputed wineries, the Newberg area also offers slightly more out-of-the-ordinary entertainment, with tours of nine llama ranches and the Pacific Northwest's largest hot-air-balloon company. St. Paul, a historic town with a population of about 325, is about 8 mi south of Newberg and 20 mi north of Salem. Every July, St. Paul holds a professional rodeo.

George Fox University, founded by the Quakers in 1884, is on a 75-acre shady campus in a residential neighborhood. Centennial Tower is surrounded by a campus quad and academic buildings, the library, and the student commons. Hess Creek Canyon cuts through the campus. ⊠*414 N. Meridian St., 97132* ☎*503/538–8383* ⊛*www.georgefox. edu* ⊠*Free* ⊙*Daily.*

The oldest and most significant of Newberg's original structures is the **Hoover-Minthorn House Museum,** the boy-hood home of President Herbert Hoover. Built in 1881, the preserved frame house still has many of its original fur-nishings. Outside is the woodshed that no doubt played an important role in shaping young "Bertie" Hoover's charac-ter. ⊠*115 S. River St.* ☎*503/538–6629* ⊠*$3* ⊙*Mar.–Nov., Wed.–Sun. 1–4; Dec. and Feb., weekends 1–4.*

The drive-in is a perpetual novelty, and **99W Drive-in** is a good bet for a double feature. Ted Francis built this one in 1953 and operated it until his death at 98; the business is now run by his grandson. The first film begins at dusk. Kids 6–11 get in for $4, and children 5 and under are free. ⊠*Hwy. 99 W, Portland Rd., just west of Springbrook Rd. intersection* ☎*503/538–2738* ⊛*www.99w.com* ⊠*$7 per person, $11 minimum vehicle charge* ⊙*Fri.–Sun.*

DUNDEE & YAMHILL

6 mi southwest of Newberg on Hwy. 99 W.

William Reid traveled to Oregon from Dundee, Scotland. As he became interested in the railway business, he got support from his homeland to finance the Oregon Railway Co., Ltd. After the city was incorporated in 1895, Dundee was named after Reid's hometown in recognition of its support.

The lion's share (more than 90%) of the U.S. hazelnut crop is grown in Dundee, a haven of produce stands and wine-tasting rooms. The 25 mi of Highway 18 between Dundee and Grande Ronde, in the Coast Range, roll through the heart of the Yamhill Valley wine country. What used to be a pleasant drive through quaint Dundee is now a traffic bottleneck nightmare; as the one road is the main artery from Lincoln City to suburban Portland. Until the Dundee bypass is built, weekday visits are best.

WINERIES

Merlot, chardonnay, and gewürztraminer are among the wines made at **Duck Pond Cellars** (⌧23145 Hwy. 99 W ☞Box 429, 97115 ☎503/538–3199 or 800/437–3213 ⊕www.duckpondcellars.com). Select free tastings and other vintages for $2. Picnicking in the outdoor seating area is encouraged. The winery is open October–April, daily 11–5, and May–September, daily 10–5.

Pinot noir, chardonnay, and sparkling wines are among the specialties vintaged at **Argyle Winery** (⌧691 Hwy. 99W, 97115 ☎503/538–8520 or 888/427–4953 ⊕www.argylewinery.com). The winery is open daily 11–5.

★ **Sokol Blosser** (⌧5000 Sokol Blosser La., 3 mi west of Dundee off Hwy. 99 W ☎503/864–2282 or 800/582–6668 ⊕www.sokolblosser.com), one of Oregon's oldest and largest wineries, has a tasting room and walk-through vineyard with a self-guided tour that explains the grape varieties—pinot noir and chardonnay, among others. Open daily 10–4.

WHERE TO EAT

★ Fodor'sChoice ✕**Tina's.** Chef–proprietors Tina and David
$$$–$$$$ Bergen bring a powerful one-two punch to this Dundee favorite that often lures Portlanders away from their own restaurant scene. The couple shares cooking duties—Tina does the baking and is often on hand to greet you—and David brings his experience as a former caterer and employee of nearby Sokol Blosser Winery to the table, ensuring that you have the right glass of wine—and there are many—to match your course. Fish and game vie for attention on the country French menu—entrées might include grilled Oregon salmon or Alaskan halibut, or a braised rabbit, local lamb, or tenderloin. Avail yourself of any special soups, particularly if there's corn chowder in the house. A lunch menu includes soup, sandwiches, and Tina's grilled hamburger, made with free-range beef. Service is as intimate and laid-back as the interior. A double fireplace divides the dining room, with heavy glass brick shrouded by bushes on the highway side, so you're not bothered by the traffic on Highway 99. ⌧760 Hwy. 99W, 97115 ☎503/538–8880 ⊗No lunch Sat.–Mon. ▭AE, D, MC, V ⊕www.tinasdundee.com.

8

$–$$$ ✕**Dundee Bistro.** This highly regarded, 80-seat restaurant by
the Ponzi wine family uses Northwest organic foods such
as Draper Valley chicken and local foods such as locally
produced wines, fruits, vegetables, nuts, mushrooms, fish,
and meats. Vaulted ceilings provide an open feeling inside,
warmed by abundant fresh flowers and the works of local
Oregon artists. ⊠*100-A S.W. 7th St., Dundee 97115*
☎*503/554–1650* ⊟*AE, DC, MC, V.*

MCMINNVILLE

14 mi south of Newberg on Hwy. 99 W.

The Yamhill County seat, McMinnville, lies at the center of
Oregon's burgeoning wine industry. There's a larger con-
centration of wineries in Yamhill County than in any other
area of the state, and the vineyards in the McMinnville
area, including some in the town of Dayton to the east,
also produce the most award-winning wines. Among the
varieties are chardonnay, pinot noir, and pinot gris. Most
of the wineries in the area offer tours and tastings. McMin-
nville's downtown area, with a pleasantly disproportionate
number of bookstores and art galleries for its size, is well
worth exploring; many of the historic district buildings,
erected 1890–1915, are still standing and are remarkably
well-maintained.

★ Fodor'sChoice The claim to fame of the **Evergreen Aviation
Museum** is the Hughes (H-4) HK-1 Flying Boat, better
known by its more sibilant nickname, the *Spruce Goose,* on
permanent display here. The famous plane, which eccentric
millionaire Howard Hughes flew only once—on Novem-
ber 2, 1947—was moved to Portland in 1992 from Long
Beach, California, and eventually shipped to McMinnville
in pieces. If you can take your eyes off the Spruce Goose
there are also more than 45 historic planes and replicas
here from the early years of flight and World War II, as well
as the postwar and modern eras. Among the aircraft are a
Spitfire, a C-47 "Gooney Bird," a Messerschmitt Bf 109,
and the sleek SR-71 Blackbird, which set both speed and
high-altitude records as "the world's fastest spy plane."
Among the replicas are a Wright 1903—the craft the
Wright brothers used for the first sustained powered flight.
If you're curious to know which of these planes are still fly-
able, look for the telltale oil pan resting on the floor under-
neath the aircraft. There's a museum store and café—the
Spruce Goose Café, of course—and there are ongoing edu-

cational programs and special events. ✉*500 N.E. Michael King Smith Way, 97128* ☎*503/434–4180* ⊕*www.spruce goose.org* ☜*$13* ☉*Daily 9–5, closed holidays.*

A perennial football powerhouse in NCAA Division III, **Linfield College** is an outpost of brick and ivy amid McMinnville's farmers'-market bustle. The college, founded in 1849 and the second oldest in Oregon, hosts the **International Pinot Noir Celebration** (☎*503/883–2200*) at the end of July and beginning of August (⊕www.ipnc.org/) ✉*900 S.E. Baker St.* ⊕*www.linfield.edu.*

NEED A BREAK? Try Tillamook Ice Cream on a waffle cone at Serendipity Ice Cream (✉*502 N.E. 3rd St.* ☎*503/474–9189*), an old-fashioned ice-cream parlor in the former Cook's Hotel; the building was constructed in 1886.

WINERIES

★ Its original tasting area was the back of a 1952 Ford pickup. Its Gamay noir label notes that the wine gives "more enjoyment to hamburgers [and] fried chicken." And the winery's current architecture still includes a trailer affectionately referred to as the "mobile chateau," already on the property when winemaker Myron Redford purchased the winery in 1974. These modest and whimsical touches underscore what seems to be Redford's philosophy for **Amity Vineyards** (✉*18150 Amity Vineyards Rd. SE, Amity* ☎*503/835–2362* ⊕*www.amityvineyards.com*): take your winemaking a lot more seriously than you take yourself. Taste the pinot blanc for Redford's take on the grape, and also linger in the tasting room to sample the pinot noir and the gewürztraminer, among other varieties. Chocolates made with Amity's pinot noir and other products are available for sale. Hours are daily, October–May noon–5 and June–September 11–5.

In Dundee's Red Hills, **Domaine Serene** (✉*6555 N.E. Hilltop La., Dayton* ☎*503/864–4600* ⊕*www.domaineserene. com*) is a world-class five-level winery and a well-regarded producer of Oregon pinot noir, as well as chardonnay and Syrah. It's open Wednesday–Sunday 11–4.

If Oregon presents the problem of so many wines, so little time, the **Oregon Wine Tasting Room and The Bellevue Market** (✉*19690 S.W. Hwy. 18, 97128* ☎*503/843–3787* ⊕*www. oregonwinetastingroom.com*) provides a handy one-stop tasting venue, with 150 wines from 70 Oregon wineries, some of which rarely open to the public. There are also a gallery and deli on the premises (Daily 11–5:45)

WHERE TO STAY & EAT

$$–$$$$ ✕ **Joel Palmer House.** Joel Palmer was an Oregon pioneer, and his 1857 home in Dayton is now on the National Register of Historic Places. There are three small dining rooms, each seating about 15 people. The chef specializes in wild-mushroom dishes; a popular starter is Heidi's three-mushroom tart. Entrées include rib eye au poivre, rack of lamb, breast of duckling, and coq au vin; desserts include apricot-walnut bread pudding and crème brûlée. Or, if you really, really like mushrooms, have your entire table order Jack's Mushroom Madness Menu, a five-course extravaganza for $75 per person. ⊠ *600 Ferry St., Dayton* ☎ *503/864–2995* ⊕ *www.joelpalmerhouse.com* ⊟ *AE, D, DC, MC, V* ⊘ *Closed Sun.–Mon. No lunch.*

$$$ ✕ **Nick's Italian Cafe.** Modestly furnished but with a volu-
★ minous wine cellar, Nick's is a favorite of area wine makers. The food is spirited and simple, reflecting the owner's northern Italian heritage. The five-course prix-fixe menu changes nightly for $45. À la carte options are also available. ⊠ *521 N.E. 3rd St.* ☎ *503/434–4471* ⌂ *Reservations essential* ⊟ *AE, MC, V* ⊘ *Closed Sun. and Mon. No lunch.*

★ Fodor'sChoice ☑ **Mattey House Bed & Breakfast.** Built in 1982
$$–$$$ by English immigrant Joseph Mattey, a local butcher, this Queen Anne Victorian mansion—on the National Register of Historic Places—has several cheerful areas that define it. Downstairs is a cozy living room jammed with antiques, dual dining areas—a parlor with white wicker and a dining room with elegant furniture—and a porch with a swing. The four upstairs rooms are whimsically named after locally grown grape varieties—Riesling, chardonnay, pinot noir, and Blanc de Blanc—and are decorated in keeping with the character of those wines: the chardonnay room, for instance, has tall windows and crisp white furnishings, and pinot noir has dark-wood pieces and reddish wine accents. A small balcony off the upstairs landing is perfect for sipping a glass of wine on a cool Yamhill Valley evening. Proprietors Jack and Denise will ensure you're comfortably ensconced, familiar with the local history, surrounding vineyards, and the antiquing scene, and holding that glass of wine: in case you don't remember where you are, the house, on 10 acres, is bound by an orchard and its own vineyard, which the couple maintains. If your

imprudent enough to duck out before the fine full breakfast, which might include poached pears with raspberry sauce, frittatas, and Dutch-apple pancakes, Denise or Jack will have pastry and hot coffee available before you set off. A rule barring children under 10 is waived if you're renting the entire house. ⊠*10221 N.E. Mattey La., off Hwy. 99 W, ¼ mi south of Lafayette, 97128* ☎*503/434–5058* ⊕*www. matteyhouse.com* ⇗*4 rooms* &*In-room: No phone. In-hotel: No-smoking rooms* ≡*AE, MC, V* ⎮⊙⎮*BP.*

¢–$$ ▥**Hotel Oregon.** Built in 1905, this historic facility—the former Elberton Hotel—was rescued from decay by the McMenamins chain, renovated in 1998, and reopened the following year. It's four stories of brick; rooms have tall ceilings and high windows. The hotel is outfitted in late Victorian furnishings, but its defining design element is its art. The hotel is whimsically decorated by McMenamins's half-dozen staff artists: around every corner, even in the elevator, you'll find art—sometimes serene, often times bizarre and haunting—as well as photos and sayings scribbled on the walls. The Oregon has a first-floor pub serving three meals a day, a rooftop bar with an impressive view of Yamhill County, and a cellar wine bar, resembling a dark speakeasy, that serves only area vintages. ⊠*310 N.E. Evans St., 97128* ☎*503/472–8427 or 888/472–8427* ⊕*www.mcmenamins.com* ⇗*42 rooms* &*In-hotel: Bars* ≡*AE, D, DC, MC, V.*

8

WILLAMETTE VALLEY & WINE COUNTRY ESSENTIALS

BY CAR

I–5 runs north–south the length of the Willamette. Many Willamette Valley attractions lie not too far east or west of I–5. Highway 22 travels west from the Willamette National Forest through Salem to the coast. Highway 99 travels parallel to I–5 through much of the Willamette Valley. Highway 34 leaves I–5 just south of Albany and heads west, past Corvallis and into the Coast Range, where it follows the Alsea River. Highway 126 heads east from Eugene toward the Willamette National Forest; it travels west from town to the coast.

VISITOR INFORMATION

Contacts **Chehalem Valley Chamber of Commerce (Newberg, Dundee, and St. Paul)** (⊠*415 E. Sheridan, 97132* ☎*503/538–2014* ⊕*www.chehalemvalley.org*).

McMinnville Chamber of Commerce (✉ *417 N.W. Adams St., 97128* ☎ *503/472–6196* ⊕ *www.mcminnville.org*).

Oregon Wine Country/ Willamette Valley Visitors Association (✉ *553 N.W. Harrison Blvd., Corvallis 97330* ☎ *866/548–5018* ⊕ *www. oregonwinecountry.org*).

Yamhill Valley Visitors Association (✉ *Box 774, McMinnville 97128* ☎ *503/883–7770* ⊕ *www.yamhillvalley.org*).

THE COLUMBIA GORGE & MT. HOOD AREA

Updated by Kimberly Gadette

Volcanoes, lava flows, Ice Age floodwaters, and glaciers were Nature's tools of choice to carve a breathtaking 80-mi landscape now called the Columbia River Gorge. Proof of human civilization here reaches back 31,000 years, and excavations near the Dalles have uncovered evidence that salmon fishing is a 10,000-year-old tradition in these parts.

In 1805 Lewis and Clark discovered the Columbia River to be the only waterway that led to the Pacific. Their first expedition was a treacherous route through wild, plunging rapids, but their successful navigation set a new exodus in motion. By the 1850s, almost 12,000 new settlers arrived in the Oregon Territory.

Sightseers, hikers, and skiers have long found contentment in this robust region, officially labeled a national scenic area in 1986. Highlights of the Columbia River Gorge include Multnomah Falls, Bonneville Dam, and the rich orchard land of Hood River—a windsurfing hub. To the south of Hood River are all the alpine attractions of the 11,245-foot-high Mt. Hood. From Portland, the Columbia Gorge–Mt. Hood Scenic Loop is the easiest way to see the gorge and the mountain. Take I-84 east to Troutdale and follow U.S. 26 to Bennett Pass (near Timberline), where Highway 35 heads north to Hood River; then follow I-84 back to Portland. Or make the loop in reverse.

Winter weather in the Columbia Gorge and the Mt. Hood area is much more severe than in Portland and western Oregon. At times I-84 may be closed because of snow and ice. If you're planning a winter visit, be sure to carry plenty of warm clothes. Note that chains are a requirement for traveling over mountain passes. In spring the Gorge's 77 waterfalls, including 11 that cascade over 100 feet, are especially energetic—and photogenic. In early fall, look for maple, tamarack, and aspen trees fairly bursting with brilliant red and gold color. But no matter the season, the basalt cliffs, the acres of lush forest, and that glorious expanse of water make the Gorge worth visiting time and again.

Points of interest can be found on The Columbia Gorge map.

TROUTDALE

13 mi east of Portland on I–84.

Troutdale's nomenclature comes courtesy of captain of industry and sea, John Harlow, who bought a substantial portion of the town's original land claim in 1872 to build his country home. Harlow raised trout in the ponds surrounding his estate and called his place "Troutdale." But Captain John was also a farmer who needed to transport his produce, so he convinced the railroad to build a depot near his home. Or, rather, at the exact site of his home. Therefore, when the train pulled up to its new destination, it would always be known as Troutdale. Called the gateway to the Columbia River Gorge, Troutdale is still known for its great fishing spots, as well as antique stores and the Columbia Gorge Premium Outlets.

Continuing eastward, as the Gorge widens, is the 22-mi-long **Historic Columbia River Highway,** U.S. 30 (also known as the Columbia River Scenic Highway and the Scenic Gorge Highway). The oldest scenic highway in the U.S., it's a construction marvel that integrates asphalt path with cliff, ocean, and forest landscapes. Paralleling the highway on the south side of I–84, the road climbs to forested riverside bluffs high above the Interstate. Completed in 1922, the serpentine highway was the first paved road in the Gorge built expressly for automotive sightseers. (Keep an eye out for five waterfalls along the way.)

A few miles east of Troutdale on U.S. 30 is **Crown Point State Scenic Corridor,** a 730-foot-high bluff with an unparalleled 30-mi view down the Columbia River Gorge. **Vista House,** the two-tier octagonal structure on the side of the cliff, opened its doors to visitors in 1916; the rotunda has displays about the Gorge and the highway. Vista House's architect Edgar Lazarus is the brother to Emma Lazarus, the author of the poem residing at the base of the Statue

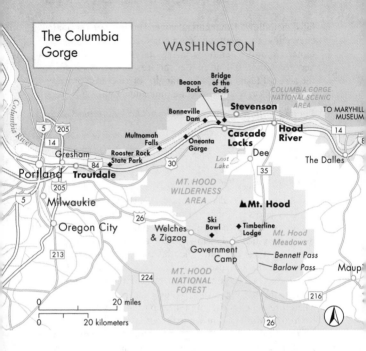

The Columbia Gorge

WASHINGTON

Beacon Rock

Bridge of the Gods

Bonneville Dam

Stevenson

COLUMBIA GORGE NATIONAL SCENIC AREA

TO MARYHILL MUSEUM

Multnomah Falls

Oneonta Gorge

Cascade Locks

Hood River

Rooster Rock State Park

Lost Lake

Dee

The Dalles

Gresham

Portland

Troutdale

Milwaukie

Oregon City

MT. HOOD WILDERNESS AREA

Welches & Zigzag

Ski Bowl

Mt. Hood

Timberline Lodge

Mt. Hood Meadows

Government Camp

Bennett Pass

Barlow Pass

Maup

MT. HOOD NATIONAL FOREST

0   20 miles

0   20 kilometers

of Liberty. ✉*U.S. 30* ☎*503/695–2261 or 800/551–6949* ⊕*www.oregonstateparks.org/park_150.php* ⊟*Free* ⊘*Daily* ♿*ADA accessible.*

About 4 mi east of the Troutdale bridge, **Dabney State Park** has boating, hiking, and fishing. There's also a popular summer swimming hole and an 18-hole disc golf course. A boat ramp is open year-round. ✉*U.S. 30, 4 mi east of Troutdale* ☎*800/551–6949* ⊕*www.oregonstateparks.org/park_151. php* ⊟*Day use $3 per vehicle* ⊘*Daily dawn–dusk.*

The most famous beach lining the Columbia River, **Rooster Rock State Park** is below Crown Point; access is from the Interstate only. Three miles of sandy beaches, panoramic cascades, and a large swimming area makes this a popular spot. True naturists appreciate that one of Oregon's two designated nude beaches is at the east end of Rooster Rock, and that it's not visible to conventional sunbathers. ✉*I–84, 7 mi east of Troutdale* ☎*503/695–2261* ⊕*www.oregon stateparks.org/park_175.php* ⊟*Day use $3 per vehicle* ⊘*Daily 7–dusk.*

WHERE TO STAY & EAT

$–$$$$ ✕**Black Rabbit Restaurant & Bar.** Chef John Zenger's grilled rib-eye steak, old-fashioned roasted chicken, and sesame-crusted salmon are popular entrées at this McMenamins Hotel restaurant. Vivid murals depicting the Gorge's history enrich your view as you linger over dinner in a high-backed wooden booth. Enjoy an Edgefield wine or any one of five McMenamins brews (made on-site, approximately 50 yards away!). Patio seating is available, with plenty of heaters to handle the unpredictable Oregon weather. Top off your meal with a homemade dessert and, wouldn't you know?, a McMenamins' home-roasted cup of coffee. ⊠*2126 S.W. Halsey St., 97060* ☎*503/492–3086* ⊕*www.mcmenamins. com/index.php?loc=114* ▤*AE, D, DC, MC, V.*

★ Fodor'sChoice 🔲**McMenamins Edgefield.** As you explore the
$–$$ grounds of this Georgian Revival manor, you'll feel like you've entered a European village filled with activity and beauty. Wander through 38 acres of gardens, orchards, and vineyards with a drink in your hand. Enjoy complimentary movies in the Edgefield theater, live music in the Winery, and golf at the 17-hole course. There are three restaurants and six bars to choose from, as well as a pool hall and distillery. Ruby's Spa offers an amplitude of body treatments. Be sure to make reservations ahead of time for the Black Rabbit restaurant and Ruby's Spa. Pros: Plenty of choices for eating and drinking. A large variety of rooms and prices to choose from. Cons: Crowds can get large at this busy place. ⊠*2126 S.W. Halsey St., 97060* ☎*503/669–8610 or 800/669–8610* ⊕*www.mcmenamins.com* ➷*114 rooms, 24 beds in men's/women's hostels* ♿*In-room: No a/c (some), no phone, no TV. In-hotel: 3 restaurants, bars, golf course, spa, public Wi-Fi, parking (no fee)* ▤*AE, D, DC, MC, V.*

EN ROUTE. **From Crown Point, the Columbia River Highway heads downhill over graceful stone bridges built by Italian immigrant masons and winds through quiet forest glades. More than a dozen waterfalls pour over fern- and lichen-covered cliffs in a 10-mi stretch. Latourell, Bridal Veil, Wahkeena, and Horsetail falls are the most impressive. All have parking areas and hiking trails.**

8

MULTNOMAH FALLS

20 mi east of Troutdale on I–84 or Historic Columbia River Hwy. (U.S. 30).

Multnomah Falls, a 620-foot-high double-decker torrent, the second highest year-round waterfall in the nation, is by far the most spectacular of the cataracts east of Troutdale. The scenic highway leads down to a parking lot; from there, a paved path winds to a bridge over the lower falls. A much steeper trail climbs to a viewing point overlooking the upper falls.

WHERE TO EAT

$–$$$ ✕**Multnomah Falls Lodge.** Vaulted ceilings, stone fireplaces,
★ and exquisite views of Multnomah Falls are complemented by wonderful service and an extensive menu at this restaurant, which is listed on the National Register of Historic places. Consider the halibut fish-and-chips, the lemon and herb roasted wild salmon, or ancho chile and espresso-cured flat iron steak. Breakfast favorites include blueberry, buttermilk, or huckleberry pancakes. A particular pleaser for out-of-town guests, the champagne Sunday brunch is held 8–2. For a treat during warmer months sit on the patio and get close to the Falls without feeling a drop. ⊠*Exit 31 off I–84, 50000 Historic Columbia River Hwy., Bridal Veil 97010* ☎*503/695–2376* ⊕*www.multnomahfallslodge.com* ⊟*AE, D, MC, V.*

ONEONTA GORGE

2 mi east of Multnomah Falls on Historic Columbia River Hwy.

Following the old highway east from Multnomah Falls, you come to a narrow, mossy cleft with walls hundreds of feet high. Oneonta Gorge is most enjoyable in summer, when you can walk up the streambed through the cool green canyon, where hundreds of plant species—some found nowhere else—flourish under the perennially moist conditions. At other times of the year, take the trail along the west side of the canyon. The clearly marked trailhead is 100 yards west of the gorge, on the south side of the road. The trail ends at Oneonta Falls, about ½ mi up the stream. Bring boots or submersible sneakers—plus a strong pair of ankles—because the rocks are slippery. East of Oneonta Gorge, the scenic highway returns to I–84.

CASCADE LOCKS

7 mi east of Oneonta Gorge on Historic Columbia River Hwy. and I–84, 30 mi east of Troutdale on I–84.

In pioneer days, boats needing to pass the bedeviling rapids near the town of Cascade Locks had to portage around them. The locks that gave the town its name were completed in 1896, allowing waterborne passage for the first time. Native Americans still use the locks for their traditional dip-net fishing.

✪ The first federal dam to span the Columbia, **Bonneville Dam** was dedicated by President Franklin D. Roosevelt in 1937. Its generators (visible from a balcony during self-guided powerhouse tours) have a capacity of nearly a million kilowatts, enough to supply power to more than 200,000 single-family homes. There's a modern visitor center on Bradford Island, complete with underwater windows for viewing migrating salmon and steelhead as they struggle up fish ladders. The best viewing times are between April and October. In recent years the dwindling runs of wild Columbia salmon have made the dam a subject of much environmental controversy. ⊠*Bonneville Lock and Dam, U.S. Army Corps of Engineers, from I–84 take Exit 40, head northeast, and follow signs 1 mi to visitor center, Cascade Locks* ⊕*www.nwp.usace.army.mil/op/b/home.asp* ☎*541/374–8820* ☜*Free* ☼*Visitor center daily 9–5.*

✪ Below Bonneville Dam, the ponds at the **Bonneville Fish Hatchery** teem with fingerling salmon, fat rainbow trout, and 6-foot-long sturgeon. The hatchery raises chinook and coho salmon; from mid-October to late November, you can watch as staff members spawn the fish, beginning a new hatching cycle, or feed the trout with food pellets from a coin-operated machine. ⊠*From I–84 take Exit 40 and follow signs northeast 1 mi to Hatchery, 70543 N.E. Herman Loop* ☎*541/374–8393* ☜*Free* ☼*Hatchery grounds daily dawn–dusk, spawning room daily 7:30–4:30.*

✪ Cascade Locks is the home port of the 600-passenger stern-wheeler *Columbia Gorge*. Between mid-June and early October the relic ship churns upriver, then back again, on two-hour excursions through some of the Columbia River Gorge's most impressive scenery. The ship's captain will talk about the gorge's fascinating 40-million-year geology and about pioneering spirits and legends, such as Lewis and Clark, who once triumphed over this very same river.

8

Group bookings and private rentals available. Call sales department at 800/224–3901 for rates. ✉*Cruises leave from Marine Park in Cascade Locks. Marine Park, 355 Wanapa St.* ☎*541/374–8427 or 800/224-3901* ⊕*www. sternwheeler.com* ⚓*Reservations essential* ✉*Prices vary, depending on choice of excursion: sightseeing, brunch, dinner, or Landmarks of the Gorge cruises, $25–$80* ☉*Cruises offered mid-June–early Oct., call for cruise schedule* ▭*AE, MC, V.*

WHERE TO STAY & EAT

$–$$$ ✕**Pacific Crest Pub.** A woodsy tavern with cedar-shake walls, historical photos, and a stone fireplace provides hearty servings of starters, salads, and main courses, including on-site-smoked salmon chowder and oven-roasted chicken accompanied by house-specialty horseradish. If you like feta cheese with your pizzas, try the house favorite, the Greek "Pizza of the Gods." During warmer months, sit outside in the adjacent courtyard and take in mountain and river views while sipping one of 13 featured microbrews, including Full Sail and Walking Man. ✉*500 Wanapa St.* ☎*541/374–9310* ▭*D, MC, V* ☉*Closed Mon.*

STEVENSON, WASHINGTON

Across the river from Cascade Locks via the Bridge of the Gods and 4 mi east on Hwy. 14.

For a magnificent vista 135 feet above the Columbia, as well as a speedy route between Oregon and Washington, $1 will pay your way over the grandly named **Bridge of the Gods** (⊕*www.portofcascadelocks.org/bridge.htm*). Slightly west of the bridge, hikers gain access to the Oregon-Washington link of the Mexico-to-Canada **Pacific Crest Trail.** Travel east on Highway 14 for about 10 minutes to reach the small town of Stevenson, with several antiques shops and good places to grab a bite.

★ For several hundred years, 848-foot **Beacon Rock** was a landmark for river travelers, including Native Americans, who recognized this point as the last rapid of the Columbia River. Lewis and Clark are thought to have been the first white men to see the volcanic remnant. Picnic atop old lava flows after hiking a 1-mi trail, steep but safe, which leads to tremendous views of the Columbia Gorge and river. A round-trip hike takes 45–60 minutes. The site is a few miles west of the Bridge of the Gods.

NEED A BREAK? Funky and fun, '60s Haight-Ashbury meets Native American art, **Bahma Coffee Bar** is the place in Stevenson for Wi-Fi (with purchase) and, of course, coffee. Or choose from grilled panini sandwiches, soups, fresh carrot juice, wine, sake, tea, and tasty homemade pastries. Scrabble tournaments, games aplenty, reading material, and live music on some weekends. All this, and a super staff. ⊠ *256 S.W. 2nd St., Hwy. 14, 98648* ☎ *509/427–8700* ⊕ *www.bahmacoffeebar.com* ▭ *MC, V* ⊙ *Daily 8:30–5.*

☋ A petroglyph whose eyes seem to look straight at you, "She Who Watches" or "Tsagaglalal" is the logo for the **Columbia Gorge Interpretive Center.** Sitting among the dramatic basaltic cliffs on the north bank of the Columbia River Gorge, the museum explores the life of the Gorge: its history, culture, architecture, legends, and much more. The younger crowd may enjoy the reenactment of the Gorge in the Creation Theatre. Or a 37-foot high fishwheel from the 19th century. Historians will appreciate studying the water route of the Lewis & Clark Expedition. There's also an eye-opening exhibit that examines current environmental impacts on the area. ⊠ *990 S.W. Rock Creek Dr., Stevenson, WA 98648* ⊹ *1 mi east of Bridge of the Gods on Hwy. 14* ☎ *509/427–8211 or 800/991–2338* ⊕ *www.columbiagorge.org* ▧ *$7* ⊙ *Daily 10–5* ☞ *Handicapped accessible.*

WHERE TO STAY & EAT

$$$$ ▨ **Skamania Lodge.** "Skamania," the Chinook word for "swift water," overlooks exactly that with its 175 acres sitting to the north of the Columbia River Gorge. So big you need a map to get around, the Lodge impresses with its multitude of windows that take in the surrounding forests and Gorge, Montana slate tiling, Native American artwork, and an immense word-burning fireplace. Outstanding recreational facilities include an 18-hole, par-70 golf course, 3 hiking trails, large indoor pool and even a sand volleyball court. The accommodating staff will pack you a box lunch if you're going out to explore for the day. Pros: Addresses the active guest as well as the kids. U.S. Forest Service has a kiosk in the lobby. Well-suited to handle large events, conferences, weddings. Cons: Costs can quickly multiply for a large family; can get crowded, sometimes there's a wait for table-seating in the dining room. ⊠ *Skamania Lodge Way north of Hwy. 14, 1½ mi east of Bridge of the Gods 1131 S.W. Skamania Lodge Way, 98648* ☎ *509/427–7700 or*

800/221–7117 ⊕www.skamania.com ⌁254 rooms ☐In-room: Wi-fi, ethernet. In-hotel: 3 restaurants, bars, golf course, tennis courts, pool, gym, spa, bicycles, concierge, executive floor, public Wi-Fi, parking (no fee), some pets allowed ⊟AE, D, DC, MC, V.

GRAPE EXPECTATIONS? The Columbia Gorge Winemakers Association is credited with the catchy slogan, "A World of Wine in 40 Miles." Representing three different regions, there's a 40-square mi area within the Gorge that varies in soil and climate, supporting more than 22 wineries. Though vintners state that in Europe, a similar variety of wines would encompass 1,200 square mi, they swear that the Gorge can do it all, from rieslings to nebbiolos, from pinot noirs to pinot gris. Meaning that whatever the weather, the weather's just "vine."

$$$–$$$$ ☐**Bonneville Hot Springs Resort and Spa.** Enter an architec-
★ tural wonderland of wood, iron, rock, and water, water everywhere. Owner Pete Cam and his five sons built the resort to share their love of these historic mineral springs with the public, especially those seeking physical renewal. The three-story lobby, with its suspended black-iron trestle, Paul Bunyon–size river-rock fireplace, and floor-to-ceiling arched windows, is magnificent to behold. The unique redwood-paneled, 25-meter indoor lap pool is adjacent to an immaculate European spa, offering more than 40 candlelighted treatments (mineral baths, body wraps, massages). Rooms are spacious, with upscale furnishings. Pros: Glorious grounds, amazing architectural detail, attentive and knowledgeable spa staff. Cons: Must reserve spa appointments separately from room reservations. The dull, boxy exterior belies what's inside. ⊠*1252 E. Cascade Dr., North Bonneville, WA 98639 ✛3 mi west of Bridge of the Gods on Hwy. 14, right on Hot Springs Way, right on E. Cascade Dr. follow for ½ mi ☎509/427–7767 or 866/459–1678 ⊕www.bonnevilleresort.com ⌁78 rooms ☐In-room: Refrigerator. In-hotel: Restaurant, bar, pool, spa, concierge, public Wi-Fi ⊟AE, D, MC, V.*

HOOD RIVER

17 mi east of Cascade Locks on I–84.

For years the incessant easterly winds blowing through the town of Hood River were nothing more than a nuisance.

Then somebody bolted a sail to a surfboard, waded into the fat part of the Gorge, and a new recreational craze was born. A fortuitous combination of factors—mainly the reliable gale-force winds blowing against the current—has made Hood River the self-proclaimed boardsailing capital of the world. Especially in summer, this once-somnolent town swarms with colorful "boardheads," from as far as Europe and Australia. Not just content to surf the water, others are boosting their hang time with another craze, the kiteboard. In winter many of these same athletes stay in town, but turn south to ski on mountain slopes that are only a short drive away. Other outdoor enthusiasts find the area's fishing, boating, swimming, and hiking venues the best in the region.

Hood River's rich pioneer past is reflected in its downtown historic district. The City of Hood River publishes a free self-guided walking tour (available through the City of Hood River government office or the Hood River Chamber of Commerce), which will take you on a tour of more than 40 civic and commercial buildings dating from 1893 to the 1930s, some of which are listed in the National Register of Historic Places.

Either by car or bicycle, tour Hood River valley's **Fruit Loop,** whose vast orchards surround the Hood River. You'll see apples, pears, cherries, and peaches fertilized by volcanic soil, pure glacier water, and a conducive harvesting climate. Along the 35 mi of farms are a host of delicious baked goods, wines, flowers, and nuts. Festive farm activities from April to November also give a taste of the agricultural life. While on the loop, consider stopping at the town of **Parkdale** to lunch, shop, and snap a photo of Mt. Hood's north face. There are well-marked signs on the entire 35-mi loop. ✉*Rte. begins on Hwy. 35* ⊕*www. hoodriverfruitloop.com.*

On a 2-acre National Historic Site, the **Hutson Museum** exhibits Native American dolls, taxidermy, and a rare rock collection, which includes thousands of rough specimens, polished slabs, spheres, and eggs. More than 2,500 arrow and spear points, stone bowls, mortars, grinding tools, and specialized tools are prized for their regional geological and historical value. The Mt. Hood excursion train terminates at the museum. ✉*4967 Baseline Dr., Parkdale* ☎*541/352–6808* ⚟*$1* ☉*Apr.–Oct..*

An efficient and relaxing way to survey Mt. Hood and the Hood River, the **Mt. Hood Scenic Railroad and Dinner Train** was established in 1906 as a passenger and freight line. Chug alongside the Hood River through vast fruit orchards before climbing up steep forested canyons, glimpsing Mt. Hood along the way. There are four trip options: a four-hour excursion (serves light concessions with two daily departures, morning and afternoon), dinner, brunch, and a themed murder-mystery dinner. Choose from brunch fare such as raspberry crepes, omelets, eggs Benedict. Favorite dinner selections include huckleberry-sauced salmon, sun-dried tomato ravioli, and chicken picatta. Exceptional service is as impressive as the scenery. ⊠*110 Railroad Ave.* ☎*541/386–3556 or 800/872–4661* ⊕*www. mthoodrr.com* ⊟*AE, D, MC, V* ⊡*$25–$80* ☉*Apr.–Dec., call for schedule.*

NEED A BREAK? A glass-walled microbrewery with a windswept deck overlooking the Columbia, the **Full Sail Tasting Room and Pub** (⊠*506 Columbia St.* ☎*541/386-2247*) has won major awards at the Great American Beer Festival. Savory snack foods complement fresh ales. The Taster Tray, seven 4-ounce samples for $5, is a great way to explore the many varieties of Full Sail brews. On-site brewery tours available.

Half art museum, half theater, the **Columbia Center for the Arts** promotes professional and novice artists alike, both visual and theatrical. The successful blend of the 28-year-old Columbia Arts Stage Troupe (CAST) and the Columbia Art Galley happened by coincidence, when both realized they were looking for a home in 2003. Combining their efforts and fundraising, they renovated a 10,000 square foot American Legion Hall, and opened as one in 2005, calling themselves the Columbia Center for the Arts. Call or check the Web site for updates on exhibits and theater. ⊠*215 Cascade Ave., 97031* ☎*541/387–8877* ⊕*www.columbiaarts.org* ☉*Gallery hrs Wed.–Sun. 11–5 and by appointment.*

Awarded the Oregon Winery of the Year in 2007 by the Northwest Wine Press, **Cathedral Ridge Winery** has a 6-acre vineyard. Popular varietals include Riesling, pinot gris, and Syrah. The tasting room is open 11–5 daily. ⊠*4200 Post Canyon Dr., 97031* ☎*800/516-8710* ⊕*www.cathedral ridgewinery.com* ⊡*Free* ☉*Daily 11–5.*

Sauvignon blanc, cabernet sauvignon, and merlot are among the varieties produced at the 12-acre, family-owned **Hood River Vineyards,** which overlook the Columbia River Gorge and the Hood River valley. Bottles are sold individually; best sellers are the pinot noir and chardonnay. ✉ *4693 Westwood Dr.* ☎ *541/386–3772* ⊕ *www.hoodrivervineyards.us* ⊡ *Free* ☉ *Apr.–Oct., daily 11–5; Nov.–Mar., Wed.–Sun. 11–5.*

OFF THE BEATEN PATH. One of the most photographed sights in the Pacific Northwest, the waters of Lost Lake reflect towering Mt. Hood and the thick forests that line its shore. Cabins are available for overnight stays, and because no motorboats are allowed on Lost Lake, the area is blissfully quiet. ✉ *Lost Lake Rd., take Hood River Hwy. south from Hood River to town of Dee and follow signs; also accessible from Lolo Pass* ☎ *541/386–6366* ⊡ *Day use $5.*

WHERE TO STAY & EAT

★ **Fodor's**Choice ✕**Stonehedge Gardens.** It's not just the cuisine
$$$ that's out of this world—Stonehedge is of another time and place, surrounding you with 7 acres of lush English gardens that gracefully frame its multitude of stone terraces and trickling fountains. Each of the four dining rooms in the restored 1898 home has a distinct personality, from cozy to verdant to elegant. The curry shiitake mushroom soup is a *Bite of the Gorge* favorite. The homemade pecan vinaigrette dressing, and the fresher-than-fresh seafood and meat, melded with sauces and spices that heighten rather than smother. Just when you think your meal is complete, along comes the flaming bread pudding. ✉ *3405 Cascade Ave.* ☎ *541/386–3940* ⊟ *AE, MC, V* ☉ *No lunch.*

$$$ ✕⊡**Columbia Gorge Hotel.** One selling point of this grande dame of gorge hotels is the view of a 208-foot-high waterfall. Rooms with plenty of wood, brass, and antiques overlook the formal gardens. Rates include a seven-course breakfast, dubbed the World Famous Farm Breakfast (nonguests pay $24.95). While watching the sun set on the Columbia River, you can dine in the hotel's restaurant, also open to nonguests, where selections might include breast of pheasant with pear wine, hazelnuts, and cream, as well as grilled venison, breast of duck, Columbia River salmon, or sturgeon. ✉ *4000 Westcliff Dr., 97031* ⊹ *off I–84 Exit 62* ☎ *541/386–5566 or 800/345–1921* ⊕ *www.*

columbiagorgehotel.com ⇆46 rooms ⌂In-hotel: restaurant, bar ▤AE, D, DC, MC, V ⏘BP.

$$$ ▦**Lakecliff Bed & Breakfast.** Perched on a cliff overlooking
★ the Columbia Gorge, this beautiful 1908 summer home
has long been a favorite spot for weddings. Designed by
architect A.E. Doyle (who also created the Multnomah
Falls Lodge), this 3-acre magical land of ferns, fir trees,
and water is a stunner. There are a deck at the back of
the house, fireplaces and river views in three of the rooms,
and top-notch service, including hot coffee right outside
your door in the morning. "Large, spoiling breakfasts,"
says the owner, referring to her poached pears, blueberry
pancakes, and butterscotch pecan rolls. For summer, make
reservations as far ahead as possible. Pros: Glorious views,
friendly and accommodating staff, the B&B can handle
receptions 50–150 guests. Cons: No king-size beds, need
to book months in advance. ✉3820 Westcliff Dr., head
east from I–84 Exit 62, 97031 ☏541/386–7000 ⊕www.
lakecliffbnb.com ⇆4 rooms ⌂In-room: No phone, no TV.
In-hotel: No elevator, no kids under 18 ▤MC, V.

MT. HOOD

About 60 mi east of Portland on I–84 and U.S. 26, 65 mi
from the Dalles, west on I–84 and south on Hwy. 35 and
U.S. 26.

Majestically towering 11,245 feet above sea level, Mt.
Hood is what remains of the original north wall and rim
of a volatile crater. Although the peak no longer spews
ash or fire, active steam vents can be spotted high on the
mountain. Native Americans in the area named it Wy'east,
after a great chief who mystically became the mountain.
In anger, Wy'east spouted flames and threw rocks toward
the sky. The name was changed in 1792 when a crew of
the British Royal Navy, the first recorded Caucasians sailing
down the Columbia River, spotted the mountain and
named it after a famed British naval officer by the name
of—you guessed it—Hood.

Mt. Hood offers the only year-round skiing in the lower
48 states, with three major ski areas and 26 lifts, as well as
extensive areas for cross-country skiing and snowboarding.
Many of the ski runs turn into mountain bike trails in
summer. The mountain is also popular with climbers and

hikers. In fact, some hikes follow parts of the Oregon Trail, and signs of the pioneers' passing are still evident.

★ The highest mountain in Oregon and the fourth-highest peak in the Cascades, towering at 11,235 feet and crowned by year-round snow, "the Mountain" is a focal point of the 1.1-million-acre **Mt. Hood National Forest,** an all-season playground attracting more than 7 million visitors annually. Twenty miles southeast of Portland, it extends south from the Columbia River Gorge for more than 60 mi and includes 189,200 acres of designated wilderness. These woods are perfect for hikers, horseback riders, mountain climbers, and cyclists. Within the forest are more than 80 campgrounds and 50 lakes stocked with brown, rainbow, cutthroat, brook, and steelhead trout. The Sandy, Salmon, and other rivers are known for their fishing, rafting, canoeing, and swimming. Both forest and mountain are crossed by an extensive trail system for hikers, cyclists, and horseback riders. The **Pacific Crest Trail,** which begins in British Columbia and ends in Mexico, crosses at the 4,157-foot-high Barlow Pass. As with most other mountain destinations within Oregon, weather can be temperamental, and snow and ice may affect driving conditions as early as October and as late as May. Bring tire chains and warm clothes as a precaution.

For a glimpse into the area's vivid history stop at the **Mt. Hood Information Center** and pick up a copy of *The Barlow Road.* This is a great navigational map of the first emigrant road over the Cascades where pioneers traveled west via ancient Indian trails to avoid the dangers of the mighty Columbia River. Since this forest is close to the Portland metro area, campgrounds and trails are potentially crowded over the summer months, especially on weekends. If camping, contact the forest service desk while you're at the Mt. Hood Information Center. Prepare yourself by gathering information about the more than 80 campgrounds, including a string of neighboring campgrounds that rest on the south side of Mt. Hood: Trillium Lake, Still Creek, Timothy Lake, Little Crater Lake, Clackamas Lake, Summit Lake, Clear Lake, and Frog Lake. Each varies in what it offers and in price. The mountain is overflowing with day-use areas, and passes can be obtained for $5. There are also Mt. Hood National Forest maps with details about well-marked trails. ✉ *24403 E. Welches Rd., 97067* ☎ *503/622–4822 or 888/622–4822* ⊕ *www.mthood.info* ✉ *Day use free–$5, campsites $12–*

8

$14 ⊙*Information center weekdays 9–5, weekends 9–4, most campgrounds open year-round.*

WHERE TO STAY & EAT

$$$–$$$$ ×**Cascade Dining Room.** If the wall of windows aren't coated
★ with snow, you may get a good look at some of the neigh-
boring peaks. Vaulted wooden beams and a wood-plank
floor, handcrafted furniture, hand-woven drapes, and a
lion-size stone fireplace set the scene. Executive chef Leif
Benson has been going strong since 1979, incorporating
Mt. Hood–grown morels in his "campfire spice" wild
salmon, pistachios in his basmati rice, and truffles with
his pheasant. A four-course tasting menu (including house
favorite, crème brûlée) is always a delightful option. Open
for breakfast, lunch, and dinner, look for the clever mix of
lobster with macaroni and cheese at the noon hour. Sunday
brunch buffet, an all-you-can-eat affair, is almost as big
as the fireplace. ⊠*Timberline Rd., Timberline* ☎*503/622–
0700 or 800/547–1406* ⊕*www.timberlinelodge.com/din-
ing/cascade_room.php* ▤*AE, D, MC, V.*

$$–$$$$ 🏨**Timberline Lodge.** The approach alone, an unforgettable
⏱ 6-mi ascent that circles Mt. Hood, is reason enough to
★ visit the magnificent Timberline Lodge. Now you see it,
now you don't: Mt. Hood teases you the whole way up,
then quite unexpectedly, the Lodge materializes out of the
mist and you momentarily forget about the snow-capped
peak. It's no wonder that Stanley Kubrick used shots of
the Lodge's exterior for the film "The Shining." Built to
complement the size and majesty of Mt. Hood, the massive
structure was erected from the timber and rock donated by
the forests of the mountain itself. More than 500 men and
women toiled in 1936–37 forging metal for furniture and
fixtures, sculpting old telephone poles into beams and ban-
isters, weaving, looming, sawing. But for once, the historical artifacts are not displayed behind a glass wall—they're
the chairs you sit on, the doors you walk through, the
floors you step on. Enjoy the restaurants, the snow sports,
the hiking paths; relax by the lobby's massive fireplace with
a 96-foot stone chimney. But also take in the marvelously
detailed 22-minute film (on the lower level) to learn about
the building's genesis—it'll "heighten" your appreciate of
Timberline all the more! Pros: A thrill to stay on the mountain itself, great proximity to all snow activity, plush feather
beds, amazing architecture throughout, fun dining places.
Cons: Rooms are small, no a/c in summer, prepare yourself
for carloads of tourists. ⊠*Timberline, Timberline Lodge,*

OR 97028 ☎503/231–5400 or 800/547–1406 ⊕www. timberlinelodge.com ⇆60 rooms ☖In-room: No a/c. In-hotel: Restaurant, bar, pool, gym, elevator, concierge, parking (no fee) ⊟AE, D, MC, V.

SPORTS & THE OUTDOORS

SKIING

One of the longest ski seasons in North America unfolds at **Timberline Lodge Ski Area** (⊠*Off U.S. 26, Timberline* ☎*503/272–3311*). The U.S. ski team conducts summer training at this full-service ski area. It's the only ski area in the lower 48 states that's open year-round (except for two weeks in late September), and that also welcomes snowboarders. Timberline is famous for its Palmer chairlift, which takes skiers to a high glacier for summer skiing. There are five double chairs and two high-speed quad chairs. The top elevation is 8,500 feet, with a 3,600-foot vertical drop, and the longest run is 3 mi. Facilities include a day lodge with fast food and a ski shop; lessons and equipment rental and repair are available. Parking requires a Sno-Park permit. Lift tickets per day are $54 peak, $49 regular. The area is open Sunday–Tuesday 9–5 and Wednesday–Saturday 9 AM–10 PM; the lift is also open June–August, daily 7 AM–1:30 PM.

THE COLUMBIA GORGE & MT. HOOD ESSENTIALS

BY CAR

I–84 is the main east–west route into the Columbia River Gorge. U.S. 26, heading east from Portland and northwest from Prineville, is the main route into the Mt. Hood area. Portions of I–84 and U.S. 26 that pass through the mountains pose winter-travel difficulties, though the state plows these roadways regularly. The gorge is closed frequently during harsh winters due to ice and mud slides. Extreme winds can also make driving hazardous and potentially result in highway closures.

The Historic Columbia River Highway (U.S. 30) from Troutdale, to just east of Oneonta Gorge, passes Crown Point State Park and Multnomah Falls. I–84/U.S. 30 continues on to the Dalles. Highway 35 heads south from the Dalles to the Mt. Hood area, intersecting with U.S. 26 at Government Camp.

VISITOR INFORMATION

Contacts **Columbia River Gorge Visitors Association** (✉️*404 W. 2nd St., The Dalles 97058* ☎️*800/984–6743* ⊕*www.crgva.org*).

Hood River County Chamber of Commerce (✉️*405 Portway Ave., 97031* ☎️*541/386–2000 or 800/366–3530* ⊕*www.hoodriver.org*).

Mt. Hood Chamber of Commerce (✉️*24403 E. Welches Rd., Welches 97067* ☎️*503/622–3017* ⊕*www.mthood.org*).

Mt. Hood Information Center (✉️*24403 E. Welches Rd., Welches 97067* ☎️*503/622–4822* ⊕*mthood.info*).

Mt. Hood National Forest Ranger Stations (✉️*6780 Hwy. 35, Mt. Hood 97041* ☎️*541/352–6002* ✉️*Superintendent, 16400 Champion Way, off U.S. 26, Sandy 97055* ☎️*503/668–1700*).

Oregon Tourism Commission (✉️*775 Summer St. NE, Salem 97301-1282* ☎️*503/986–0000 or 800/547–7842* ⊕*www.travel oregon.com*).

Portland
Essentials

There are planners and there are those who, excuse the pun, fly by the seat of their pants. We happily place ourselves among the planners. Our writers and editors try to anticipate all the issues you may face before and during any journey, and then they do their research. This section is the product of their efforts. Use it to get excited about your trip to Portland, to inform your travel planning, or to guide you on the road should the seat of your pants start to feel threadbare.

GETTING STARTED

We're really proud of our Web site: Fodors.com is a great place to begin any journey. Scan Travel Wire for suggested itineraries, travel deals, restaurant and hotel openings, and other up-to-the-minute info. Check out Booking to research prices and book plane tickets, hotel rooms, rental cars, and vacation packages. Head to Talk for on-the-ground pointers from travelers who frequent our message boards. You can also link to loads of other travel-related resources.

▌RESOURCES

ONLINE TRAVEL TOOLS

Whether you prefer indoor or outdoor activities, historical or cultural slants, social or solo pursuits, the Portland Oregon Visitor Association (POVA) has information about specialty trips and tours. Here you can find guides for sports enthusiasts, the gay community, wine and beer aficionados, environmentalists, bicyclers, hikers, and more. POVA assists with tips on getting around and making the most of your visit. Go to ⊕*www.travelportland.com* to traverse the lay of the land.

The Oregon Coast Visitors Association provides information on coastal towns as well as a helpful FAQ on driving tours and beach etiquette at ⊕*www.visittheoregoncoast.com*. The Columbia

River Gorge Visitors Association Web site, ⊕*www.crgva.org*, has tons of links to help you find outfitters, events, and accommodations in Oregon's most-popular recreation area. Before you head to Mt. Hood to hike or ski, go to ⊕*www.mthoodterritory.com* to find everything from driving tour maps to agritourism suggestions. Oregon's wine country is a big attraction, and the Willamette Valley Visitor's Association does a good job of cataloging the state's sizable number of wineries by region or by experience at ⊕*www.oregonwinecountry.org*.

If you're eager to get outdoors, ⊕*www.gorp.com* has information on adventure travel—everything from weekend city escape ideas to the logistics of camping in old fire lookouts.

Safety Transportation Security Administration (TSA; ⊕www.tsa.gov).

Time Zones Timeanddate.com (⊕www.timeanddate.com/worldclock) can help you figure out the correct time anywhere.

Weather Accuweather.com
(⊕www.accuweather.com) is an
independent weather-forecasting
service with good coverage of hur-
ricanes. **Weather.com** (⊕www.
weather.com) is the Web site for the
Weather Channel.

Other Resources **CIA World
Factbook** (⊕www.odci.gov/cia/
publications/factbook/index.html)
has profiles of every country in the
world. It's a good source if you need
some quick facts and figures.

VISITOR INFORMATION
Contacts **Portland Oregon
Visitors Association** (✉1000
S.W. Broadway, Suite 2300, 97205
☎800/962-3700 ⊕www.travel
portland.com).

**Portland Oregon Visitors As-
sociation Information Center** (✉Pioneer Courthouse Sq.
☎503/275-8355 or 877/678-5263).

BOOKING YOUR TRIP

Unless your cousin is a travel agent, you're probably among the millions of people who make most of their travel arrangements online.

But have you ever wondered just what the differences are between an online travel agent (a Web site through which you make reservations instead of going directly to the airline, hotel, or car-rental company), a discounter (a firm that does a high volume of business with a hotel chain or airline and accordingly gets good prices), a wholesaler (one that makes cheap reservations in bulk and then re-sells them to people like you), and an aggregator (one that compares all the offerings so you don't have to)?

Is it truly better to book directly on an airline or hotel Web site? And when does a real live travel agent come in handy?

▌ ONLINE

You really have to shop around. A travel wholesaler such as Hotels.com or HotelClub.net can be a source of good rates, as can discounters such as Hotwire or Priceline, particularly if you can bid for your hotel room or airfare. Indeed, such sites sometimes have deals that are unavailable elsewhere. They do, however, tend to work only with hotel chains (which makes them just plain useless for getting hotel reservations outside of major cities) or big airlines (so that often leaves out upstarts like jetBlue and some foreign carriers like Air India).

Also, with discounters and wholesalers you must generally prepay, and everything is non-refundable. And before you fork over the dough, be sure to check the terms and conditions, so you know what a given company will do for you if there's a problem and what you'll have to deal with on your own.

▇ TIP → **To be absolutely sure everything was processed correctly, confirm reservations made through online travel agents, discounters, and wholesalers directly with your hotel before leaving home.**

Booking engines like Expedia, Travelocity, and Orbitz are actually travel agents, albeit high-volume, online ones. And airline travel packagers like American Airlines Vacations and Virgin Vacations—well, they're travel agents, too. But they may still not work with all the world's hotels.

An aggregator site will search many sites and pull the best prices for airfares, hotels, and rental cars from them. Most aggregators compare the major travel-booking sites such as Expedia, Travelocity, and Orbitz; some also look at airline Web sites, though rarely the sites of smaller budget airlines. Some aggregators also compare other travel products, including complex packages—a good thing, as you can sometimes get the best overall deal by booking an air-and-hotel package.

▌ WITH A TRAVEL AGENT

If you use an agent—brick-and-mortar or virtual—you'll pay a fee for the service. And know that the service you get from some online agents isn't comprehensive. For example Expedia and Travelocity don't search for prices on budget airlines like jetBlue, Southwest, or small foreign carriers. That said, some agents (online or not) *do* have access to fares that are difficult to find otherwise, and the savings can more than make up for any surcharge.

A knowledgeable brick-and-mortar travel agent can be a godsend if you're booking a cruise, a package trip that's not available to you directly, an air pass, or a complicated itinerary including several overseas flights. What's more, travel agents that specialize in a destination may have exclusive access to certain deals and insider information on things such as charter flights. Agents who specialize in types of travelers (senior citizens, gays and lesbians, naturists) or types of trips (cruises, luxury travel, safaris) can also be invaluable.

■TIP➔ Remember that Expedia, Travelocity, and Orbitz are travel agents, not just booking engines. To resolve any problems with a reservation made through these companies, contact them first.

The Pacific Northwest is a do-it-yourself region in spirit, and you'll find it's fairly easy to book all travel on your own, especially if you're using Portland as a base.

Agent Resources **American Society of Travel Agents** (☎703/739–2782 ⊕www.travelsense.org).

▌ AIRLINE TICKETS

Most domestic airline tickets are electronic; international tickets may be either electronic or paper. With an e-ticket the only thing you receive is an e-mailed receipt citing your itinerary and reservation and ticket numbers.

The greatest advantage of an e-ticket is that if you lose your receipt, you can simply print out another copy or ask the airline to do it for you at check-in. You usually pay a surcharge (up to $50) to get a paper ticket, if you can get one at all.

The sole advantage of a paper ticket is that it may be easier to endorse over to another airline if your flight is canceled and the airline with which you booked can't accommodate you on another flight.

■TIP➔ Discount air passes that let you travel economically in a country or region must often be pur-

Online Booking Resources

AGGREGATORS		
Kayak	www.kayak.com	looks at cruises and vacation packages.
Mobissimo	www.mobissimo. com	examines airfare, hotels, cars, and tons of activities.
Qixo	www.qixo.com	compares cruises, vacation packages, and even travel insurance.
Sidestep	www.sidestep.com	compares vacation packages and lists travel deals and some activities.
Travelgrove	www.travelgrove. com	compares cruises and vacation packages and lets you search by themes.
BOOKING ENGINES		
Cheap Tick- ets	www.cheaptickets. com	discounter.
Expedia	www.expedia.com	large online agency that charges a book- ing fee for airline tickets.
Hotwire	www.hotwire.com	discounter.
lastminute. com	www.lastminute. com	specializes in last-minute travel; the main site is for the U.K., but it has a link to a U.S. site.
Luxury Link	www.luxurylink. com	has auctions (surprisingly good deals) as well as offers on the high-end side of travel.
Onetravel. com	www.onetravel. com	discounter for hotels, car rentals, airfares, and packages.
Orbitz	www.orbitz.com	charges a booking fee for airline tickets, but gives a clear breakdown of fees and taxes before you book.
Priceline.com	www.priceline.com	discounter that also allows bidding.
Travel.com	www.travel.com	allows you to compare its rates with those of other booking engines.
Travelocity	www.travelocity. com	charges a booking fee for airline tickets, but promises good problem resolution.
ONLINE ACCOMMODATIONS		
Hotelbook. com	www.hotelbook. com	focuses on independent hotels world- wide.
Hotel Club	www.hotelclub.net	good for major cities and some resort areas.

Online Booking Resources

Hotels.com	www.hotels.com	big Expedia-owned wholesaler that offers rooms in hotels all over the world.
Quikbook	www.quikbook.com	offers "pay when you stay" reservations that allow you to settle your bill when you check out, not when you book; best for trips to U.S. and Canadian cities.
OTHER RESOURCES		
Bidding For Travel	www.biddingfor-travel.com	good place to figure out what you can get and for how much before you start bidding on, say, Priceline.

chased before you leave home. In some cases you can only get them through a travel agent.

The least expensive airfares to the Pacific Northwest are often priced for round-trip travel and usually must be purchased in advance. Airlines generally allow you to change your return date for a fee; most low-fare tickets, however, are nonrefundable. America West sometimes offers specials deals and packages around the region. Air Canada is the only airline that offers a regional flight pass, which covers 10 one-way trips between cities in the western United States and western Canada. The pass is nontransferable, so it only makes sense if you're planning to do a lot of flying or to make multiple trips to the region within a year.

You can also save money on your car rental (a must for most Pacific Northwest itineraries) by booking a fly/drive package through your airline. Many airlines offer deals on rental cars if you book through them.

▌ RENTAL CARS

It's possible to get around Portland by public transportation and taxis, but once you go outside city limits, your options are limited. National lines like Greyhound do provide service between major towns, and Amtrak has limited service between Washington and Oregon (allowing you to get from, say, Portland to Seattle, by train), but it's nearly impossible to get to and around the major recreation areas and national parks of each state without your own wheels.

Rates in Portland begin at $30 a day and $138 a week, not including the 12.5% tax.

All the major agencies are represented in the region. If you're planning to cross the U.S.–Canadian border with your rental car, discuss it with the agency to see what's involved.

In the Pacific Northwest you must be 21 to rent a car. Car seats are compulsory for children under four years *and* 40 pounds;

older children are required to sit in booster seats until they're eight years old *and* 80 pounds. In the United States nonresidents need a reservation voucher, passport, driver's license, and insurance for each driver.

When you reserve a car, ask about cancellation penalties, taxes, drop-off charges (if you're planning to pick up the car in one city and leave it in another), and surcharges (for being under or over a certain age, for additional drivers, or for driving across state or country borders or beyond a specific distance from your point of rental). All these things can add substantially to your costs. Request car seats and extras such as GPS when you book.

Rates are sometimes—but not always—better if you book in advance or reserve through a rental agency's Web site. There are other reasons to book ahead, though: for popular destinations, during busy times of the year, or to ensure that you get certain types of cars (vans, SUVs, exotic sports cars).

■ TIP→ **Make sure that a confirmed reservation guarantees you a car. Agencies sometimes overbook, particularly for busy weekends and holiday periods.**

CAR RENTAL RESOURCES

Automobile Associations **U.S.: American Automobile Association** (AAA ☎315/797-5000 ⊕www.aaa.com); most contact with the organization is through state and regional members. **National Au-**tomobile Club (☎650/294-7000 ⊕www.thenac.com); membership is open to California residents only.

Major Agencies **Alamo** (☎800/462-5266 ⊕www.alamo.com). **Avis** (☎800/331-1212 ⊕www.avis.com). **Budget** (☎800/527-0700 ⊕www.budget.com). **Hertz** (☎800/654-3131 ⊕www.hertz.com). **National Car Rental** (☎800/227-7368 ⊕www.nationalcar.com).

CAR-RENTAL INSURANCE

Everyone who rents a car wonders whether the insurance that the rental companies offer is worth the expense. No one—including us—has a simple answer. It all depends on how much regular insurance you have, how comfortable you are with risk, and whether or not money is an issue.

If you own a car and carry comprehensive car insurance for both collision and liability, your personal auto insurance will probably cover a rental, but read your policy's fine print to be sure. If you don't have auto insurance, then you should probably buy the collision- or loss-damage waiver (CDW or LDW) from the rental company. This eliminates your liability for damage to the car.

Some credit cards offer CDW coverage, but it's usually supplemental to your own insurance and rarely covers SUVs, minivans, luxury models, and the like. If your coverage is secondary, you may still be liable for loss-of-use costs from the car-rental company (again, read the fine print). But no credit-card insurance is valid unless you use that card for *all* transactions, from reserving to paying the final bill.

■TIP→ Diners Club offers primary CDW coverage on all rentals reserved and paid for with the card. This means that Diners Club's company—not your own car insurance—pays in case of an accident. It *doesn't* mean that your car-insurance company won't raise your rates once it discovers you had an accident.

You may also be offered supplemental liability coverage; the car-rental company is required to carry a minimal level of liability coverage insuring all renters, but it's rarely enough to cover claims in a really serious accident if you're at fault. Your own auto-insurance policy will protect you if you own a car; if you don't, you have to decide whether you are willing to take the risk.

U.S. rental companies sell CDWs and LDWs for about $15 to $25 a day; supplemental liability is usually more than $10 a day. The car-rental company may offer you all sorts of other policies, but they're rarely worth the cost. Personal accident insurance, which is basic hospitalization coverage, is an especially egregious rip-off if you already have health insurance.

■TIP→ You can decline the insurance from the rental company and purchase it through a third-party provider such as Travel Guard

(⊕www.travelguard.com)—$9 per day for $35,000 of coverage. That's sometimes just under half the price of the CDW offered by some car-rental companies.

■ VACATION PACKAGES

Packages *are not* guided excursions. Packages combine airfare, accommodations, and perhaps a rental car or other extras (theater tickets, guided excursions, boat trips, reserved entry to popular museums, transit passes), but they let you do your own thing. During busy periods packages may be your only option, as flights and rooms may be sold out otherwise.

Packages will definitely save you time. They can also save you money, particularly in peak seasons, but—and this is a really big "but"—you should price each part of the package separately to be sure. And be aware that prices advertised on Web sites and in newspapers rarely include service charges or taxes, which can up your costs by hundreds of dollars.

■TIP→ Some packages and cruises are sold only through travel agents. Don't always assume that you can get the best deal by booking everything yourself.

Each year consumers are stranded or lose their money when packagers—even large ones with excellent reputations—go out of business. How can you protect yourself?

First, always pay with a credit card; if you have a problem, your credit-card company may help you resolve it. Second, buy trip insurance that covers default. Third, choose a company that belongs to the United States Tour Operators Association, whose members must set aside funds to cover defaults. Finally, choose a company that also participates in the Tour Operator Program of the American Society of Travel Agents (ASTA), which will act as mediator in any disputes.

You can also check on the tour operator's reputation among travelers by posting an inquiry on one of the Fodors.com forums.

Organizations American Society of Travel Agents (ASTA ☎703/739–2782 or 800/965–2782 ⊕www.astanet.com). **United States Tour Operators Association** (USTOA ☎212/599–6599 ⊕www.ustoa.com). ■TIP➔ Local tourism boards can provide information about lesser-known and small-niche operators that sell packages to only a few destinations.

▌ GUIDED TOURS

Guided tours are a good option when you don't want to do it all yourself. You travel along with a group (sometimes large, sometimes small), stay in prebooked hotels, eat with your fellow travelers (the cost of meals sometimes included in the price of your tour, sometimes not), and follow a schedule.

But not all guided tours are an if-it's-Tuesday-this-must-be-Belgium experience. A knowledgeable guide can take you places that you might never discover on your own, and you may be pushed to see more than you would have otherwise. Tours aren't for everyone, but they can be just the thing for trips to places where making travel arrangements is difficult or time-consuming (particularly when you don't speak the language).

Whenever you book a guided tour, find out what's included and what isn't. A "land-only" tour includes all your travel (by bus, in most cases) in the destination, but not necessarily your flights to and from or even within it. Also, in most cases prices in tour brochures don't include fees and taxes. And remember that you'll be expected to tip your guide (in cash) at the end of the tour.

TRANSPORTATION

▮ BY AIR

It takes about 5 hours to fly non-stop to Portland from New York, 4 hours from Chicago, and 2½ hours from Los Angeles. Flying from Seattle to Portland takes just under an hour; flying from Portland to Vancouver takes an hour and 15 minutes.

Even if your final destination is in another city in Oregon, you may choose to fly into Portland and rent a car to get there, because all other airports in the state are small regional airports with limited service. It is possible, however, to get a connecting flight from Portland International Airport (PDX) to smaller cities in Oregon. Portland Airport is served by all major airlines as well as by several smaller regional carriers.

▮TIP➔ If you travel frequently, look into the TSA's Registered Traveler program. The program, which is still being tested in several U.S. airports, is designed to cut down on gridlock at security checkpoints by allowing prescreened travelers to pass quickly through kiosks that scan an iris and/or a fingerprint. How sci-fi is that?

Airlines & Airports **Airline and Airport Links.com** (⊕www.airlineandairportlinks.com) has links to many of the world's airlines and airports.

Airline Security Issues **Transportation Security Administration** (⊕www.tsa.gov) has answers for almost every question that might come up.

AIRPORTS

Portland International Airport (PDX) is a sleek, modern airport with service to many national and international destinations. It's easily accessible from downtown Portland.

▮TIP➔ Long layovers don't have to be only about sitting around or shopping. These days they can be about burning off vacation calories. Check out ⊕www.airportgyms.com for lists of health clubs that are in or near many U.S. and Canadian airports.

Airport Information **Portland International Airport** (✉N.E. Airport Way at I–205 ☎877/739–4636 ⊕www.flypdx.com/).

GROUND TRANSPORTATION

TriMet trains and buses serve the airport. A 5½-mi extension of the MAX light-rail system runs from the Gateway Transit Center (at the intersection of I–84 and I–205) directly to and from the airport. Trains arrive at and depart from inside the passenger terminal near the south baggage-claim area. The trip takes about 35 minutes from downtown. TriMet Bus 12, which runs about every 15 minutes, also serves the airport. The fare to or from the airport on MAX or the bus is $1.75.

Contacts **TriMet/MAX** (✉6th
Ave. and Morrison St., Downtown
☎503/238-7433 ⊕www.trimet.org).

FLIGHTS

Many international carriers serve
the Pacific Northwest, includ-
ing Air France, British Airways,
KLM, Lufthansa, and Qantas.
U.S. carriers include Alaska Airlines, Continental, Delta, Northwest, and United. JetBlue has
daily flights from New York's
JFK airport to Portland. US Airways flies from Portland to Las
Vegas, Phoenix, Charlotte, and
Philadelphia. Big Sky, Frontier
Airlines, Horizon Air, and United
Express provide frequent service
between cities in Washington,
Oregon, Idaho, Montana, and
California. Southwest Airlines
has frequent service to Portland
from cities in California, Nevada,
Idaho, and Utah as well as some
other parts of the country.

Airline Contacts **Alaska Airlines**
(☎800/252-7522 or 206/433-3100
⊕www.alaskaair.com). **American
Airlines** (☎800/433-7300 ⊕www.
aa.com). **ATA** (☎800/435-9282
or 317/282-8308 ⊕www.ata.
com). **Continental Airlines**
(☎800/523—3273 for U.S. and
Mexico reservations, 800/231-0856
for international reservations
⊕www.continental.com). **Delta
Airlines** (☎800/221-1212 for U.S.
reservations, 800/241-4141 for
international reservations ⊕www.
delta.com). **jetBlue** (☎800/538-
2583 ⊕www.jetblue.com). **Northwest Airlines** (☎800/225-2525
⊕www.nwa.com). **Southwest
Airlines** (☎800/435-9792 ⊕www.
southwest.com). **Spirit Airlines**

NAVIGATING PORTLAND

Geographically speaking, Portland
is relatively easy to navigate. It's
mapped out into quadrants with
the Willamette River dividing east
and west into halves and Burnside Street separating the north
from south:

■ Northwest: north of Burnside,
west of the river;

■ Southwest: south of Burnside,
west of the river;

■ Northeast: north of Burnside,
east of the river; and

■ Southeast: south of Burnside,
east of the river.

It's handy to know that while
you travel around the Portland
metropolitan area, a general rout-
ing rule is that named east and
west streets intersect numbered
avenues, which are north-south
adjacent to, and begin at, each
side of the river. For instance,
Southwest 12th Avenue is 12
blocks west of the Willamette.
Most of downtown's streets run in
one-way directions, which keeps
the traffic grid flowing.

(☎800/772-7117 or 586/791-7300
⊕www.spiritair.com). **United
Airlines** (☎800/864-8331 for
U.S. reservations, 800/538-2929
for international reservations
⊕www.united.com). **USAirways**
(☎800/428-4322 for U.S. and Canada reservations, 800/622-1015 for
international reservations ⊕www.
usairways.com).

▌ BY BOAT

From Portland, the *Portland Spirit, Willamette Star,* and *Crystal Dolphin* make sightseeing and dinner cruises on the Willamette and Columbia rivers. America West also uses paddle-wheel boats for overnight historic tours along the Columbia and Snake rivers. Departing from Cascade Locks, Oregon (45 minutes east of Portland), the sternwheeler *Columbia Gorge* cruises the Columbia Gorge and the Willamette River (December only). To view the rich wildlife along the western edge of the Columbia River, you can take an ecologically focused cruise or an estuary tour, both of which depart from Astoria, Oregon.

Information Columbia Gorge (☎503/224–3900 or 800/224–3901 ⊕www.sternwheeler.com). Portland Spirit (☎503/224–3900 or 800/224–3901 ⊕www.portland spirit.com).

▌ BY BUS

Greyhound is a good way to get between destinations in Oregon for a reasonable price if you don't have a car at your disposal. Portland is the main hub for nearly all routes in the state, making it the most practical starting and ending point for most bus excursions. Keep in mind that many small towns in Oregon may not be regularly accessible by bus and that there may be no public transportation or car-rental locations in many towns you visit. Buses arrive at and depart from the Greyhound terminal next to the Amtrak station in Old Town.

Greyhound's domestic and international Discovery Passes allow unlimited bus travel in North America—including Canada and Mexico—for periods of 7 to 60 days.

For bus travel within the city, see ⇨ *By TriMet/MAX,* below.

Bus Information Greyhound Terminal (✉550 N.W. 6th Ave., Old Town ☎503/243–2310 or 800/231–2222, 503/243–2337 baggage, 503/243–2361 customer service).

▌ BY CAR

I–5 enters Portland from the north and south. I–84, the city's major eastern corridor, terminates in Portland. U.S. 26 and U.S. 30 are primary east–west thoroughfares. Bypass routes are I–205, which links I–5 and I–84 before crossing the Columbia River into Washington, and I–405, which arcs around western downtown. Most city-center streets are one-way only, and Southwest 5th and 6th avenues between Burnside and Southwest Madison streets are limited to bus traffic.

From the airport to downtown, take I–205 south to westbound I–84. Drive west over the Willamette River and take the City Center exit. If going to the airport, take I–84 east to I–205 north; follow I–205 to the airport exit.

Traffic on I–5 north and south of downtown and on I–84 and I–205 east of downtown is heavy between 6 AM and 9 AM and between 4 and 8 PM. Four-lane U.S. 26 west of downtown can be bumper-to-bumper any time of the day going to or from downtown.

GASOLINE

Gas stations are plentiful in major metropolitan areas and along major highways like I–5. Most stay open late, except in rural areas, where Sunday hours are limited and where you may drive long stretches without a refueling opportunity. This is particularly true in Oregon, where you are not allowed to pump your own gas, and therefore won't be able to find an automated pump in an emergency.

■TIP→ **Keep an eye on the gauge when traveling to national parks and off-the-beaten-path trails, particularly if you'll be heading down Forest Service roads. A good rule of thumb is to fill up before you get off (or too far away) from a major highway like I–5 or I–90.**

PARKING

Though there are several options, parking in downtown Portland can be tricky and expensive. If you're parked for more than several hours, your most afford-able and accessible option is to park in one of seven city-owned "Smart Park" lots. Rates start at $1.25 per hour (short-term parking, four hours or less) to $3 per hour (long-term parking, week-days 5 AM–6 PM), with a $15 daily maximum; weekends and evenings have lower rates. The best part about Smart Park is that hundreds of participating merchants will validate tickets and cover the first two hours of parking when you spend at least $25 in their stores.

There are numerous privately owned lots around the city as well; fees for those vary and add up quickly.

Street parking is metered only and requires you to visibly display a sticker on the inside of your curbside window. The meters that dispense the stickers take coins or credit cards (though you'll be charged a bank fee for using a debit card). Metered spaces are mostly available for 90 minutes to three hours; parking tickets for exceeding the limit are regularly issued.

Once you get out of downtown, there's plenty of nonmetered street parking available within residential areas.

ROAD CONDITIONS

Winter driving can present challenges. In coastal areas the mild, damp climate contributes to frequently wet roadways. Snowfalls generally occur only once or twice a year, but when it does fall, traffic grinds to a halt and roadways become treacherous and stay that way until the snow melts.

Tire chains, studs, or snow tires are essential equipment for winter travel in mountain areas. If you're planning to drive into high elevations, be sure to check the weather forecast beforehand. Even the main highway mountain passes can close because of snow conditions. In winter state and provincial highway departments operate snow advisory telephone lines that give pass conditions.

ROADSIDE EMERGENCIES

For **police, ambulance,** or **other emergencies** dial 911.

Other Contacts **Oregon State Police** (☎503/378–3720 or 800/452–7888).

▌BY TAXI

Taxi fare is $2.50 at flag drop plus $2.10 per mile. The first person pays by the meter, and each additional passenger pays $1. Cabs cruise the city streets, but it's better to phone for one. The major companies are Broadway Cab, New Rose City Cab, Portland Taxi Company, and Radio Cab. The trip between downtown Portland and the airport takes about 30 minutes by taxi. The fare is about $30.

Taxi Companies **Broadway Cab** (☎503/227–1234). **New Rose City Cab** (☎503/282–7707). **Portland Taxi Company** (☎503/256–5400). **Radio Cab** (☎503/227–1212).

▌BY TRAIN

Amtrak, the U.S. passenger rail system, has daily service to Union Station from the Midwest and California. The *Empire Builder* takes a northern route through Minnesota and Montana from Chicago to Spokane, from where separate legs continue to Seattle and Portland. The *Coast Starlight* begins in Los Angeles; makes stops throughout California, western Oregon, and Washington; and terminates in Seattle.

Amtrak's *Cascades* trains travel between Seattle and Vancouver and between Seattle, Portland, and Eugene. The trip from Seattle to Portland takes roughly 3½ hours and costs $28–$44 for a coach seat; this is a pleasant alternative to a mind-numbing drive down I–5. The *Empire Builder* travels between Portland and Spokane (7 hours, $75), with part of the route running through the Columbia River gorge. From Portland to Eugene, it's a 3-hour trip; the cost is $21–$35.

▐TIP→ **Book Amtrak tickets at least a few days in advance, especially if you're traveling between Seattle and Portland on the weekend.**

Information **Amtrak** (✉800 N.W. 6th Ave., Old Town ☎800/872–7245).

▌BY TRIMET/MAX

TriMet operates an extensive system of buses, streetcars, and light-rail trains. The Central City streetcar line runs between Legacy Good Samaritan hospital in Nob Hill, the Pearl District, downtown, and Portland State University. To Nob Hill it travels along 10th Avenue and then on Northwest Northrup; from Nob Hill it runs along Northwest Lovejoy and then on 11th Avenue. Trains stop every few blocks.

Metropolitan Area Express, or MAX, links the eastern and western Portland suburbs with downtown, Washington Park and the Oregon Zoo, the Lloyd Center district, the Convention Center, and the Rose Quarter. From downtown, trains operate daily 5:30 AM–1 AM, with a fare of $1.75 for travel through one or two zones, $2.05 for three zones, and $4.25 for an unlimited all-day ticket. A seven-day visitor pass is also available for $19. Trains run about every 10 minutes Monday–Saturday and every 15 minutes on Sunday and holidays.

Bus, MAX, and streetcar fare is $1.75 for one or two zones, which covers most places you'll have cause to go, and $2.05 for three zones, which includes all of the outlying areas of the city. Ask the driver if you're uncertain whether you're traveling within Zones 1 and 2. A "fareless square" extends from downtown all the way to the Lloyd Center on the east side. If you're riding only within this area, your ride is free.

Day passes for unlimited system-wide travel cost $4.25. Three-day and monthly passes are available. As you board the bus, the driver will hand you a transfer ticket that is good for one to two hours, depending on the time of day, on all buses and MAX trains. Be sure to hold on to it whether you're transferring or not; it also serves as proof that you have paid for your ride. MAX trains run every 10 minutes Monday–Saturday before 8 PM and every 15 minutes after 8 PM and all day Sunday and holidays. Buses can operate as frequently as every five minutes or once an hour. Bikes are allowed on designated areas of MAX trains, and there are bike racks on the front of all buses that everyone is free to use.

Information TriMet/MAX (✉6th Ave. and Morrison St., Downtown ☎503/238–7433 ⊕www.trimet.org).

ON THE GROUND

▌ COMMUNICATIONS

INTERNET
Portland is well wired, and it's difficult to find a hotel that doesn't offer either Ethernet connections, Wi-Fi, or both. (Whether those services are free, however, is another issue.)

Coffeehouses almost always have reliable Wi-Fi and the service is often free (assuming, of course, that you at least buy a cup of coffee); a few have a communal computer or two if you didn't bring the laptop, but often your best bet for dedicated computer stations is either your hotel's business center or public library branches.

For a list of wired coffee shops in Portland, check out ⊕*http://portland.wifimug.org*. For more Portland hot spots, check out ⊕*www.wifipdx.com*.

Contacts **Cybercafes** (⊕www.cybercafes.com) lists more than 4,000 Internet cafés worldwide.

▌ DAY TOURS & GUIDES

BOAT TOURS
Sternwheeler Riverboat Tours' *Columbia Gorge* departs year-round from Tom McCall Waterfront Park on two-hour excursions of the Willamette River; there are also Friday-night dinner cruises. In summer the sternwheeler travels up the Columbia River.

For the more adventurous, Willamette Jetboat Excursions offers whirling, swirling one- and two-hour tours along the Willamette River that include an up-close visit with Willamette Falls.

Tour Operator **Sternwheeler Riverboat Tours** (⊠S.W. Naito Pkwy. and Stark St., Riverfront Park ☎503/223–3928). **Willamette Jetboat Excursions** (⊠S.E. Marion St. ☎888/538–2628).

BUS TOURS
Gray Line operates City of Portland and Pacific Northwest sightseeing tours, including service to Chinook Winds Casino in Lincoln City, from April through October; call for departure times and tours.

Tour Operator **Gray Line** (☎503/684–3322 Ext. 2 ⊕www.grayline.com).

TROLLEY TOURS
The Willamette Shore Trolley company operates vintage double-decker electric trolleys that provide scenic round-trips between suburban Lake Oswego and downtown, along the west shore of the Willamette River. The 7-mi route, which the trolley traverses in 45 minutes, passes over trestles and through Elk Rock tunnel along one of the most scenic stretches of the river. The line, which opened in 1885, was electrified in 1914, and Southern Pacific Railway oper-

ated dozens of trips daily along this route in the 1920s. Passenger service ended in 1929, and the line was taken over by the Oregon Electric Railway Historical Society. Reservations are recommended. The trolley ($8 round-trip) departs Lake Oswego at noon and 2:30 PM and Portland at 1 and 3:15 on weekends from May through October. Charters are available year-round.

Contacts **Willamette Shore Trolley** (✉311 N. State St., Lake Oswego ✉South of RiverPlace Marina, at Sheridan and Moody Sts., Portland ☎503/697-7436).

WALKING TOURS

The Portland Oregon Visitors Association (⇨ *Visitor Information*), which is open weekdays 9–5 and Saturday 9–4, has brochures, maps, and guides to art galleries and select neighborhoods.

▌ HOURS OF OPERATION

In Oregon, store hours can be erratic, a testament to the laid-back nature of the region. Major department stores or shops generally follow the 10-to-6 rule, but you should always phone ahead if you have your heart set on visiting a smaller shop. Never assume a store is open on Sunday; many smaller shops have truncated Saturday hours as well. To make matters more confusing, most smaller stores close one day during the week (usually Monday or Tuesday, but it varies), and some stores don't open until 11 AM, noon, or even 1 PM. Thankfully, coffeehouses tend to keep regular and long hours, so you'll have no problem finding one to kill time in if you have to wait for a store to open.

Bars in Oregon close at 2 AM, with last call coming as early as 1:30.

▌ MONEY

Meals in Portland are generally a little less expensive than in other major North American regions. Prices for first-class hotel rooms are high in summer ($250–$400), though the same rooms become surprisingly affordable in low season ($100 to $200 a night). Unless you're willing to stay in rundown motels, the cheapest rooms you'll find start at $75–$90 a night. Though you'll get some great deals on food and other on-the-ground expenses (fewer sights charge prohibitive fees), you'll find that some urban "necessities," like taxi rides, are frustratingly expensive.

Debit cards and major credit cards are accepted almost everywhere—some cafés will even let you charge a single cup of coffee—so don't worry about carrying around wads of cash. It's a good idea to keep handy a few small bills and coins for parking meters.

ITEM	AVERAGE COST
Cup of Coffee	$1.50
Glass of Wine	$6–$9
Glass of Beer	$4–$6
Sandwich	$5–$8
One-Mile Taxi Ride	$4.50
Museum Admission	$10–$15

CREDIT CARDS

Throughout this guide, the following abbreviations are used: **AE**, American Express; **D**, Discover; **DC**, Diners Club; **MC**, MasterCard; and **V**, Visa.

It's a good idea to inform your credit-card company before you travel, especially if you're going abroad and don't travel internationally very often. Otherwise, the credit-card company might put a hold on your card owing to unusual activity—not a good thing halfway through your trip. Record all your credit-card numbers—as well as the phone numbers to call if your cards are lost or stolen—in a safe place, so you're prepared should something go wrong. Both MasterCard and Visa have general numbers you can call (collect if you're abroad) if your card is lost, but you're better off calling the number of your issuing bank, since MasterCard and Visa usually just transfer you to your bank; your bank's number is usually printed on your card.

Reporting Lost Cards **American Express** (☎800/528–4800 in the U.S. or 336/393–1111 collect from abroad ⊕www.americanexpress.com). **Diners Club** (☎800/234–6377 in the U.S. or 303/799–1504 collect from abroad ⊕www.dinersclub.com). **Discover** (☎800/347–2683 in the U.S. or 801/902–3100 collect from abroad ⊕www.discovercard.com). **MasterCard** (☎800/627–8372 in the U.S. or 636/722–7111 collect from abroad ⊕www.mastercard.com). **Visa** (☎800/847–2911 in the U.S. or 410/581–9994 collect from abroad ⊕www.visa.com).

▌ SAFETY

The Pacific Northwest is generally a safe place to visit. Portland is the least gentrified of the three major cities, though it doesn't necessarily have more problems with crime than Seattle or Vancouver. You'll often see people in coffeehouses leave laptops and bags unattended when they head up to the counter for a refill. That said, it's better to be safe than sorry, so keep an eye on your belongings in public places.

Always lock rental cars. Try not to leave any valuables inside the car; if you must do so, put them in the trunk. Car break-ins are common in Portland, even in seemingly peaceful residential areas.

The Great Outdoors pose the most dangerous element of the Northwest. Don't hike alone, and make sure you bring enough water plus basic first-aid items. If you're not an experienced hiker, stick to tourist-friendly spots like the more accessible parts of the national parks; if you have to drive 30 mi down a Forest Service road to reach a trail, it's possible you might be the only one hiking on it.

TAXES

Oregon has no sales tax, although many cities and counties levy a tax on lodging and services. Room taxes, for example, vary from 6% to 9½%.

TIME

Portland is in the Pacific time zone. Daylight savings time is observed from early April to late October.

TIPPING

Tips and service charges are usually not automatically added to a bill. If service is satisfactory, customers generally give waitstaff 15%–20% of the total bill. Hairdressers, taxi drivers, and other service specialists receive 10%–20%. Bellhops, doormen, and porters at airports and railway stations are generally tipped $1–$2 for each item of luggage.

When visiting coffeehouses, throw your change or $1 into the tip jar on the counter—like waiters, baristas depend on tips to supplement their wages.

TIPPING GUIDELINES FOR PORTLAND	
Bartender	$1 per drink per round
Bellhop	$1 to $2 per bag, depending on the level of the hotel
Hotel Concierge	$5 or more, if he or she performs a service for you
Hotel Doorman	$1–$2 if he helps you get a cab
Hotel Maid	$1–$3 a day (either daily or at the end of your stay, in cash)
Hotel Room-Service Waiter	$1 to $2 per delivery, even if a service charge has been added
Skycap at Airport	$1 to $3 per bag checked
Taxi Driver	15%–20%, but round up the fare to the next dollar amount
Valet Parking Attendant	$1–$2, but only when you get your car
Waiter	15%–20%, with 20% being the norm at high-end restaurants.

INDEX

NOTES

NOTES

ABOUT OUR WRITERS

Janna Mock-Lopez, the primary writer of this guide, is enamored of the spirit, beauty, and vitality of Portland and the Northwest. She believes that when it comes to providing a well-rounded life of culture, art, and nature, there's no better place than the City of Roses to share these with her husband, daughter, and son. Mock-Lopez is also a publisher of *Portland Family* magazine (⊕www.portlandfamily.com) which distributes over 40,000 copies locally each month around the greater Metropolitan area. She's previously contributed to several Fodor's guides, *Travel Oregon* and *Sunset* magazines, and other publications. She's honored to be able to highlight the uniqueness of what this city offers to all those around the world who may come to visit one day.

Kimberly Gadette's writings encompass travel, film, politics, sports, dating, and dogs (though it's funny, dogs seldom date).

Her first novel, *So Much for Love*, is debuting this year. Aside from her ongoing movie column, "The Screen Savor" with www.livepdx.com, she's been published more than 300 times in the last three years, in publications from the West Coast to the East, from *The Oregonian* to the *Boston Globe*. Though no one's ever asked to see it, she has an MFA from UCLA. She covered the Columbia Gorge and Mt. Hood area.

Portland-based writer Deston Nokes enjoys escaping the Oregon clouds to write about compelling cultures and provocative people. Raised in a family of journalists, he grew up traveling, having lived in Old San Juan, Buenos Aires and along the eastern seaboard. Deston specializes in Hawaiian, Pacific Northwest, Caribbean and Latin American travel, and his two teenage kids often come along for the ride. He covered the Oregon Coast and Willamette Valley.